Fashion and Textile Design with Photoshop and Illustrator

Fairchild Books
An imprint of Bloomsbury Publishing Plc
Imprint previously known as AVA Publishing

50 Bedford Square   1385 Broadway
London   New York
WC1B 3DP   NY 10018
UK   USA

www.bloomsbury.com

**FAIRCHILD BOOKS, BLOOMSBURY and the Diana logo are
trademarks of Bloomsbury Publishing Plc**

**Adobe®, Illustrator®, and Photoshop® are registered trademarks
of Adobe Systems Incorporated in the United States and
other countries.**
Fashion and Textile Design with Photoshop and Illustrator is not
authorized, endorsed, or sponsored by Adobe Systems Incorporated,
Publisher of Adobe Photoshop® and Adobe Illustrator®.
**PANTONE® and other Pantone trademarks are the property
of Pantone LLC.**

© Bloomsbury Publishing Plc, 2016

**British Library Cataloguing-in-Publication Data
A catalogue record for this book is available from the
British Library.**

ISBN: PB: 978-1-4725-7875-4
          ePDF: 978-1-4725-7876-1

Library of Congress Cataloging-in-Publication Data
Hume, Robert.
Fashion and textile design with Photoshop and Illustrator: professional
creative practice / Robert Hume.
pages cm
Includes index.
ISBN 978-1-4725-7875-4 (pbk.) -- ISBN 978-1-4725-7876-1 (epdf)
1. Fashion design--Data processing. 2. Adobe Photoshop.
3. Adobe Illustrator (Computer file)
4. Computer-aided design. I. Title.
TT507.H77 2016
746.9'20285--dc23
2015019776

Typeset by Roger Fawcett-Tang
Printed and bound in China

Fashion and Textile Design with Photoshop and Illustrator

Professional Creative Practice

Robert Hume

Fairchild Books
An imprint of Bloomsbury Publishing Plc

BLOOMSBURY

LONDON · OXFORD · NEW YORK · NEW DELHI · SYDNEY

CONTENTS

INTRODUCTION   **6**

LEVEL ONE   **10**

LEVEL TWO   **62**

LEVEL THREE **154**

SHARING, COMMUNICATION, AND OUTPUT **236**

APPENDIX **248**

HOW TO USE THIS BOOK

As a reader you may not be inclined to diligently work your way through every section of this book from start to finish. The projects are devised so that you can dip into them and learn the particular skills you need. However, if you have the opportunity I recommend that you do work through all the sections in sequence. The beginner can miss some fundamental tools in Photoshop and Illustrator when their significance may not be apparent. Quite a few Photoshop users have plugged away without learning the pen tool, for example, and have really reduced the opportunities available with the application. Clipping paths are extremely useful in both Photoshop and Illustrator but to discover their power you may have to be directed to them. So stick with the projects, and their relevance will start to materialize.

Creating work from scratch in the applications is so important to developing fluency and expressing yourself freely. Because creating from scratch is so important, working with scanned-in artwork is relegated to later on in the course of projects. Photoshop and Illustrator are wonderful tools to be used in any combination and in any order with other tools and processes, but experience has shown that too much reliance on material grabbed from elsewhere can become a straitjacket to creativity. By delaying the use of scans and working through the earlier projects you will find that it can be easy to generate material from scratch in a direct and rapid way. Both applications are rich in resources for new ways of drawing, painting, and designing.

Subsequent projects practice and reinforce the techniques introduced in previous projects, while introducing further methods and skills. A project may involve a technique that has been covered in more detail in an earlier project, so even if you don't read every project, it makes sense to look at the projects in a particular section in order. The projects develop skills in Photoshop and Illustrator for real-world applications in textiles and fashion.

The emphasis of this book is solidly on developing creativity and professional ability in parallel. The three levels loosely follow the course structure of a degree course with projects increasing in complexity and ambition. By the end you will have developed skills in Photoshop and Illustrator that are equivalent to those of a professional designer.

All the material needed to complete the projects is available on the accompanying website, **www.bloomsbury.com/hume -textile-design**. I recommend you follow through what you have learned in the specific project by applying the techniques to design material of your own as reinforcement. This way the applications will quickly allow you to reflect your personal creativity.

The case studies showcase some of the work and creative thinking of a number of professional designers. They reflect on the appeal of Illustrator and Photoshop for them and provide some inspiration for developing your personal creative practice in the applications.

Robert Hume

INTRODUCTION

Why choose Photoshop and Illustrator for designing for textiles and fashion? Well the very fact that you are reading this introduction indicates you likely know how popular they are in the textile and fashion industry. Adobe® Photoshop® and Illustrator® have become essential tools for textile and fashion design professionals. Though not devised specifically for those activities the brilliant design of the applications, their ease of use and constant evolution has eclipsed many specialist textile and fashion systems. The complexity of Photoshop and Illustrator can be intimidating at first: the novice learning on the same "industrial strength" application as those used intensively by professionals the world over. However the applications are well suited to the creative user and the fundamentals—those elements that gave the applications their advantages and attractions in the earliest incarnations—are very flexible and easy to use. This book aims to rapidly get you to grips with those fundamentals.

If you are new to Photoshop and Illustrator then this book is ideal for you because it will take you through the key processes for working in Photoshop and Illustrator up to a professional level. If you are already experienced with Photoshop and Illustrator then this book offers the opportunity to learn additional techniques and possible alternatives to your current methods. It is understandable that professional designers with the demands of day-to-day work don't always have the opportunity to investigate for themselves some of the latest tools and techniques.

Photoshop and Illustrator continue to evolve. Whether you have an earlier version or the most recent of these applications the elements emphasized in the projects remain key to their effective and creative use. Core aspects such as paths, selections and transformations are introduced successively in the early projects and familiarity with these tools and their use in combination enable more complex tasks to be tackled further on in the book.

Creating work from scratch and expressing yourself freely with new ways of drawing, painting and designing is very important to developing a facility with the applications and this approach is emphasized in the early projects. Experience has taught that creating work from scratch in the applications rather than considering them merely as a means of adding treatments to material generated elsewhere is a more fruitful way of learning how to use the applications. Routine resorting to stock techniques, such as filters used to make photos look painted, can severely restrict your creativity and produce very generic work—work that is more about Photoshop and Illustrator than it is about you.

Supportive material accompanying the projects deals with subjects such as effective colorways and principles of good repeat work. Case studies show professionals using the applications creatively in real-world situations and in diverse practices. The projects revolve around gaining confidence with the key tools of Photoshop and Illustrator; these fundamentals then act as springboards to the more complex tasks required to design textiles and fashion in Photoshop and Illustrator.

Photoshop and Illustrator continue to evolve. Whether you have an earlier version or the most recent of these applications the elements emphasized in the projects remain key to their effective and creative use.

WHY USE PHOTOSHOP AND ILLUSTRATOR
FOR TEXTILES AND FASHION?

The underlying difference between the two applications is that Photoshop is a raster, or bitmap, application and Illustrator is a vector application. This distinction, over time, has become a little diluted, as Photoshop now incorporates vector elements and Illustrator can handle raster image effects. Photoshop though is still principally tailored for raster images. These images are composed of an array or map of bits within a rectangular grid of pixels or dots. Each bit is a discrete element with a specific location and color value within the document. Illustrator works with vector objects described by lines, shapes, and other graphic image components defined only by mathematical formulas. Vector graphics maintain crisp edges and lose no detail when resized because their shape is recalculated afresh and wholly resolution independent. Bitmap images allow for subtle delicate nuances and painterly qualities, and vector images allow for precise edges and curves to shapes and for perfect resizing and transformations.

Photoshop is often favored for textile design and Illustrator for fashion illustration, but such is the versatility of the programs that there are no hard and fast rules. The projects in this book will help you explore their strengths. Photoshop is dealt with first because it is the less obviously technical of the two applications. However some people find Illustrator much more preferable to use and click with Illustrator in a way they don't with Photoshop. Familiarity with paths and the pen tool, important tools in Photoshop, is excellent preparation for the introduction of Illustrator in Project Eight. There is a lot of similarity in the interface of the two and Adobe makes the applications very consistent. It is very common practice for the professional designer to treat the two as companions and to have both applications open at the same time, switching between the two as the specific task dictates.

THE PROJECTS

The projects are devised to rapidly give you confidence in the tools and processes required for real-world digital design for fashion and textiles. They reflect contemporary practice but are not intended to be prescriptive. In Photoshop and Illustrator there is normally at least one other way of achieving the same effects through a different route. That is one of the ways the applications allow you to reflect your individuality. However the process chosen in a project is often there for a specific reason so be careful about substituting a different method at first viewing.

And don't forget to practice. It may not make perfect but it does make intuitive.

Photoshop is often favored for textile design and Illustrator for fashion illustration, but such is the versatility of the programs that there are no hard and fast rules.

LEVEL ONE

This chapter gets you to grips with some of the fundamentals of effective and creative design in Photoshop, gaining a proficiency that is readily transferred to Illustrator. You will practice on-screen drawing, manipulation of preparatory drawings and creating designs completely from scratch.

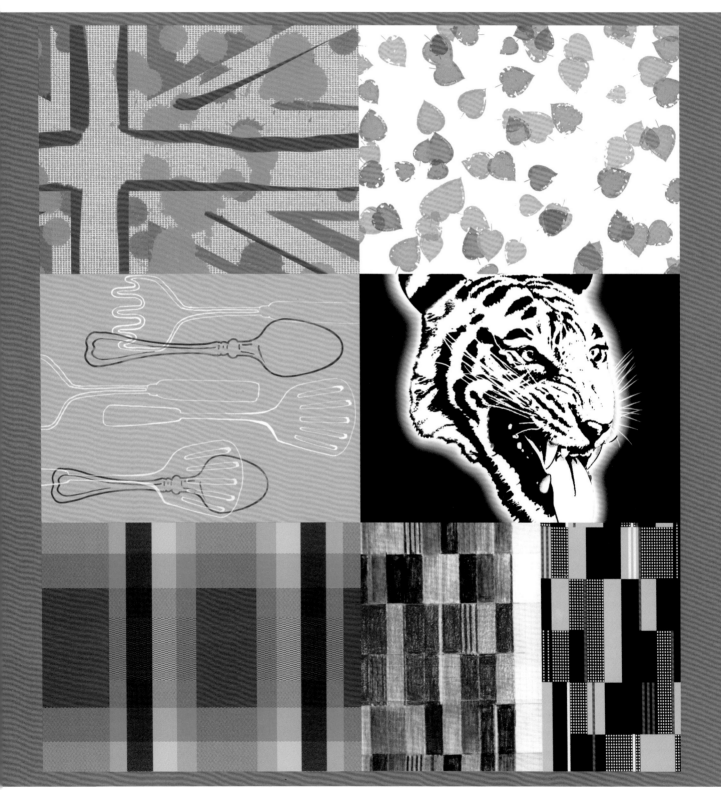

A BRIEF EXPLANATION
OF PHOTOSHOP

This section provides a brief explanation of the Photoshop layout and some specific technical terms you will encounter in this book followed by projects that introduce you to working with some of the core aspects of Photoshop.

Photoshop is an image manipulation application that has gained wide appeal in areas very different from its original purpose. Many current elements still evoke Photoshop's original purpose; for example, the Dodge and Burn tools reference manual darkroom techniques. However, Photoshop has gradually taken on the mantle, too, of a paint program and now offers such excellent drawing and painting tools that it has rendered obsolete many of the specialist paint applications that once existed. Getting bigger and better has also meant getting more complex; but, the fundamentals remain the same. The user works on a document that has at minimum one layer; this, by default, is the *background layer*. Other layers can be added in a stack and the design is seen with the various layers sitting one upon the other. The typical Photoshop collaged image is created by varying the visual interaction of these layers, with some layers at times being seen partially through others. Layers typically contain the material (or data) in an image, but they can also contain no material and instead have the special function of changing the appearance of the material in a layer that they are assigned to. The material is not actually edited; only its appearance is changed. This allows for nondestructive editing and for the possibility of always reverting to the original appearance. These adjustment layers become a sort of distorting glass through which the image is seen. They are ideal for creating colorways, as the image is preserved in its original colors with data neither changed permanently nor degraded through multiple changes.

Selections, which are made great use of in this book, are used to define for Photoshop the areas you want to manipulate. When a selection is saved it becomes stored as a grayscale image known as an alpha channel. You can edit these alpha channels like any other image using painting tools, editing tools, or filters. Areas in black are outside the selection and are protected and areas painted white are inside and editable. Some confusion may arise in the beginning because images in Photoshop already have channels and these are required to construct the image.

Color models describe the colors that we see and work with in digital images. Each color model represents a different method for describing color. An image defined by the RGB color model is composed of red, green, and blue channels while an image defined by the CYMK model is composed of cyan, yellow, magenta, and black channels. These channels are accessible through the Channels window alongside the alpha channels. If you edit an alpha channel you need to make sure afterward that the RGB or CYMK composite channel is visible and active in order to allow you to see and edit your image.

A BRIEF
EXPLANATION
OF PHOTOSHOP

PROJECT ONE—
PHOTOSHOP:
LAYERS AND
CUSTOM BRUSHES

PROJECT TWO—
PHOTOSHOP:
NEW WAYS OF
DRAWING

PROJECT THREE—
PHOTOSHOP:
SCANNING
DRAWINGS FOR
EDITING AND
RECOLORING

PROJECT FOUR—
PHOTOSHOP:
VECTOR DRAWING
AND BRUSHES
APPLIED AS
STROKES

PROJECT FIVE—
PHOTOSHOP:
STRIPES AND
WEAVES

CASE STUDY:
WALLACE SEWELL

Terms

Terms for various on-screen elements of Photoshop (and of Illustrator) do vary and Adobe itself uses varying terms for the same elements. This book tries to be consistent with the naming of elements. The bar with text commands that forms the header of the Application window is called the Menu bar. Clicking and holding on one of the menu titles produces a drop-down menu that shows commands and further submenus. The strip of tool icons that by default appears on the left-hand side of the document window is the Toolbar. As for other elements in the application interface, this book avoids calling some things palettes and other things panels or windows, as this can be confusing. For our purposes, all will be called windows because they are opened from the Window menu. Some windows float and are displayed permanently, and some windows open temporarily while you make some change. Many options are available in these windows, usually through text boxes, tick boxes, or sliders. Commands are also accessible from these windows by very small buttons at the top right that open lists of commands in a drop-down menu.

Symbols for tools are by convention called icons and little pictures of the content of a layer are called thumbnails (derived from thumbnail sketch). Two colors are always displayed in the Toolbar—the foreground color and the background color. The foreground color, shown uppermost, is the color a painting tool will apply, and the background color is the color that erasing and deleting will reveal on the background layer only. Foreground color and background color also feature in creating the color range of a graduated fill and in the colors used in some effects in the filter gallery.

Shortcuts

Where the + symbol appears in the text of this book it indicates that the key commands being described are done simultaneously. For example, "command + T" means that the command key and the T key on the keyboard are pressed down together, and the actual "plus" key itself is not involved. Photoshop and Illustrator are very consistent in feel whether on a Mac or on a PC, but there are variations in the keyboard shortcuts. For example, the command key on a Mac is the same as the control key on a PC and this key is indicated by command/control in the text. Keyboards vary around the world. The alt key can also be labeled the option key and vice versa, hence the combined name: option/alt. These are keys for shortcuts that you are going to use a lot. The most important shortcuts are the ones you can do with one hand while keeping the mouse or digital pen in the other hand and working on the image. These shortcuts cluster together conveniently at the extreme left of the keyboard.

PROJECT ONE—PHOTOSHOP: LAYERS AND CUSTOM BRUSHES

Project One immediately introduces you to working with some of the core aspects of Photoshop for professional use—selections and layers. You will quickly experience Photoshop's potential for generating variations and possible colorways.

Spreading the elements of a design across different layers is a fundamental way of working in Photoshop. Layers give great flexibility to, and control of, the specific elements of a design. By default, a Photoshop document has a background layer at the outset. The designer then creates additional layers as necessary. If you delete or erase material on the background layer you then get the background color in those areas. All other layers sit on top of the background layer. Deleting or erasing material on these layers leaves transparent space.

Altering the quality of a specific area, for example the color, requires you to define it with a selection. Photoshop then knows the area to alter. Selections are a second core aspect of Photoshop. Various tools and techniques are used for making selections to suit the situation or to suit your preference. Some selection techniques are based on criteria that you enter in the tolerances of a tool and others are more manual, and based on a path you have drawn. Further projects will familiarize you with ways of refining selections.

One of the ways Photoshop can reflect your individual creativity is through customizing. In this project you will add custom brushes, which are supplied on the supporting website, to those brushes available in Photoshop "out of the box." Many excellent brushes are supplied with Photoshop. Despite this, designers may create a whole library of their own to get just the effects they want.

A BRIEF
EXPLANATION
OF PHOTOSHOP

PROJECT ONE—
PHOTOSHOP:
LAYERS AND
CUSTOM BRUSHES

PROJECT TWO—
PHOTOSHOP:
NEW WAYS OF
DRAWING

PROJECT THREE—
PHOTOSHOP:
SCANNING
DRAWINGS FOR
EDITING AND
RECOLORING

PROJECT FOUR—
PHOTOSHOP:
VECTOR DRAWING
AND BRUSHES
APPLIED AS
STROKES

PROJECT FIVE—
PHOTOSHOP:
STRIPES AND
WEAVES

CASE STUDY:
WALLACE SEWELL

PHOTOSHOP: LAYERS AND CUSTOM BRUSHES

In this project you will:
- Generate a design in Photoshop by combining and manipulating existing artwork and drawing additional material with a custom brush.
- Practice some simple color adjustments.
- Use a selection to modify a specific area.
- Start working with layers—a key aspect of Photoshop.

Outcome
You should have created a fashion-orientated, graphic image in which colors are easily editable.

Aim
This initial project immediately introduces you to some of the core aspects of Photoshop for professional use—selections and layers. You will quickly experience Photoshop's potential for generating variations on an original image and possible colorways.

The illustrations of Photoshop in this and all other projects show the appearance of the application set to light gray. The interface color is a user preference in Creative Cloud applications. Setting it to light gray makes the tools and windows easier to see and to find in the application. Also, because many drop-down menus and dialog boxes remain light gray, regardless of the appearance color set in preferences, the light gray choice keeps the application consistent and settled in aspect. To change your version of Photoshop to match the one here you can change the interface color in preferences.

**Project files are available at
www.bloomsbury.com/hume-textile-design**

1.1

Launch Photoshop. Photoshop displays transparency, or the absence of material, as a gray checkerboard. The checkerboard can sometimes be both an advantage and a disadvantage. It can be turned off in Preferences. Preferences, as mentioned earlier, is where the default settings for Photoshop can be adjusted to how you want them. In a number of the projects, the checkerboard will interfere with evaluating the look of a design so you are going to turn it off.

1.2

Go → **Photoshop → Preferences** (or **File → Preferences** on a PC) and select Transparency and Gamut from the drop-down menu. In the Transparency Settings change Grid Size to None in the drop-down menu. Click Okay to exit.

1.3

Go → **File → Open** and then navigate to the Project One folder and open the file Union Flag.

You will see how easy it is to adjust colors in Photoshop and start getting dramatic results.

1.4

Go → **Image → Adjustments → Hue/ Saturation**. In the window that opens ensure the preview box is ticked. Move the Hue, Saturation, and Lightness sliders and note how the colors change in the document. Create a new color version using the settings in the accompanying image. **(fig. 1)**

Next you will paint in the white area of the flag that is currently empty of material. This introduces you to selections. Most Photoshop involves selections. They isolate one or more parts of the image. By selecting specific areas you can modify portions of your image while leaving the unselected areas untouched. Use the Magic Wand as your selection tool. **(fig 2)**

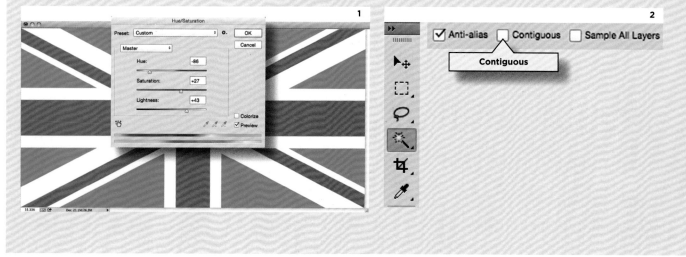

A BRIEF
EXPLANATION
OF PHOTOSHOP

**PROJECT ONE—
PHOTOSHOP:
LAYERS AND
CUSTOM BRUSHES**

PROJECT TWO—
PHOTOSHOP:
NEW WAYS OF
DRAWING

PROJECT THREE—
PHOTOSHOP:
SCANNING
DRAWINGS FOR
EDITING AND
RECOLORING

PROJECT FOUR—
PHOTOSHOP:
VECTOR DRAWING
AND BRUSHES
APPLIED AS
STROKES

PROJECT FIVE—
PHOTOSHOP:
STRIPES AND
WEAVES

CASE STUDY:
WALLACE SEWELL

1.5

Select the Magic Wand tool. In your version of Photoshop this tool may be hidden behind the Quick Selection tool. Press the tool icon down in the Toolbar to expand the tool choices. (A small triangle at the lower right of the tool icon signals the presence of hidden tools.) Select the alternative option of the Magic Wand by releasing the mouse over its icon. In the Magic Wand tool options make sure that Contiguous is off. (Contiguous confines your selection to connected areas of the same color.) With the Magic Wand tool click in the white area of the flag to select it. **(fig. 3)**

1.6

Use the Eyedropper tool to select the mauve in the image to draw with. Clicking the Eyedropper tool on a location in the document samples that color and places it in the Foreground color selection box within the Toolbox, like a pipette sucking up a sample of color. The Brush tool and the Pencil tool paint with the current foreground color. You can temporarily switch to the Eyedropper tool while using any Paint tool by holding down the **option/alt** key and selecting the color. Release the **option/alt** key and you are back with the Paint tool.

Now you will create a new layer to paint on. Working on separate layers allows you to preserve and rearrange elements of the design.

1.7

Go to Layer in the Application menu bar (**New → Layer...**) and click Okay in the dialog window that opens. If the Layer window or panel is not open go to Window in the header and select it from the drop-down menu. You should now have two layers—the original layer with the flag and above this, an empty new layer. Highlighting should indicate that the new layer—Layer 2—is the active layer. If you start painting, this, being the active layer, is where the material will go.

The Brush Presets window contains the various brush tip shapes currently available. You can modify existing brushes and create new custom brushes (which you will do in Project Two). The Brush window contains the many possible options for the current selected brush tip. Although not devised as a paint program, the flexibility of the paint tools in Photoshop makes it excellent for all sorts of expressive mark-making. As well as the additional selections supplied in the Brushes folder of the Photoshop applications many original brush presets are available for download from the internet. In the next section you will learn how to load a custom brush into the brush library of your copy of Photoshop.

1.8

If the Brush Preset window is not open go to Window in the Application menu bar and select it from the drop-down menu. (In older versions of Photoshop you should open the Brushes Panel.)

1.9

In the Brush Presets window select the drop-down menu in the extreme right-hand, top corner. Click on Load Brushes... , navigate to the Project One folder, and select the file Splat Brushes.abr, then click Open. **(fig. 4)**

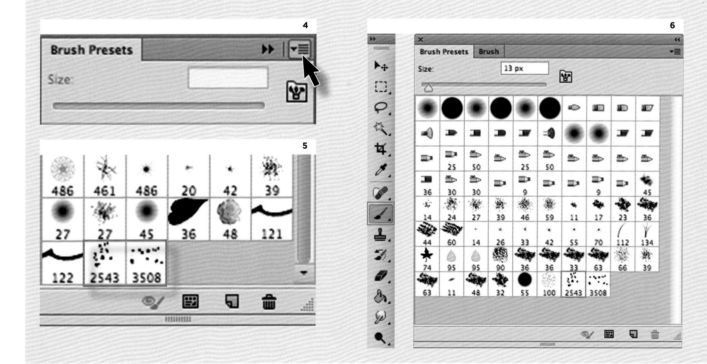

A BRIEF
EXPLANATION
OF PHOTOSHOP

**PROJECT ONE—
PHOTOSHOP:
LAYERS AND
CUSTOM BRUSHES**

PROJECT TWO—
PHOTOSHOP:
NEW WAYS OF
DRAWING

PROJECT THREE—
PHOTOSHOP:
SCANNING
DRAWINGS FOR
EDITING AND
RECOLORING

PROJECT FOUR—
PHOTOSHOP:
VECTOR DRAWING
AND BRUSHES
APPLIED AS
STROKES

PROJECT FIVE—
PHOTOSHOP:
STRIPES AND
WEAVES

CASE STUDY:
WALLACE SEWELL

1.10

If you select the Paintbrush tool the Brush Preset window becomes active and you should see your two new brushes added after the existing sample brushes. If there are a number of brushes in the Brush Preset window you may need to scroll down to the bottom of the window to see the last entries in brush tips. **(fig. 5)**

1.11

Select the Paintbrush tool and then click on the first brush you loaded to select it. **(fig. 6)**

1.12

Click on one of the brush tips to select it and draw some splatters onto Layer 2. **(fig. 7)**

TIP You now have a third layer—the linen texture—sitting above the previous two layers. Now change the weave color of the linen image to match the viridian green in the flag. It will be easier to use the Eyedropper tool to select the green color if you zoom into the image. Shortcuts are extremely useful in Photoshop, and knowing a shortcut for zooming in means you don't need to change the tool. The shortcuts done with a single hand are preferable, as the other hand can continue to hold the mouse or pen. Hold down **spacebar + command/control** and then click the mouse for zooming in and **spacebar + option/alt + command/control** and click the mouse for zooming out from the position of the cursor.

7

1.13

Now introduce a second texture. Open the Linen file in the Project One folder in Photoshop. With the Linen document active Go → **Select** → **Select All** (shortcut **command/control + A**) then go to **Edit** → **Copy** (shortcut **command/control + C**) and switch to the Union flag document. Go **Edit** → **Paste** (shortcut **command/control + V**). You can also "Place" other files directly into documents, but the copy and paste method is the simplest for this first project.

1.14

With the Eyedropper tool click on the green on the flag to make this the foreground color. The Eyedropper tool should be set to sample all layers. If it happens not to be, then change the setting under Tool options. Make the Linen layer visible again by clicking on the visibility column. **(fig.8)**

1.15

Use the Magic Wand tool to select the weave texture by clicking on one of the black squares. All black squares should then be selected. If only one square is selected it is because the Contiguous setting is ticked in the Magic Wand tool options. Click in the Contiguous options box to remove the tick and then click again on the black squares in the image. **(fig.9)**

1.16

Now use the shortcut **option/alt + delete** to fill the current selection with the foreground color. **(fig. 10)**

Reordering the layers of a design can be a very direct way of changing the composition.

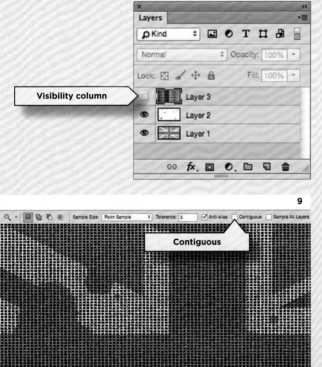

8

Visibility column

9

Contiguous

10

A BRIEF
EXPLANATION
OF PHOTOSHOP

PROJECT ONE—
PHOTOSHOP:
LAYERS AND
CUSTOM BRUSHES

PROJECT TWO—
PHOTOSHOP:
NEW WAYS OF
DRAWING

PROJECT THREE—
PHOTOSHOP:
SCANNING
DRAWINGS FOR
EDITING AND
RECOLORING

PROJECT FOUR—
PHOTOSHOP:
VECTOR DRAWING
AND BRUSHES
APPLIED AS
STROKES

PROJECT FIVE—
PHOTOSHOP:
STRIPES AND
WEAVES

CASE STUDY:
WALLACE SEWELL

1.17

Click and hold the cursor on Layer 3 in the Layers window, drag Layer 3 down, and release the mouse or pen when the layer is between Layer 2 and Layer 1. For a second variation move Layer 1 to the top of the layer stack. **(fig. 11–12)**

1.18

Save your new document; select Photoshop as the format. This format ensures all aspects of the design, such as paths, layers, and saved selections, are preserved. Other formats such as JPEG can create smaller files that are readable by everyone and that may be more convenient for sending as attachments, but the Photoshop-specific elements, such as Layers, will be discarded and only an image will be saved.

PROJECT REVIEW

REVIEW

In this project you have altered the colors of an image and combined two documents into one file to create a very different design. Using a custom brush has added more interest, as has reordering the layers. The image now could be used as a T-shirt graphic or placement print.

PRACTICE

Practice using Hue/Saturation adjustments on the individual layers. Click on an individual layer in the Layers window to transfer that to the active layer.

Use the Magic Wand tool to select different parts of the flag and then create a new layer and fill this area with a new color. Note that the selection can be made on one layer and by switching the active layer the fill can be applied to the new layer.

Paint into a selection on a new layer. See how your marks are constrained within the selection. **(fig. 13)**

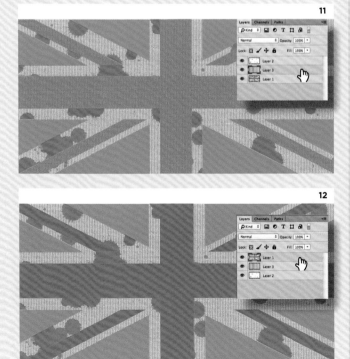

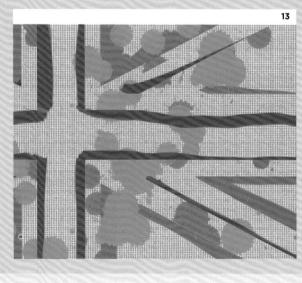

PROJECT TWO—PHOTOSHOP: NEW WAYS OF DRAWING

2

Textile and fashion design rely on drawing at many stages of the creation process.

Drawing as a discipline: analyzing and demarcating the qualities of the subject of your attention.

Drawing as imagination: giving form to your ideas and to your intuitions.

Drawing for utility: clarifying your ideas for others and creating the guidelines for the creation of something.

The varied ways of drawing have been extended by new technology, offering exciting additional possibilities. However, the ability to edit and refine your drawing continues to be essential. Using photography as the starting point for your drawing is fine as long as you are able to continue to refine and develop the result and you are not held captive by reliance on the original photographic image. Drawing from scratch yields dividends and becomes a tool that will continue to develop and inspire.

Digital drawing does not replace pencil and paper—these continue to be the direct and immediate tools they always were. Digital drawing can be combined with paper and pen at any stage of design development. Digital drawing, in particular, brings us the freedom of nondestructive work and unlabored precision. You can experiment in any direction without sacrificing the original work and you can always draw with vigorous economy. Access to color is uniquely immediate. As a new medium, digital drawing also brings its own native ways of mark-making.

The freedom in Photoshop and Illustrator is so wide that the distinction between drawing and painting and other forms of mark-making is easily blurred.

Adobe Illustrator is defined as a drawing application, using the very specific definition of drawing as formation of a line by drawing from point to point. Those point-to-point lines however can have very painterly strokes drawn along them.

The precise way of drawing in Illustrator is very useful for fashion; it enables clear and convincing descriptions of garment shapes and of details. Illustrator has become the most common tool for garment drawings or "flats." It is also the ideal tool for outline drawings of other 3D objects such as accessories and housewares. Illustrator technical drawings are commonly used as the guides for manufacturing samples. However it is often easier at the outset to become comfortable with digital drawing by starting your mark-making first in Photoshop.

In Photoshop and Illustrator there are drawing tools and, separately, there are brushes that can be selected as the brush tips for these drawing tools, for example, the Eraser tool can be given a watercolor brush tip to erase with. In this way these tools provide great choice in mark-making and the expressive options are enormous.

Drawing a line with a mouse is unlikely to be as fluid as drawing a line on paper with a pencil, but with a digital pen and tablet it can be. The tablet can respond to pressure and to the angle of the pen, or stylus, and so reflects a much more natural way of working. Digital pens and graphic tablets have the edge over standard tablets and phone apps for drawing, whether with fingers or styluses, because graphic tablets are so sensitive and responsive to the smallest movement.

Trying to reproduce exactly the way you draw and paint outside of Photoshop and Illustrator is unlikely to be a productive use of your time. It is better to capitalize on the new possibilities offered by the medium. Project Two introduces you to new ways of drawing that derive from the opportunities available in Photoshop. Drawing in Illustrator will be practiced in later projects.

Project Two explores some of the opportunities available in digital work—drawing half an element and then flipping a copy of it to create the second half, painting inside a drawn shape and turning that shape into a brush tip to paint with.

PHOTOSHOP: NEW WAYS OF DRAWING

In this project you will:

- Work fast and efficiently in Photoshop to generate material in ways that differ from the traditional.
- Create a design entirely from scratch from one element.
- Practice with layers and learn a second selection tool—Lasso.
- Use the Transform tool to flip a motif and be introduced to the Free-Transform tool and hidden variations.
- Be reminded of the importance of keyboard shortcuts for fluid working and be introduced to a new selection method—Select by Layer.
- Use selections for painting effects, create a custom brush for more personal handwriting, and look at the wide variety of possibilities using the Brush Dynamics window to alter motifs as you draw.

Outcome

You will have easily created a detailed motif. This motif can be developed into a textile pattern design.

Aim

This project immediately introduces you to some native ways of drawing in Photoshop, building confidence without the need for photographic or scanned source material to create a design from scratch. You will gain practice in the use of layers and transformation, to understand the principle of lipping a copy of half a drawing to build up a garment drawing.

Project files are available at
www.bloomsbury.com/hume-textile-design

KEY TERMS

Photoshop is predominantly used for bitmap images, and Illustrator is used for vector images, although both applications can support either format.

Bitmap images, also called **raster** images, are constructed from a rectangular grid of picture elements—pixels. Bitmap images are resolution dependent, that is, they contain a fixed number of pixels to a physical area, usually defined as pixels per inch. Enlargement of an image requires either the original pixels to be multiplied, which can result in the original pixel pattern becoming very obvious (pixelation), or additional transitional pixels to be added, which makes the image soft and blurry. So it is better to have a sufficient pixel-per-inch resolution (ppi) from the start. Specifying too high a resolution—more pixels per inch than the output device can produce—increases the file size at no benefit and can slow the printing of the artwork.

Vector images are made up of lines and curves defined by mathematical objects called vectors. Vectors describe an image through its geometric characteristics. Vector images are resolution independent, graphical elements that can be moved or scaled without any loss of sharpness because the geometric characteristics are simply recalculated.

A BRIEF
EXPLANATION
OF PHOTOSHOP

PROJECT ONE:
PHOTOSHOP –
LAYERS & CUSTOM
BRUSHES

PROJECT TWO—
PHOTOSHOP:
NEW WAYS OF
DRAWING

PROJECT THREE—
PHOTOSHOP:
SCANNING
DRAWINGS FOR
EDITING AND
RECOLORING

PROJECT FOUR—
PHOTOSHOP:
VECTOR DRAWING
AND BRUSHES
APPLIED AS
STROKES

PROJECT FIVE—
PHOTOSHOP:
STRIPES AND
WEAVES

CASE STUDY:
WALLACE SEWELL

2.1

Create a new document with dimensions of 4 inches by 4 inches (or 10 centimeters by 10 centimeters), a resolution of 200 pixels per inch, and color mode RGB.

File ➔ New ➔ name the file Leaf. Type 4 into the width and height fields and select inches in the units drop-down menu. Or, if using metric units, type 10 into the width and height fields and select centimeters from the units drop-down menu. Type 300 into the resolution field and select pixels/inch in the resolution units drop-down menu. Have RGB color in the Colour Mode drop-down menu and 8 Bit in the Bit Depth drop-down menu (the menu to the right of Color Mode). Set the Background Contents to White.

2.2

By default, the image has one layer—the background layer.

This is important: Create a new layer to draw on rather than the background layer. **(fig. 14)**

2.3

If the Layers window is not open, select it from the drop-down menu of Window in the Menu bar (across the top of the work space). Or press the **F7 key** to bring up the Layers window. Press the very small, down-facing triangle on the extreme left of the Layers window to open the drop-down menu and select **New Layer**. This new layer should be the active one—indicated by the highlighting of the layer in the Layer window.

Draw a large leaf onto this new layer, about 2.3 inches (or 6 centimeters) tall, using the Brush tool. Make sure you do not draw on the background layer because this makes it harder to select the leaf later. Use a large brush tip to draw out the basic shape and switch to a smaller tip to make the indentations in the leaf edge. You only need to draw indentations on one side of the leaf, as you will copy this first side to make the other side. **(fig. 15)**

14

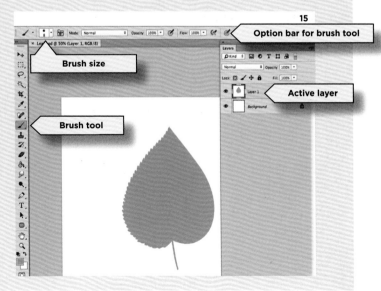

15

2.4

With the Lasso tool select the completed half of the leaf. Draw down the centerline and around the edge coming back to the start point to close the selection. **(fig. 16)**

2.5

Go **Edit → Copy → Edit → Paste**. This puts a copy of the half leaf that was selected onto a new layer, Layer 2. **(fig. 17)**

2.6

Use the Move tool to move the leaf half over to the opposite side of the original leaf's center and **Edit → Transform → Flip Horizontal** to flip the active layer's content—the leaf half—so it faces the correct way. **(fig. 18)**

A convincing leaf does not have exact bilateral symmetry. You will use **Free Transform** to create a realistic leaf.

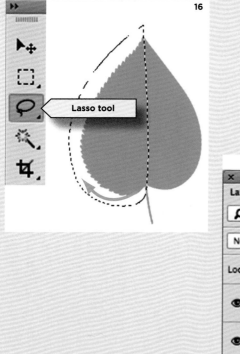

16

Lasso tool

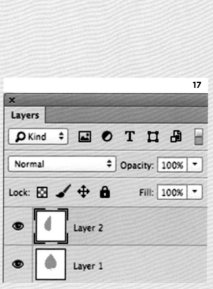

17

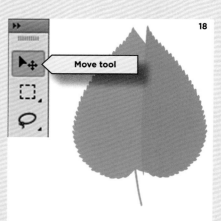

18

Move tool

A BRIEF
EXPLANATION
OF PHOTOSHOP

PROJECT ONE:
PHOTOSHOP –
LAYERS & CUSTOM
BRUSHES

**PROJECT TWO—
PHOTOSHOP:
NEW WAYS OF
DRAWING**

PROJECT THREE—
PHOTOSHOP:
SCANNING
DRAWINGS FOR
EDITING AND
RECOLORING

PROJECT FOUR—
PHOTOSHOP:
VECTOR DRAWING
AND BRUSHES
APPLIED AS
STROKES

PROJECT FIVE—
PHOTOSHOP:
STRIPES AND
WEAVES

CASE STUDY:
WALLACE SEWELL

2.7

Go → **Edit** → **Free Transform**. The control points of the bounding box that appears allow you to rotate, resize, and freely transform the selection. As you move the cursor near the point or line it will change its shape to indicate the specific means of transformation. **(fig. 19)**

TIP

Further forms of transformation are available by holding down keys while selecting a point on the transformation box. This is very typical of how Photoshop works, where many tools have further permutations that are accessible with modifier keys. If you start moving a corner point on the transformation box and then hold down the **command/control** key the individual corner can be distorted on its own.

The two halves of the leaf are still on separate layers and you want them on a single layer, so you will merge two layers. Before merging the layers, use the Eraser tool to remove any unwanted overlap between the two leaf halves.

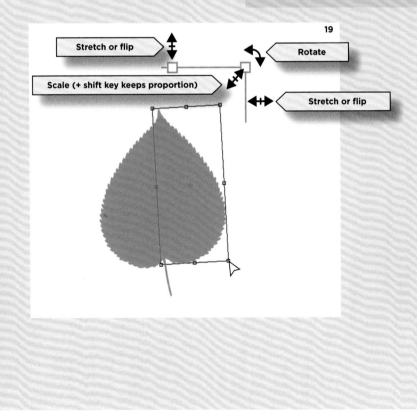

19

Stretch or flip

Rotate

Scale (+ shift key keeps proportion)

Stretch or flip

2.8

One layer will already be active. To select the second layer hold down the shift key and click to highlight in the Layer window.

2.9

Press down on the tiny triangle in the top corner of the Layer window. In the drop-down menu select **Merge Layers**. The selected layers become merged as one. You are now going to add more detail to the leaf. By using another form of selection—that of selecting everything on a layer— you can constrain your painting to be within the exact leaf shape. This is one of the reasons for not drawing on the background layer, as it is a solid layer and this selection command will be of no use.

2.10

To select everything on an individual layer, in this case, the leaf, hold down the **command/control** key and click over the layer thumbnail. **(fig. 20)**

By painting within the selection, the shape is kept crisp. Draw within the outline to create some interesting patina in the leaf.

You will now make a duplicate layer that allows you to shrink the leaf and to practice another form of copying—the form that does not create additional layers.

2.11

On the Layer window drop-down menu select **Duplicate Layer...** You will now practice spreading leaves that are rotated in various directions across the image.

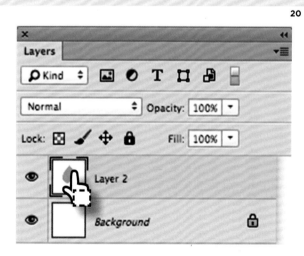

20

A BRIEF
EXPLANATION
OF PHOTOSHOP

PROJECT ONE:
PHOTOSHOP –
LAYERS & CUSTOM
BRUSHES

**PROJECT TWO—
PHOTOSHOP:
NEW WAYS OF
DRAWING**

PROJECT THREE—
PHOTOSHOP:
SCANNING
DRAWINGS FOR
EDITING AND
RECOLORING

PROJECT FOUR—
PHOTOSHOP:
VECTOR DRAWING
AND BRUSHES
APPLIED AS
STROKES

PROJECT FIVE—
PHOTOSHOP:
STRIPES AND
WEAVES

CASE STUDY:
WALLACE SEWELL

2.12

In the Layer window turn off the eye icon beside the original layer's thumbnail by clicking on it; this makes that layer invisible. Select the new duplicate layer (it should now be highlighted). Using Free Transform, shrink the leaf to 20 percent of its original size. The transformation box will automatically snap around the selection. You can drag a corner handle of the transformation box while holding down the shift key to retain the proportions while scaling and read off the changing size from the measurement boxes in the Tools Options bar below the Menu bar. Or, for a more precise and easier method, click on the link button in Tools Options bar to lock the proportions and then enter 20 percent into either the height or width box. Press **return/enter** to accept the change. **(fig. 21)**

Earlier, when you copied and pasted this resulted in the leaf-half landing on a new layer. Now you will look at a second way of copying, which, in contrast, keeps the copy on the same layer. To keep the copy on the same layer requires the original to be selected at the outset, otherwise the copies will each get their own layer. With the leaf still selected, hold down **command/ control + option/alt** and drag the leaf away with the cursor. The original is left in position and a duplicate is created. Each move will create a fresh copy. Only the leaf is copied and not the white space because the leaf exists on its own on the layer.

Use the shortcut **command/ control + T** to bring up the Free Transform box and change the direction of the leaves. Note that the latest copied leaf is the one selected. To go back and transform a leaf that was copied earlier you will need to select it with the Lasso tool. If you don't make any selection and use **command/control + option/ alt** to drag and copy then the entire contents of the layer will be copied. **(fig. 22)**

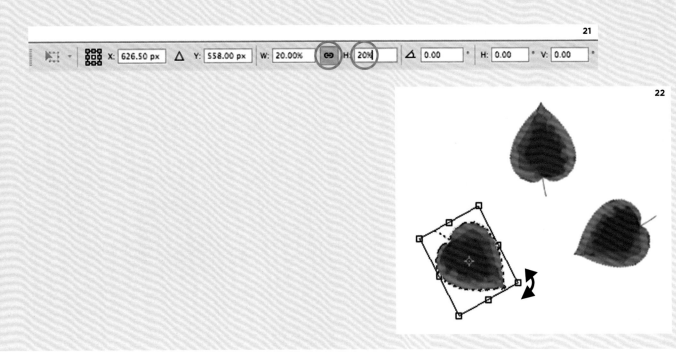

21

X: 626.50 px   Y: 558.00 px   W: 20.00%   H: 20%   0.00   H: 0.00   V: 0.00

22

2.13

When you have drawn sufficient numbers of leaves, repeat what you did before to select everything on an individual layer: press the **command/control** key and click over the layer thumbnail. Paint within this selection to create more variation in the leaves. You can hide the selection/marquee without losing it using **command/control + H**. These same keystrokes make the selection visible again. This is also available under **View → Extras**. Note that a one-time alert dialog box may appear the first time you use this shortcut, offering you the option to assign the **command/control + H** shortcut to the extras in Photoshop (the most useful option) or to assign it to the Hide Photoshop command.

Creating a Custom Brush

You can define one of the leaf shapes as a brush tip. Brushes are saved as grayscales with the black in the brush tip equivalent to 100 percent of the foreground color. For a good result with the brush, the image that is to become the brush tip needs contrast and some areas approaching black. A leaf can be selected and the contrast increased by going to **Image → Adjustments → Brightness/Contrast** and then manipulating the sliders. You may need to do this more than once to get sufficient darkness depending on your artwork. **(fig. 23)**

2.14

Select the leaf with the Lasso tool marquee. Go **→ Edit → Define Brush Preset...** The brush becomes the last in the set of brush tips. **(fig. 24)**

2.15

To get started with your custom brush there are two key settings to change.

Increasing the *Spacing* on the brush tip puts space between the leaf motifs and makes them individually visible, which is a key first step.

Shape Dynamics allows for variation in Size and Angle, which is variation in the rotation of the motifs, and Roundness, which is variation in the flatness of the motif. Adding a percentage of jitter to the Roundness setting immediately gives the leaf brush a feeling of natural variation. **(fig. 25–26)**

Note: Before painting with your new brush tip you will need to deselect (**command/control + D**) the selection around the original leaf shape. Otherwise, as you now know, you will only be able to paint inside the selection.

2.16

Create a new layer for painting with the new brush tip on and turn off the eyes on the other layers to make them invisible.

23

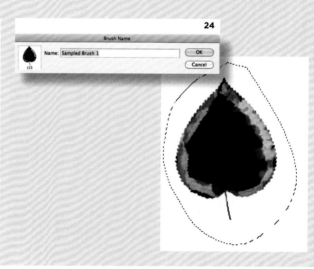

24

A BRIEF
EXPLANATION
OF PHOTOSHOP

PROJECT ONE:
PHOTOSHOP –
LAYERS & CUSTOM
BRUSHES

**PROJECT TWO—
PHOTOSHOP:
NEW WAYS OF
DRAWING**

PROJECT THREE—
PHOTOSHOP:
SCANNING
DRAWINGS FOR
EDITING AND
RECOLORING

PROJECT FOUR—
PHOTOSHOP:
VECTOR DRAWING
AND BRUSHES
APPLIED AS
STROKES

PROJECT FIVE—
PHOTOSHOP:
STRIPES AND
WEAVES

CASE STUDY:
WALLACE SEWELL

TIP There are many options available with brushes in Photoshop, accessible through the Brush window (shortcut key **F5**). Different settings in the options produce radically different and visually exciting results. Specifying an Angle Jitter rotates the leaf in different directions when drawn, Scattering moves the leaf either side of the path drawn, and Color Dynamics changes the color of successive brush strokes. If a graphic tablet and pen are attached to the computer this greatly enhances the expressive potential of the brushes, as many of the options react to pen pressure.

PROJECT REVIEW

REVIEW
You should have learned how easy it is to make changes and create variations on a motif using the powerful Free Transform tool. Following on from Project One where adding a custom brush to Photoshop was introduced, you should now see how easy it is to make your own custom brushes. You can develop these to reflect your personal visual style.

PRACTICE
Create some motifs from scratch; practice using the Free Transform tool. Reduce a motif in scale to make it suitable to be used as a brush, practice adjusting the various brush options, and explore the results. Transforming elements quickly builds up the variety in a design. In garment drawing, flipping a copy of an element such as a sleeve is frequently used to quickly build up the drawing.

PROJECT THREE—PHOTOSHOP: SCANNING DRAWINGS FOR EDITING AND RECOLORING

3

Existing artwork or inspirational material needs to be photographed or scanned to get it onto the computer. Photographed artwork, unless done in ideal circumstances, can result in vignetting, a lens defect that causes the edges, especially the corners, of an image to be darker than the central area. Scanning is a more controlled way of getting the artwork digitized. Large scanners exist for bigger pieces of work, but, as explained in this project, there is also an excellent method in Photoshop for seamless joining of scanned sections.

Resolution, as mentioned before, very much dictates the quality of the work. Best practice is gearing the scan resolution of artwork to the intended output to avoid possible problems with resizing. Scans can be converted to vector artwork in Illustrator to liberate them from resolution, but the drawing needs to be scanned at a high enough resolution in the beginning to get good results.

A BRIEF
EXPLANATION
OF PHOTOSHOP

PROJECT ONE:
PHOTOSHOP –
LAYERS & CUSTOM
BRUSHES

PROJECT TWO—
PHOTOSHOP:
NEW WAYS OF
DRAWING

**PROJECT THREE—
PHOTOSHOP:
SCANNING
DRAWINGS FOR
EDITING AND
RECOLORING**

PROJECT FOUR—
PHOTOSHOP:
VECTOR DRAWING
AND BRUSHES
APPLIED AS
STROKES

PROJECT FIVE—
PHOTOSHOP:
STRIPES AND
WEAVES

CASE STUDY:
WALLACE SEWELL

Photoshop was built as an image correction and manipulation application; therefore, it has excellent tools for adjusting scanned artwork. There are possibilities for correcting black and white and tonal balance of scans and for manipulating the contrast and tone for effect. It is very easy to introduce color to black and white sketches and to recolor all aspects of your original drawing. In fact it is common practice to draw only outline artwork and introduce the entire color in Photoshop.

In this project you will manipulate your own scanned artwork. You will see how easy it is, with some of the skills you have already learned, to take a black and white sketch and completely transform it into a multicolored design and freely explore color variations and new possibilities.

The exact procedure of scanning will not be described herein, as the commands will be specific to your scanner model. With your own scanner you may need to look for an advanced mode or to expand the settings to access the resolution settings and adjust these as necessary.

PHOTOSHOP: SCANNING DRAWINGS FOR EDITING AND RECOLORING

In this project you will:
• Return to the Magic Wand tool and explore the variations to the tool, modifiers being common to tools in Photoshop.
• Explore the use of Tolerances and the Contiguous option and their importance.
• Split artwork across layers.
• Use Hue/Saturation sliders to alter the color of elements in the artwork on their separate layers.
• Use coloration for tonal recoloring.

Outcome
This project enables you to take a black and white sketch and completely transform it into a multicolored design on a colored background.

Aim
To understand the requirements for scanning artwork and the possibilities of creating a working method of combining pencil sketching with recoloring in Photoshop.

3.1

File → Open, select your scanned document. (Your image should have been scanned at 200 ppi minimum, but ideally somewhere between 240 and 300 ppi. Resolution is the amount of image data in a given space. It is measured in pixels per inch (ppi). The more pixels per inch, the greater the resolution. Generally, the higher the resolution of your image, the better the printed image quality will be. Resolution determines the fineness of detail you can see in an image. Keep in mind the physical size of your output and make sure it will have sufficient resolution at that size. (You can scale up later, but this will likely negatively affect the appearance of your image.) If your document is not an RGB document, for example a grayscale, change it in **Image → Mode → RGB**, as it will need to be a color document.

3.2

It is usually important to adjust the Levels in a scan to have a good tonal range. Moving the Shadow, Midtone, and Highlight sliders redistributes and increases the tonal range of the image, in effect increasing the overall contrast of the image. The histogram shows the tones in the scan. By moving the Shadow slider, the black triangle, to where the mountain landscape starts means this area will start at proper black tones. Go **Image → Adjustments → Levels** to open the Levels adjustment window. **(fig. 27)**

3.3

In the example shown, and probably in your drawing, there are more very light tones in the paper area than are useful and these tones reduce the contrast between the drawn lines and the paper. The Highlight or White Point slider, the white triangle, can be used to trim the number of light tones in the image by converting many of these tones to white or close to white. Experiment with moving the slider, in stages, from the right toward the middle of the histogram to adjust your image. You will find that a scanner records an image with varying difference to the one that you see. Scanning technology looks for differences of tone and emphasizes these differences to produce detail, whereas you will tend to ignore visual information that doesn't interest you and expect detail in the visual information that does.

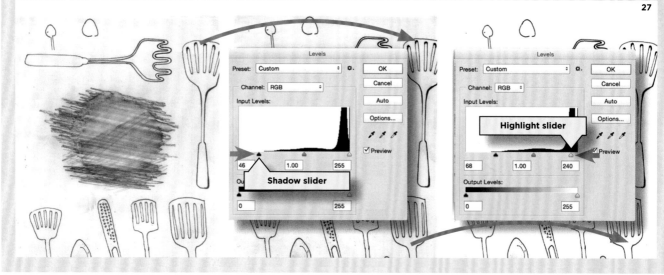

27

A BRIEF
EXPLANATION
OF PHOTOSHOP

PROJECT ONE:
PHOTOSHOP -
LAYERS & CUSTOM
BRUSHES

PROJECT TWO—
PHOTOSHOP:
NEW WAYS OF
DRAWING

**PROJECT THREE—
PHOTOSHOP:
SCANNING
DRAWINGS FOR
EDITING AND
RECOLORING**

PROJECT FOUR—
PHOTOSHOP:
VECTOR DRAWING
AND BRUSHES
APPLIED AS
STROKES

PROJECT FIVE—
PHOTOSHOP:
STRIPES AND
WEAVES

CASE STUDY:
WALLACE SEWELL

3.4

One method for extracting the drawing from the ground is to make a selection with the Magic Wand tool. The Magic Wand is in the Toolbar, sharing the position of the Quick Selection tool. The Magic Wand tool lets you select a consistently colored area (or tones in a monochrome image) without having to trace its outline. You specify the selected color range, or tolerance, relative to the original color you clicked on with the pointer. The higher the number, the wider the spread of colors or tones included will be. The Contiguous tick box constrains the selection to include only additional colors that are directly in contact with the original selection. Without Contiguous ticked all pixels of the same color in the entire image are selected. **(fig. 28)**

3.5

With the Magic Wand tool click on an area of your drawing that tonally represents the majority of the drawing. If all of your drawing becomes selected (indicated by the flashing dotted line) and no paper is included, you have successfully selected all you need, so **Edit → Copy, Edit → Paste**. If only part of your drawing is included in your selection, use the shortcut **command/control + D** to deselect, increase the tolerances in the Magic Wand tool, and click in the same area again. Make sure where you click is representative of the majority of the drawing. If paper is included in the selection then deselect and reduce the tolerance a little. The exact figures will depend on your particular drawing. **Edit → Copy, Edit → Paste** places the selected material

on a new layer, Layer 1. This layer sits above he original image, which is labeled Background. Layers are a fundamental part of the Photoshop method of working, which allows manipulation of elements on different layers and control of the ways that layers interact. **Edit → Copy, Edit → Paste** generates a new layer for each element you paste—not always what you want, so at times you need to use the **Drag Selection → Copy** method shown in Project Two. Click on the eye icon of Background layer to make it invisible. You will then see the copied material on Layer 1 on its own. Turn off transparency grid in the preferences if it is on.

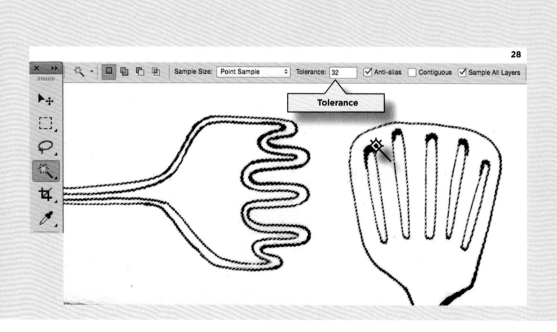

28

Tolerance

3.6

Go to Layer in the Application menu bar, select **New → Layer** from the drop down menu and click Okay in the dialog window that opens to create a new empty layer above the existing layers.

There is now a stack of three layers. Go to the Foreground and Background color boxes in the toolbox. The current foreground color appears in the upper color selection box in the toolbox; the current background color appears in the lower box. Photoshop uses the foreground color to paint, fill, and stroke selections and the background color to make gradient fills and fill in the erased areas of an image on the background layer.

3.7

Click on the foreground color box to launch the color picker window. Using the circle cursor select a dark gray (or any other color if you want to). Click Okay to accept the choice. You can also use the color slider to select colors, or enter values in the various color definition boxes. **(fig. 29)**

3.8

Go **Edit → Fill** and make sure Foreground color is the selected color in the dialog box. Click Okay. Because this extra dialog box always opens, even with the shortcut for **Edit → Fill**, a very useful alternative shortcut to learn for simply filling with the foreground color is **option/ alt + delete**. Then the layer or selection is filled instantly with the foreground color.

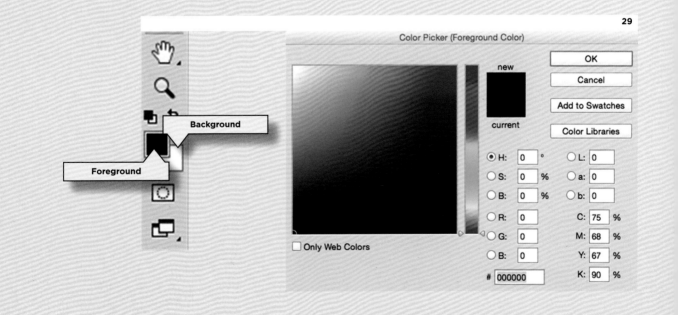

29

Background

Foreground

Color Picker (Foreground Color)

new

current

OK

Cancel

Add to Swatches

Color Libraries

☐ Only Web Colors

⦿ H: 0 °
○ S: 0 %
○ B: 0 %
○ R: 0
○ G: 0
○ B: 0
000000

○ L: 0
○ a: 0
○ b: 0
C: 75 %
M: 68 %
Y: 67 %
K: 90 %

A BRIEF EXPLANATION OF PHOTOSHOP

PROJECT ONE: PHOTOSHOP – LAYERS & CUSTOM BRUSHES

PROJECT TWO— PHOTOSHOP: NEW WAYS OF DRAWING

PROJECT THREE— PHOTOSHOP: SCANNING DRAWINGS FOR EDITING AND RECOLORING

PROJECT FOUR— PHOTOSHOP: VECTOR DRAWING AND BRUSHES APPLIED AS STROKES

PROJECT FIVE— PHOTOSHOP: STRIPES AND WEAVES

CASE STUDY: WALLACE SEWELL

3.9

Reordering layers in Photoshop is very useful. Move Layer 1 up to the top of the stack above Layer 2, the layer now filled with gray. Put the pointer in the space to the right of the layer name, and holding the mouse/pen down, push upward. A hand indicates that you are ready to move a layer. When Layer 1 is at the top of the layer stack, your drawing appears. **(fig. 30)**

3.10

Make sure Layer 1 is the active layer— indicated by highlighting (by default in blue). Go → **Image** → **Adjustments** → **Hue/Saturation**. Move the Hue, Saturation, and Lightness sliders to see all the colors or tones of black and gray in your drawing change. Move the lightness away from black first otherwise all colors will be too dark to register the change. All adjustment windows are also accessible through the Adjustment panel, a separate window in itself. **(fig. 31)**

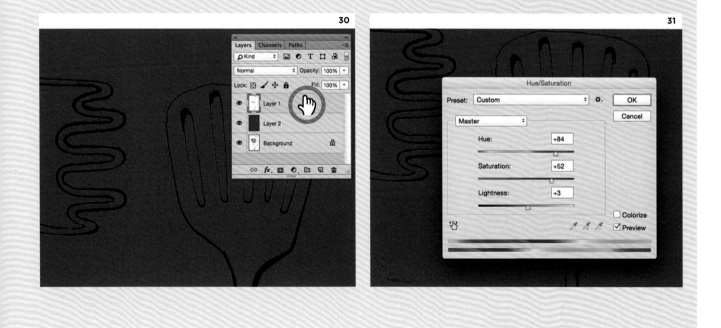

3.11

If you select elements of your drawing and copy and paste them automatically onto new layers you can then explore the Layer Blend options in the Layers window. This is a very popular way of creating the complex collage effects associated with Photoshop. A layer's blending mode determines how the pixels in that layer blend with underlying pixels in other layers of the image. You can create a variety of effects using blending modes. The colors in the layer you are adjusting interact with those of the layers below. The manner of interaction is governed by your selection of the particular mode and the additional control available on that mode. So, experiment with your artwork. **(fig. 32)**

Large Artwork and Combining Scans, an Excellent Method

It is unlikely that you would have access to a flatbed scanner larger than A3 so with larger artwork you will on occasion have to scan it in sections and then combine the separate scan files into one document. When you discover what an excellent job Photoshop does of the process of joining the separate scans you are likely to stop doing it manually.

Photomerge is one of the Automate processes in the File menu drop-down. Photomerge is a tool for creating panoramic spreads from a number of separate photos. It is also a perfect tool for combining separate sections of a large piece of artwork.

If you select the Collage option Photoshop will do all the hard work of comparing the shared areas of the artwork and rotating any sections as needed to align them perfectly. Photoshop does like a lot of shared information between the individual scans to aid it in its analysis, so you should scan in more overlap than you would need for a manual assembly. Photoshop then more easily sees how the pieces should all come together. It creates a new document with the various pieces assigned to layers and with masks to aid in the collaging. After Photoshop has done its work and everything looks okay you can collapse the layers of the document into a single layer by selecting Flatten Image in the Layer window options.

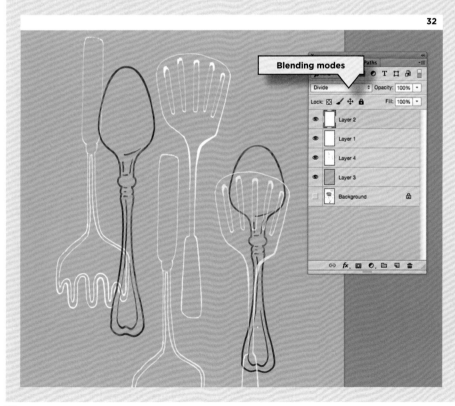

32

PROJECT REVIEW

REVIEW
You have looked at best practice regarding scanning and at the hidden tool in Photoshop for combining artwork scanned in sections with super precision. With scanning and manipulation in Photoshop you should now be able to retain the qualities you want in your paper drawing but be able to freely recolor and edit in Photoshop.

PRACTICE
Experiment with the Levels tool to adjust the look of your drawing, and experiment with dramatic changes. Reverse all darks to light and lights to dark in your drawing either using Levels or with color changes. Start transforming your objective drawing into a textile design.

When you discover what an excellent job Photoshop does of the process of joining separate scans you are likely to stop doing it manually.

PROJECT FOUR—PHOTOSHOP: VECTOR DRAWING AND BRUSHES APPLIED AS STROKES

Paths are vector outlines drawn with the Pen tool in Photoshop. Paths can be used to make selections or you can fill the path with color or stroke the path itself with a brush tip. Paths are a very particular way of drawing involving anchor points and control arms to define and edit the shape of the path. Paths offer the precision and economy of vector work allowing you to draw elements such as perfectly smooth curves in a way not easily done otherwise. This style of drawing involving points and control arms, where the appearance of a path, its stroke, is inherently a separate element, is very much the way of working in Illustrator and so Paths in Photoshop offers good preparation. The skills you learn with the Pen tool and Paths can be applied in exactly the same way in Illustrator. Outlines drawn with the Pen tool in Illustrator are the most common way of creating technical flats for fashion. Paths offer precision, and once you learn how the system works, great freedom in editing what you draw.

As Paths are common to Illustrator and Photoshop, you can freely copy and paste them between applications. A path drawn in Photoshop can be used to clip a photograph or an image imported into the other application.

A BRIEF
EXPLANATION
OF PHOTOSHOP

PROJECT ONE:
PHOTOSHOP -
LAYERS & CUSTOM
BRUSHES

PROJECT TWO—
PHOTOSHOP:
NEW WAYS OF
DRAWING

PROJECT THREE—
PHOTOSHOP:
SCANNING
DRAWINGS FOR
EDITING AND
RECOLORING

PROJECT FOUR—
PHOTOSHOP:
VECTOR DRAWING
AND BRUSHES
APPLIED AS
STROKES

PROJECT FIVE—
PHOTOSHOP:
STRIPES AND
WEAVES

CASE STUDY:
WALLACE SEWELL

The path is made up of one or more straight or curved segments. Anchor points that "work like pins holding a wire in place" mark the beginning and end of each segment. Control arms extend out from an anchor point and you change the shape of a path as it approaches and leaves the anchor point by dragging and changing the direction of its control arms or you can drag the path segment itself. It is better to draw a path with as few points as needed to define the shape as this makes any editing easier. Less is definitely more. It is also easier to draw the path as close to what you want in one continuous flow and then go back and adjust or remove superfluous points. This ensures the path is continuous and not broken into smaller sections.

Modifier keys really come into their own with the Path tool—switching it temporarily to the various options and enabling you to efficiently edit your path. Paths are always editable but you should save your Work Path as it is only temporary and will be replaced by the next Work Path that you draw. Paths add nothing to the file size and, as they are vector, if you have to resize the file they will produce perfect results at the new size.

Paths allow you to draw in a way that is very hard to do freehand, and if you don't use a digital pen then without them drawing smooth curves will be almost impossible. You can draw precise technical fashion flats with Paths but you will probably want to migrate your facility to Illustrator because there are greater possibilities in that application.

PHOTOSHOP: VECTOR DRAWING AND BRUSHES APPLIED AS STROKES

In this project you will:
- Use paths as a vector way of drawing in Photoshop.
- Draw a path with the Pen tool, manipulating the path with the vector Selection tool and Direct Selection tool, This is preparation for the same tools in Illustrator.
- Apply varying brushes to the same paths, and examine other vector tools in Photoshop.

Outcome
You should have created a fashion-orientated, graphic image with sophisticated painting techniques.

Aim
This project introduces you to another core aspect of Photoshop for professional use—Paths—a new style of drawing and selecting that is essential to professional design work.

Project files are available at
www.bloomsbury.com/hume-textile-design

4.1

From the Project Four Resources folder open the file named Tiger in Photoshop. You will find the graphic has two layers, one for the tiger head and a second reserved for the whiskers. The reason for this will become clear later. Turn the eye off on the whisker layer to make it invisible.

4.2

In this project the tiger is to appear on a black ground with an airbrushed halo around it. You will draw a path around the tiger and then apply the airbrush as a brush tip to that path. Ensure that the Paths window is displayed and if it is docked with the Layers window drag that off so that both are visible simultaneously. Click on the Pen tool. Ensure that the Pen tool mode is Path. **(fig. 33)**

4.3

Zoom in on the tiger by at least 200 percent to the area below its left ear, as that is the starting point for your path. By using the shortcut **spacebar + command/control** there is no need to change tools. Click the Pen tool just beside the tiger's fur to establish the first anchor point and with short clicks draw a continuous path of short segments alongside the fur following its general shape. Do not drag as you click, as this will create curved segments, which you don't want yet. **(fig. 34)**

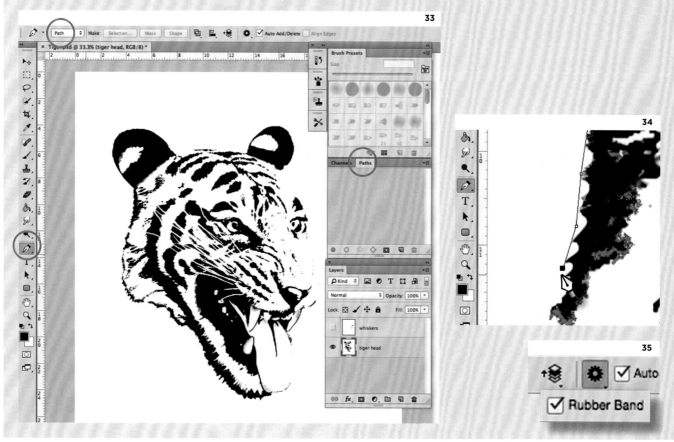

A BRIEF
EXPLANATION
OF PHOTOSHOP

PROJECT ONE:
PHOTOSHOP -
LAYERS & CUSTOM
BRUSHES

PROJECT TWO—
PHOTOSHOP:
NEW WAYS OF
DRAWING

PROJECT THREE—
PHOTOSHOP:
SCANNING
DRAWINGS FOR
EDITING AND
RECOLORING

PROJECT FOUR—
PHOTOSHOP:
VECTOR DRAWING
AND BRUSHES
APPLIED AS
STROKES

PROJECT FIVE—
PHOTOSHOP:
STRIPES AND
WEAVES

CASE STUDY:
WALLACE SEWELL

Note that successive segments will not be visible until you click the next anchor point. You can select the Rubber Band option in the tool options to preview the path segments. **(fig. 35)**

If the control arms appear because you accidentally dragged the Pen tool then click **command/control + z** to undo and carry on. If you want to alter the position of a point you can hold down the **command/control** key and temporarily change the tool to the Direct Selection tool. With this you can move the individual point. Release the **command/control** key to revert to the path tool. Stop when you reach the tiger's tongue. **(fig. 36)**

TIP | **IDENTIFYING THE COMPONENTS OF A PATH**

Paths are defined by anchor points and the connecting segments between them. The path segments can be straight or curved, and the anchor points have control arms that allow the curves to be adjusted at any time. Using the Paths in Photoshop is very good preparation for Illustrator, as the system is identical. In Illustrator you have the same two selection tool pointers: the Selection tool, for easy selection of whole objects, and the Direct Selection tool, for selection of elements of an object such as individual points or individual connecting paths. Again, the same shortcuts with selections apply in Illustrator; the **shift** key allows you to select multiple instances of whatever you want. **(fig. 37)**

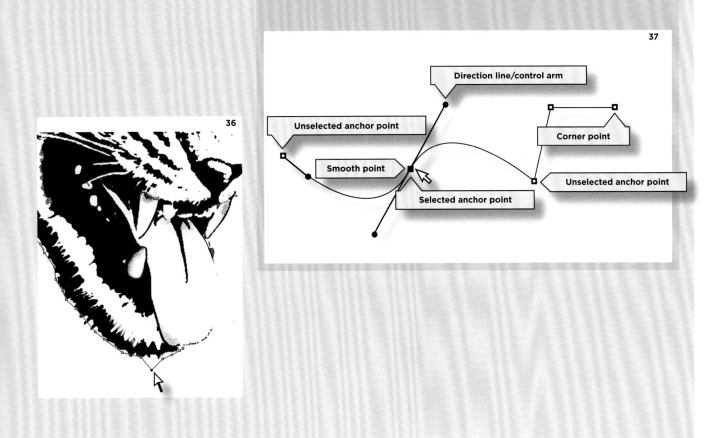

36

37

Direction line/control arm

Unselected anchor point

Smooth point

Corner point

Unselected anchor point

Selected anchor point

4.4

Now that you have reached the tiger's tongue you are ready to draw a curved path segment. This will give a clear definition to the curve of the tongue. Click the Pen tool where the right canine tooth touches the tongue and do not release the mouse (or digital pen). An anchor point appears and the Pen tool pointer changes to an arrowhead. Drag this toward the tiger's left eye and you will see a curve developing. Steer the pointer on the end of the control arm to create a curve that matches the tongue profile. Stop when it does so. **(fig. 38)**

4.5

Abrupt changes in path direction require adjustment of the curves with the Direct Selection tool. The more you practice using the Path tool, the easier it will become to understand which parts of the curve or control arms to alter. Your next click should be at the root of the canine. The curve will now change to reflect the abrupt change in direction, but you can correct this by holding down the **command/control** key and temporarily changing to the Direct Selection tool. Drag the individual control arms and the new curve running along the canine to get a good match to the profile of the tiger. It may help to understand that one control arm marks the tangent to the curve entering the point and one marks the tangent to the curve leaving the point. In addition, their length determines the height or depth of the curve. It may appear complex but practice will help you get a feel for how the system works. **(fig. 39)**

38

39

A BRIEF
EXPLANATION
OF PHOTOSHOP

PROJECT ONE:
PHOTOSHOP -
LAYERS & CUSTOM
BRUSHES

PROJECT TWO—
PHOTOSHOP:
NEW WAYS OF
DRAWING

PROJECT THREE—
PHOTOSHOP:
SCANNING
DRAWINGS FOR
EDITING AND
RECOLORING

PROJECT FOUR—
PHOTOSHOP:
VECTOR DRAWING
AND BRUSHES
APPLIED AS
STROKES

PROJECT FIVE—
PHOTOSHOP:
STRIPES AND
WEAVES

CASE STUDY:
WALLACE SEWELL

4.6

After adjusting the curve along the tongue and canine, release the **command/control key** to revert to the Pen tool. Click once by the right eye and drag the cursor to create a curve to match the cheek. The best curves are drawn with the fewest points. There should be some more adjustment of the curve as you draw around the eye and then it should be possible to draw around the head and ears with straight and curved segments with only small adjustments. When you approach your first anchor point a small circle appears next to the Pen tool pointer when it is sufficiently close. Click to close the path and click and drag if you need the final segment to be curved. **(fig. 40)**

The completed path could now be used to generate a selection, but in this project you will stroke a brush tip around the path.

4.7

In the Path window select **Save Path...** from the drop-down menu. Name it Tiger.

TIP

There is a Freeform version of the Pen tool, which is more like conventional drawing. Anchor points are added automatically as you draw and you do not determine where they are positioned. It is less precise than the standard Pen tool and you do not get the advantage of the smooth, simple curves. There is a magnetic option to aid with tracing, but with an image like the one here the tool has problems without a clear and continuous contrast. In practice it is often better to create paths entirely manually.

40

4.8

Create a new layer and move this to below the tiger head layer in the stacking order of the Layer window. Fill this new layer with black. If the Foreground color is black you can use the shortcut **option/alt + delete** to fill the layer.

4.9

Open the Brush Preset window. In the Brush Preset window, using the Options drop-down menu add Round Brushes with Size set to your current brushes. **(fig. 41)**

4.10

Now paint around the tiger head by stroking a brush tip along the path. You will paint with white so click the D key to switch the foreground and background colors to the default, black and white, and then click the X key to swap them around so that white is now the foreground color.

A BRIEF
EXPLANATION
OF PHOTOSHOP

PROJECT ONE:
PHOTOSHOP -
LAYERS & CUSTOM
BRUSHES

PROJECT TWO—
PHOTOSHOP:
NEW WAYS OF
DRAWING

PROJECT THREE—
PHOTOSHOP:
SCANNING
DRAWINGS FOR
EDITING AND
RECOLORING

**PROJECT FOUR—
PHOTOSHOP:
VECTOR DRAWING
AND BRUSHES
APPLIED AS
STROKES**

PROJECT FIVE—
PHOTOSHOP:
STRIPES AND
WEAVES

CASE STUDY:
WALLACE SEWELL

4.11

Make sure that the new Layer 1 is the active layer, because that is where you want the stroked line to go—behind the tiger's head. Select the Paintbrush tool, select the Airbrush Soft Round 200 tip, and adjust the Flow to 50 percent in the Tool options. **(fig. 42)**

4.12

You will now have Photoshop automatically draw the brush tip around the path you created. Click on the very small Stroke Path with Brush button at the bottom of the Path window. You can alternately select **Stroke Path...** from the Path window drop-down menu, but that requires you to select a specific brush, whereas the button uses the currently selected tool. When you click on the Stroke Path with Brush button you will see that an airbrush line is drawn around the tiger's head. **(fig. 43)**

Now select the Airbrush Soft Round 65, two brushes further along from the Soft Round 200 tip. Click again on the Stroke Path with Brush button to paint this brush tip along the same path. Paths are reusable, so a smaller brush can be drawn over a larger one with perfect alignment using the same path.

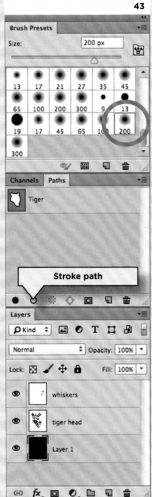

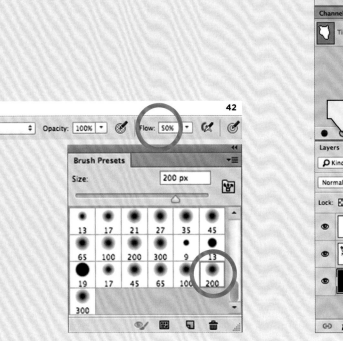

4.13

Click in the empty space below the tiger path in the Path window to make the path inactive and invisible so you can see your artwork clearly. It is good practice to turn off Paths when you are not using them. In the hierarchy of Photoshop, paths come first. So, for example, where you have an area selected and click Delete nothing will appear to happen to the area because you deleted your active path instead with the delete action. **(fig. 44)**

It would not be possible, even with a digital pen, to draw around the tiger's head and create such an even halo. Paths are ideal for this kind of controlled line. Another very important use for Paths is cutting images out from backgrounds and defining areas for pattern fills and masks. You will see some of these techniques in later projects.

4.14

What about the whiskers on the Whisker layer? Make the Whiskers layer visible. In the original black they look a bit odd now against the airbrush halo. Use the shortcut **command/control + thumbnail** to select everything on the Whisker layer. Then use the shortcut **option/ alt + delete** to fill the selection with white (as long as the foreground color is still white). This is a possible remedy. Note that these whiskers were drawn originally with the Pen tool and Paths to get the good curves. Having parts of a design on separate layers gives you opportunities for fine-tuning the image. You can better integrate the whiskers with the overall look of the graphic by using a Layer Blend Mode. **(fig. 45)**

44

Channels | Paths
Tiger

45

Layers | Channels
Kind
Normal   Opacity: 100%
Lock: Fill: 100%

Layer thumbnail → whiskers
tiger head
Layer 1

A BRIEF
EXPLANATION
OF PHOTOSHOP

PROJECT ONE:
PHOTOSHOP -
LAYERS & CUSTOM
BRUSHES

PROJECT TWO—
PHOTOSHOP:
NEW WAYS OF
DRAWING

PROJECT THREE—
PHOTOSHOP:
SCANNING
DRAWINGS FOR
EDITING AND
RECOLORING

**PROJECT FOUR—
PHOTOSHOP:
VECTOR DRAWING
AND BRUSHES
APPLIED AS
STROKES**

PROJECT FIVE—
PHOTOSHOP:
STRIPES AND
WEAVES

CASE STUDY:
WALLACE SEWELL

4.15

From the Layer Blend Mode drop-down menu, which you explored in Project Three, select Soft Light as the mode. The whiskers now fade out beyond the halo in a satisfactory way. A professional tip: With layer blend modes, by duplicating the layer exactly, a slightly stronger effect can be built up. So drag the Whisker layer thumbnail in the Layers panel onto the Create a New Layer button, the Whisker layer bounces back and a copy is created, or use the shortcut **command/control + J**. (fig. 46)

46

New layer

PROJECT REVIEW

REVIEW

Drawing with the Pen tool and Paths may be uncomfortable initially, but it does enable you to work in Photoshop in a way that is not possible otherwise. In Photoshop, paths are required for professionally clipping images with irregular edges. Making smooth curved selections requires paths. Drawing with paths is also an introduction to vector drawing, which is the whole basis of work in Illustrator, the most popular choice for fashion sketching. You have learned to draw and manipulate a path and to apply a brush stroke to that path. You have seen how blending mode can enable subtle adjustments of a graphic image.

PRACTICE

Draw some paths with the Pen tool around elements in an image and apply different brush strokes to that path. Explore using some of the other tools such as Smudge and Doge and Burn. Explore the Freeform variant of the Pen tool and the Magnetic option.

PROJECT FIVE—PHOTOSHOP: STRIPES AND WEAVES

5

Weaving is even further away from either Photoshop or Illustrator's target use than print and garment design so it is understandable that there are no specific weave tools. Specialist weave plug-ins are available to add to Photoshop and Illustrator and of course there are professional entirely weave-focused applications. Be aware though that even these specialist tools vary widely in how professional they actually are. In reality some are not very practical for textile design. However you will be pleased to know that serious weave design is possible in Photoshop and Illustrator as they stand. Their sophistication and flexibility allows for this. Many professional designers (see the Wallace Sewell case study) use the applications at various stages of the design process. They rough-out initial color concepts, create accurate pick and ends simulations, and produce design files ready for conversion to loom driver files.

Although it is difficult to simulate the qualities of a particular yarn in a weave in Photoshop or Illustrator the possibilities offered for rapid color and scale experimentation are very attractive. It is easy to create ideas for stripes, checks, and weaves and simulate their color mixes with Layer Blend Mode settings. Blend Modes, described in Project Three, are available in Illustrator as well as Photoshop, but with slightly fewer options.

A BRIEF
EXPLANATION
OF PHOTOSHOP

PROJECT ONE:
PHOTOSHOP –
LAYERS & CUSTOM
BRUSHES

PROJECT TWO—
PHOTOSHOP:
NEW WAYS OF
DRAWING

PROJECT THREE—
PHOTOSHOP:
SCANNING
DRAWINGS FOR
EDITING AND
RECOLORING

PROJECT FOUR—
PHOTOSHOP:
VECTOR DRAWING
AND BRUSHES
APPLIED AS
STROKES

PROJECT FIVE—
PHOTOSHOP:
STRIPES AND
WEAVES

CASE STUDY:
WALLACE SEWELL

Blend Modes give an impression of how a weave might work, but simple layers and masks make much more accurate work possible. In Photoshop the thread structure can be drawn and then defined as a pattern. A pattern fill can then be used to generate a selection. A mask built on this selection can define the warp on one layer and the weft on another. Changing color combinations or changing the scale of the weave structure automatically shows how these look in the weave pattern.

Further refinement to the realism of the woven cloth simulation can be developed by adjusting the pixel aspect ratio. The pixel aspect ratio can be made equivalent to the picks and ends in the weave. In Photoshop, by default, the pixels in the document view are square with height and width equal. In Photoshop, to simulate different video display ratios, it is possible to display the pixels as rectangles with varying ratios between height and width. If you are designing for a weave with 42 ends and 52 picks you can divide the picks per inch by ends per inch giving a result of 1.23. That will be your new pixel aspect ratio in Photoshop. Pixel aspect ratio can be customized in the View drop-down menu. Pixel aspect ratio is a display mode for the document only and it enables any weave design you have created to be displayed at a new picks and ends ratio by translating this to a pixel ratio.

The pixel-based nature of Photoshop offers a natural correlation to the picks and ends in cloth. However, one of Photoshop's disadvantages is that it does not allow for drawing live in repeat. This update may come in future versions, but for bitmap images juggling all that information in multiple repeats is very demanding on the computer. Illustrator, however, offers the possibility of working live in repeat now (due to the different nature of vector images) and this makes for much faster appraisal of your design in repeat. (See the explanation given with Project Eleven.)

PHOTOSHOP: STRIPES AND WEAVES

In this project you will:
- Use paths as a vector way of drawing in Photoshop.
- Draw a path with the Pen tool, manipulating the path with the vector Selection tool and Direct Selection tool, This is preparation for the same tools in Illustrator.
- Apply varying brushes to the same paths, and examine other vector tools in Photoshop.

Outcome
You should have created a fashion-orientated, graphic image with sophisticated painting techniques.

Aim
This project introduces you to another core aspect of Photoshop for professional use—Paths—a new style of drawing and selecting that is essential to professional design work.

5.1

For your first weave pattern make a new file in Photoshop with dimensions of 4 pixels wide by 4 pixels high at 200 ppi. Have the color mode as RGB and change the Background Contents to Transparent. (You do not want a background color to be included in your pattern.) These dimensions will produce a very small document so you will have to zoom in a lot to be able to see it adequately.

5.2

Select the Pencil tool. It is in the same tool-set as Paint Brush, so hold the pointer on the tool icon to open the drop-down menu to reveal the other tool options and release the pointer on Pencil to select it. Change the brush to a square brush with a tip size of one pixel width. Square brushes can be loaded from the Brush Tip window drop-down menu. Select Append to add the brushes to the existing selection. Ensure that the foreground color is set to black. **(fig. 47)**

5.3

Go **View → Show → Pixel Grid**. This pixel grid helps show the edges of the individual pixels.

5.4

Follow the plan for a twill illustrated, and draw four black pixels in a diagonal line. The pixels will fit together correctly because the document is only 4 pixels by 4 pixels. **(fig. 48–49)**

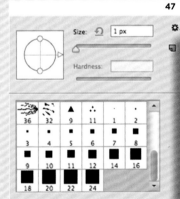

47

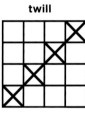

48

twill

⊠ Lifted warp thread over weft thread

☐ Lifted weft thread over warp thread

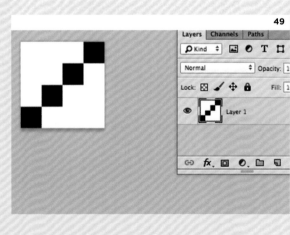

49

A BRIEF
EXPLANATION
OF PHOTOSHOP

PROJECT ONE:
PHOTOSHOP -
LAYERS & CUSTOM
BRUSHES

PROJECT TWO—
PHOTOSHOP:
NEW WAYS OF
DRAWING

PROJECT THREE—
PHOTOSHOP:
SCANNING
DRAWINGS FOR
EDITING AND
RECOLORING

PROJECT FOUR—
PHOTOSHOP:
VECTOR DRAWING
AND BRUSHES
APPLIED AS
STROKES

PROJECT FIVE—
PHOTOSHOP:
STRIPES AND
WEAVES

CASE STUDY:
WALLACE SEWELL

5.5

Go → **Edit** → **Define Pattern**. You can call the pattern Twill for reference.

5.6

Create a second document with the dimensions 8 pixels wide by 2 pixels high, Again, make it 200 ppi and with a transparent background. On this document draw pixels in black to match the weft rib layout shown. Go → **Edit** → **Define Pattern**. You can call the pattern Weft Rib for reference. **(fig. 50)**

5.7

Now having prepared your weave structures you will create your design document. Create a new document 4 inches by 4 inches and 200 ppi, with background content transparent. Click Okay to open the document. Imagine that you are designing for a weave that does not have equal picks and ends; use 42 ends and 52 picks taken from the example used in the introduction. Dividing the picks per inch by ends per inch gives a result of 1.23.

5.8

Go → **View** → **Pixel Aspect Ratio** → **Custom Pixel Aspect Ratio...** Give the custom ratio the title 42 Ends 52 picks and enter 1.23 as the Factor. You will see the document proportions change. Note this is only the display and the document itself has not been resized. You can turn the pixel aspect ratio correction off at any time by releasing the cursor on Pixel Aspect Ratio Correction in the View drop-down menu.

5.9

Go → **Edit** → **Fill...** Select the Contents as Pattern from the first drop-down menu and then select your twill custom pattern from the second drop-down menu. Make sure Blending Mode is normal and all other options are unticked. Click Okay. Layer 1 (there is no background layer) is then filled with the twill pattern. This layer will be the template for the masks for the weave layers. You may have to zoom in to see that the pattern fill has been applied.

5.10

Create a new layer, shortcut **shift + command/control + N**. Use the shortcut introduced in Project Two, Stage 10, to select all of the weave pattern, that is, hold down the **command/control key** and click over the Layer 1 thumbnail in the Layers window. This action selects all the material on a layer (the black pixels of the repeating twill only, as you made sure the pattern did not include any background white). **(fig. 51)**

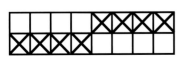

weft rib

50

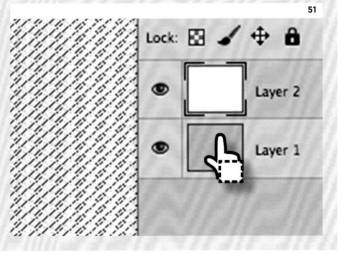

51

Lock:

Layer 2

Layer 1

5.11

Although you made a selection from Layer 1, Layer 2 should still be the active layer (the one you have just created). If not, make Layer 2 the active layer by clicking on the layer in the Layers panel. Selections can be taken from any layer and applied to the active layer. Now click on the very small Add Layer Mask button at the bottom of the Layers panel. This converts the current selection to a mask. Although Photoshop uses the term mask, remember that whatever is in the selection becomes visible and what is outside then becomes invisible, so, in reality, the selection becomes more of a window than a mask. But mask is the term both in Photoshop and Illustrator. **(fig. 52)**

5.12

Create a further new layer, Layer 3. Use the shortcut as you did in Stage 11 to select the entire weave pattern on Layer 1. This time select the inverse of the selection using the shortcut **shift + command/control + I**. The black pixels in the weave pattern represent the warp so everything that was not the black pixels in the weave structure represents the weft. This selection, being the inverse, is all that was not the black pixels and therefore can be your weft.

5.13

Make sure Layer 3 is the active layer. Click on the Make Mask button to apply a mask to Layer 3. Ensure that the active part of the layer is actually the image rather than the mask; this is indicated by the layer thumbnail, rather than the mask thumbnail, having its four corners framed. If the image thumbnail, which is always the one nearest the eye icon, does not have the corner framing, click on the thumbnail to make it the active part. **(fig. 53)**

When you start working on another layer, check that the image is the active part of the layer.

5.14

Select a color of your choosing for the foreground color. Use the Rectangle tool to start laying out your check. Draw vertical stripes on Layer 2 and horizontal stripes on Layer 3 to conform to the warp and weft structure. The Rectangle tool can draw vector shapes as well as pixel images, so make sure that Pixels is selected in the Tool options for the Rectangle tool. **(fig. 54)**

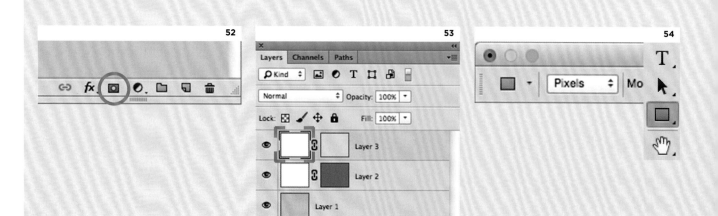

52

53

54

A BRIEF
EXPLANATION
OF PHOTOSHOP

PROJECT ONE:
PHOTOSHOP –
LAYERS & CUSTOM
BRUSHES

PROJECT TWO—
PHOTOSHOP:
NEW WAYS OF
DRAWING

PROJECT THREE—
PHOTOSHOP:
SCANNING
DRAWINGS FOR
EDITING AND
RECOLORING

PROJECT FOUR—
PHOTOSHOP:
VECTOR DRAWING
AND BRUSHES
APPLIED AS
STROKES

PROJECT FIVE—
PHOTOSHOP:
STRIPES AND
WEAVES

CASE STUDY:
WALLACE SEWELL

5.15

The masking on the layers simulates the weave structure. The rectangles appear quite different, although in the same color, depending on whether they are on Layer 2 or Layer 3.

If you have Layer 1 visible then reduce the opacity to 30 percent. It will then help indicate the weave structure in areas you have not added color to. **(fig. 55)**

5.16

To alter a color in your check you can use the Magic Wand tool. In the tool settings, make sure you have Contiguous ticked and Sample All Layers unticked in the Tool options. The Magic Wand tool selects pixels with a similar color within the tolerance range set by you. With Contiguous ticked there has to be an unbroken connection between the color clicked-on and the colors in the range then selected. When the Contiguous option is unticked, pixels of a similar color are then selected throughout the entire image. Note that in the image shown the single vertical red stripe is selected but the horizontal stripe it crosses is not selected. With Contiguous the other vertical red stripes are not included because they don't touch on their shared layer; the horizontal is not included because, although it touches, it is on a different layer. Note you only have to click the Magic Wand in the area of the stripe, as clicking in a masked area of the stripe will still allow the whole thing to be selected. **(fig. 56)**

TIP

To flip parts of a check, for example, to make a tartan plaid, do not use Copy and Paste on your selection, as this will produce a new layer for the pasted material. Use the technique that you learned in Project 2, Stage 12—**command/ control + option/alt** and drag your selection. All the copied material will stay on the same layer. Use **Edit → Transform** and either Flip Horizontal or Flip Vertical to create mirror images of your stripe.

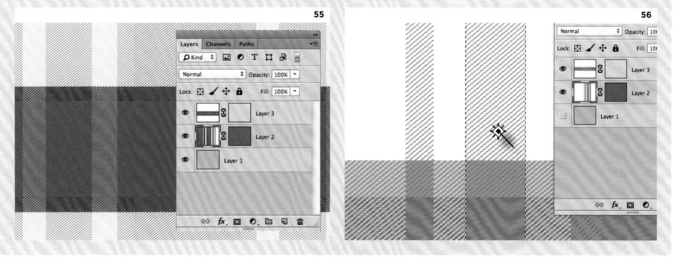

55

56

5.17

Use **Image Adjustment → Hue Saturation** to adjust the colors in the stripe. You could also use the shortcut **option/alt + delete** to fill the selection with the current foreground color. **(fig. 57)**

5.18

To change the weave structure first create a new layer and then fill this layer with your second pattern—the weft rib. Delete the existing masks controlling the appearance of your stripes. Press **control** (on a Mac) or **right click** (on a PC), click on the mask thumbnail, and select Delete from the menu. **(fig. 58)**

5.19

Make a selection from the rib pattern fill layer and, as you did in Stages 11 to 13, apply this as a mask to one stripe layer and its inverse selection as a mask to the other stripe layer. You will now see the existing stripes appear different with the alternate weave structure. **(fig. 59)**

You can experiment with different weave structures in the same design. If you select an area of the mask and delete the current fill you can then fill that area with a different weave structure pattern fill and the image will reflect the change. Remember to replace the other layer's mask with an inverted copy of this new mask, otherwise the warp and weft structure will not match. **(fig. 60)**

57

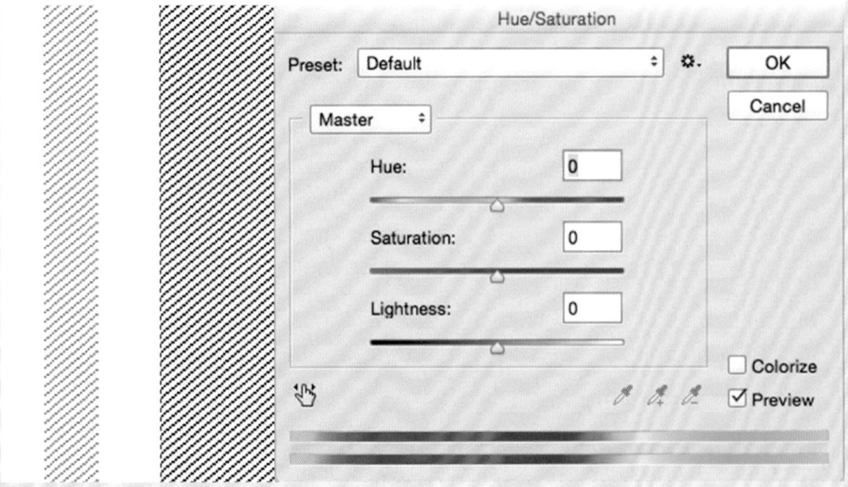

58

Notice that this weave, in reality, is only made up of green, red, and black (confirmed by the layer thumbnails), and the brown is created by the visual mix of the interweaving of the light green and red.

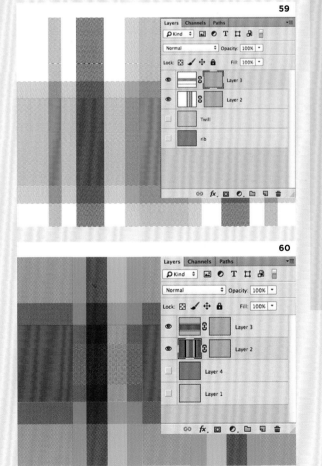

PROJECT REVIEW

REVIEW
From the exercise you should see that it is easy to make stripes and checks in Photoshop. Using layers makes these stripes and checks easy to alter. Accuracy in the woven effect can be created using pattern fills for the weave structure. The use of selections to create masks and simulate weave structure indicates again how important they are in Photoshop.

PRACTICE
Create some more weave structures and apply these as masks to some further designs. Explore the effect of changing the scale of the colored stripes in your weave design. Explore the effect of changing the scale of the weave structure in the stripes in your weave design. Create and save a number of versions as color variations. If you are confident in your weaving you might explore the Filters Gallery and apply various filters to your weave designs to give possible ideas of "fancy yarn" effects and post-weaving treatments.

CASE STUDY: WALLACE SEWELL

Wallace Sewell, the textile design studio of the designers Harriet Wallace-Jones and Emma Sewell, has long been distinguished by its woven fashion and home textiles. The studio collaborates on substantial projects with the likes of London Transport, the Tate galleries, Anthropologie, and Designtex.

In their studio, Photoshop and Illustrator are combined with pencil work and hand weaving at various stages of a design project. As Emma says, "I use CAD as another tool in the arsenal."

Photoshop and Illustrator enable the studio to explore permutations of existing weaves, reworking and recoloring elements and spinning out new designs. Compositional ideas for new designs can be developed, and mock-ups can be created in advance of actual weaving.

61

| A BRIEF EXPLANATION OF PHOTOSHOP | PROJECT ONE: PHOTOSHOP - LAYERS & CUSTOM BRUSHES | PROJECT TWO— PHOTOSHOP: NEW WAYS OF DRAWING | PROJECT THREE— PHOTOSHOP: SCANNING DRAWINGS FOR EDITING AND RECOLORING | PROJECT FOUR— PHOTOSHOP: VECTOR DRAWING AND BRUSHES APPLIED AS STROKES | PROJECT FIVE— PHOTOSHOP: STRIPES AND WEAVES | CASE STUDY: WALLACE SEWELL |

Emma Sewell:

"In a recent project for a new client, in the early stages we didn't want to invest in doing any physical sampling. It was in one of the throw qualities so I just took a picture of a tiny bit and then copied that up in order to have a big page of it in Photoshop. Then I took sections and just pushed colors around and reversed the color in order to suggest ideas for a design, and then wove up actual swatches to judge. From these I then created some artwork to indicate how the throw might look like as a final design. I then wove sections of it to show how the colors would look in reality, because I was working in Photoshop and not in an actual woven CAD program. I used it in very early stages because it was quicker to get initial ideas to show the client and to get them on board."

Wallace Sewell have worked on a number of projects for London Transport, one of the most extensive public transportation systems in the world, designing fabrics for the seating on the Underground, Overground, and Tram systems. Building on their previous success in working for the Overground and Tram networks, they competed to design fabric for the Tube network itself. They responded to the challenge of the project brief to create a design that could work across the entire Tube network. The studio's design development was a combination of paper work translated into Illustrator and Photoshop and of work done directly in the applications themselves.

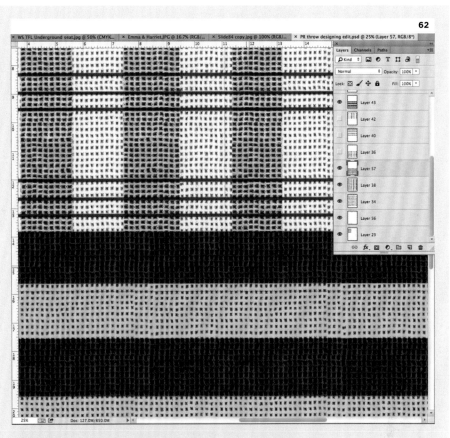

62

63

61–63
Design development for Peter Reed. Note the extensive use of layers in the development of design permutations.

Emma Sewell explains more about the project for the London Underground (known in the UK as "the Tube"):

"As we had produced designs for the Overground and Tram briefs we knew the parameters. Having worked in this area already we knew things that could succeed and what to try.

The design has to be quite a small, busy repeat. The repeat is so very tiny that it is seen as an overall effect. Something like this goes back to when I was first interested in textile design and the demands of very tight, small scale designing with very few colors. I remember when I was a teenager and the dreadful dress fabrics available. They were just not strong designs and I thought why couldn't someone create something in a small repeat with four colors that was an exciting design? Doing these projects was really interesting because they were different from what we do normally in a way because the parameters are very tight but they went back to the roots of why I became interested in textile design.

With some of them we did multiple versions. What is then fun with the program is the fact that when it is set up you can quickly change the colors around . . . for some of the later projects we have done . . . I have got it set up so that it is very easy to do colorways and try this and try that and then add this stripe and take that block out and do this and do that and, as you say, create lots of multiples, which would take days to do if you actually painted them out.

64

65

66

67

64–67
Design work in Illustrator developing a weave pattern with shapes derived from historic landmarks of London and the finished fabric in place.

**CASE STUDY:
WALLACE SEWELL**

For the design based on circles and lines, (now known as Barman after the commissioner of the first moquettes for the Underground) I sketched it out roughly, or rather elements of it, and I then started laying it over in Illustrator and built up the design that way. With other pieces, Harriet developed the initial design then I translated it into CAD artwork, and from that point we did a lot of playing around and experimenting in the application with different color balances and with some of the motifs.

There is one project we've done where it was very much balancing the colors for different lighting. We've done loads of variants, which we printed out and did do a lot of looking at them in situ under different lighting situations and got the moquettes, the actual fabric swatches, made up as well. Even if paper is different to fabric it was the balance of looking at how much red there was or how much gray and if you switched them over what was the effect, and that was very useful."

68

68
Initial design in color pencil alongside a translation into solid block colors in Illustrator as part of the development process. Wallace Sewell has an integrated use of Photoshop and Illustrator in their design process, using it where appropriate for idea development and simulation, and always with an eye on the fabric qualities of the final result.

"I remember the dreadful dress fabrics available when I was a teenager. They were just not strong designs and I thought: why can't someone create something in a small repeat with four colours to produce an exciting design?"

LEVEL TWO

2

This section begins with more advanced projects for Photoshop, building on your growing familiarity with the application. Later, projects for Illustrator are introduced, and the concluding project demonstrates both applications used in concert.

PROJECT SIX—PHOTOSHOP: REPEATS AND COLORWAYS

6

1

Repeats are intrinsic to manufactured textiles. In mass production, they are a practical necessity that has been resolved in many creative ways.

When the intended length of a patterned material is larger than a single instance of the design then the design is required to repeat. For the repeating design to be successful it must connect with itself in a visually pleasing manner. It should be possible to cut the material at any point and find an attractive balance of elements. Repeats are necessary to the manufacturing process but they are much more than a production demand and should not be thought of as a burden imposed on the design after creation but instead as an enrichment and blossoming of the design where it moves from a drawing or painting to something that gains power from the flow of repetition, from the recurrence of elements in rhythmic arrangements. Repetition is an expressive tool that has been developed to high artistic levels in textiles and across many art forms.

If you are working closely with a manufacturer you may be required to create your repeat precisely as a factor of their screen or loom dimensions. More commonly, you may only be required to indicate roughly how you expect your design to repeat, with no reference to specific sizes. Doing your own repeat work allows you to gauge how the design will appear when seen multiple times.

**PROJECT SIX—
PHOTOSHOP:
REPEATS AND
COLORWAYS**

PROJECT SEVEN —
COLOR THEORY
IN PRACTICE

PROJECT EIGHT—
PHOTOSHOP:
FILLS, TEXTURES,
AND LAYERS

PROJECT NINE—
ILLUSTRATOR:
PATHS TO FASHION

PROJECT TEN—
SIMPLE GEOMETRY
IN ILLUSTRATOR

PROJECT ELEVEN—
REPEAT PATTERNS
IN ILLUSTRATOR

CASE STUDY:
NADINE BUCHER

PROJECT TWELVE—
ILLUSTRATOR:
PHOTOSHOP AND
FILTERS

CASE STUDY:
TORD BOONTJE

2

3

Too small a repeat with too little variety in the elements and without the desirable flowing connection between repeats can result in the stiff look of a sheet of postage stamps. The computer allows work to be seen repeated many times and that should aid the designer in creating work that is less awkward and better suited for being repeated. Repeat work is definitely a design skill in itself and practice and analysis will enhance your abilities. Examining both successful and awkward repeating work will help to give you pointers. Each design is its own particular problem, or rather opportunity, but there are constants: the need to be aware of the evenness of space around elements in the design and the need to avoid design lines where too many elements line up conspicuously in a vertical, horizontal, or diagonal line. These faults catch the viewer's attention and make the design static. With repeat functions incorporated into many applications you could leave the repeat solution to an automated process, but you would no longer be a thinking designer if you did not look critically at the result.

Designs are repeated in diamond, hexagon, and rectangle structures, sometimes called tiles or nets in textiles. Other interesting forms of repeating—regular and irregular tessellations, explored particularly by mathematicians—exist but are not commonly used in textiles. In the past when wooden blocks were used for printing much ingenuity was applied to creating flowing designs of great variety within the limitations imposed by the size of a handheld block. A block would be designed so as to be able to match up with the previous impression when moved across the fabric normally and when rotated 180 degrees. Today there is less variety in repeating schemes, and designs are predominantly repeated through a step translation, which is side-by-side repeating, or by half-drop, which is where the repeat moves simultaneously sideways and down by half the height of the design. A good way to add more interest to your design is by repeating the elements in rotated and mirror arrangements within the repeat unit. This counters against too abrupt a repeat, where the identical elements occur again within a short distance resulting in unintended striping in the pattern.

Repeats can be both explicit and hidden. In an explicit repeat the repetition of the elements creates an exciting rhythm with a carefully arranged balance of elements. A tartan weave is a good example of a few elements put into a dynamic arrangement. In a hidden repeat the repetition is not so apparent and the elements appear to occur with a natural variety. A military foliage camouflage is an example of a hidden repeat. William Morris was a master of both forms and his work for textiles and wall coverings offers strong examples of dynamic repeat work.

PROJECT SIX—PHOTOSHOP: REPEATS AND COLORWAYS

PROJECT SEVEN — COLOR THEORY IN PRACTICE

PROJECT EIGHT— PHOTOSHOP: FILLS, TEXTURES, AND LAYERS

PROJECT NINE— ILLUSTRATOR: PATHS TO FASHION

PROJECT TEN— SIMPLE GEOMETRY IN ILLUSTRATOR

PROJECT ELEVEN— REPEAT PATTERNS IN ILLUSTRATOR

CASE STUDY: NADINE BUCHER

PROJECT TWELVE— ILLUSTRATOR: PHOTOSHOP AND FILTERS

CASE STUDY: TORD BOONTJE

PHOTOSHOP: REPEATS AND COLORWAYS

In this project you will:
- Create and refine a repeat.
- Balance the elements of a design to fit a suitable repeat size.
- Learn how to deal with elements that cross the repeat box.
- Use precise transformation to guarantee that the design matches up perfectly in repeat.
- Use an offset filter to evaluate spacing and balance and then define the design as a repeat unit.
- Color reduce the resulting repeat design using the index color method; be able to create colorways with specific colors matched, if need be, to color references; and be able to reorder the color table to your preferred sequence of colors.

Outcome

You should understand that repeat work is a combination of using Photoshop's powerful tools and your judgment in creating an interesting development of the design in repeat. You should be able to quickly reduce the colors in a design and create colorways.

Aim

Show that the tools introduced previously—selection, drag to copy, and transformation—enable sophisticated editing and refining of your work. Be free to create a successful arrangement for your designs in repeat whether or not elements cross the edges of the repeat box. You should not be limited by automatic repeat tools.

Project files are available at www.bloomsbury.com/hume-textile-design

6.1

Either open the document named Millefiori or create your own new document. If creating your own RGB color mode document, give the document the same dimensions as the Millefiori file—11.8 inches by 11.8 inches (30 centimeters by 30 centimeters) and 300 ppi. Create some spaced motifs in your design.

The repeat for the Millefiori design is going to be a square of 8.6 inches by 8.6 inches (22 centimeters by 22 centimeters). You will adjust the elements of the design to fit this size.

6.2

Click on the Rectangular Marquee (Selection) tool, select Fixed Size as the style to mark out a rectangle that will be 8.6 inches by 8.6 inches (22 centimeters by 22 centimeters). Enter these figures in the width and height boxes for the tool options. If you have units displayed in the units selection box other than those you are using, for example px for pixel, you can still enter 8.6 inches or 22 centimeters straight into the width and height boxes and Photoshop will accept it. Click the pointer on the document and the selection box will appear. Position the selection box, by keeping the pointer inside the box itself, so that as much of the design as possible falls within the box. **(fig. 4)**

6.3

Select **Views → Show → Smart Guides** to aid with lining up the guides in the next stage. Press **command/control + R** to display the rulers. Click in the relevant ruler and drag to pull out a horizontal or vertical guide. By holding down the **option/alt key** you can swap the orientation of the guide on the fly. Pull out guides from the rulers to line up with each side of the rectangle. Deselect the selection when the guides are in place. **(fig. 5)**

To see how the design looks in repeat make copies to surround the original. You will then be able to judge how the spacing looks and can adjust and add additional motifs as necessary.

TIP If you need to reposition a guide, use the Move tool, the topmost tool in the Toolbar, to pick up a guide and reposition it. You can use the shortcut of clicking the **V** key to switch to this tool. It has *context-sensitive* functionality and will change between the options of a Move tool, Cut and Move tool, or Move Guides tool dependent on whether it is positioned outside a selection, inside a selection, or close alongside a guide.

4

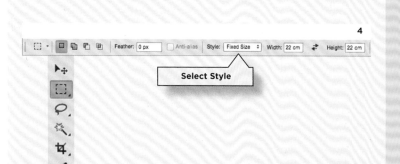

Select Style

**PROJECT SIX—
PHOTOSHOP:
REPEATS AND
COLORWAYS**

PROJECT SEVEN —
COLOR THEORY
IN PRACTICE

PROJECT EIGHT—
PHOTOSHOP:
FILLS, TEXTURES,
AND LAYERS

PROJECT NINE—
ILLUSTRATOR:
PATHS TO FASHION

PROJECT TEN—
SIMPLE GEOMETRY
IN ILLUSTRATOR

PROJECT ELEVEN—
REPEAT PATTERNS
IN ILLUSTRATOR

CASE STUDY:
NADINE BUCHER

PROJECT TWELVE—
ILLUSTRATOR:
PHOTOSHOP AND
FILTERS

CASE STUDY:
TORD BOONTJE

6.4

Make a duplicate of Layer 1 (the layer with the motifs in your design). Use the shortcut to create your duplicate by dragging the layer thumbnail over the Create Layer button at the bottom of the Layer window or, ensuring the layer is highlighted, use the shortcut of clicking **command/control + J**.

Because the design is exactly 8.6 inches (22 centimeters) square you can use the Free Transform tool to move a copy exactly 8.6 inches (22 centimeters) either vertically or horizontally as necessary.

6.5

Use **command/control + T** to bring up the Free Transform tool. Without making a selection everything on a layer will be selected, in this case all the motifs on the layer. In the options for the Free Transform tool, click on the little triangle button. This is the Use Relative Position for Reference Point option and that means the selection will move from its current position the distance you specify in the x and y boxes. Enter 8.6 inches (22 centimeters) in the x box and the design moves exactly that distance horizontally to the right (a negative value will move the selection to the left). Click **enter/return** or tick in the tool options header to accept the move. **(fig. 6)**

6.6

Make a second copy of the original layer (Layer 1 in the Millefiori design) and repeat the transform process, this time putting 8.6 inches (22 centimeters) in the *y* box and zero in the *x* box in order to move the copy down the document. Make sure you always make your copies from the original Layer 1. Make a copy for each side of the repeat. With the copies you can check that any motif that spreads outside the repeat square on one side reappears (in the copy) on the other.

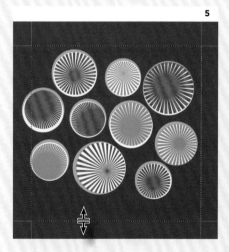

5

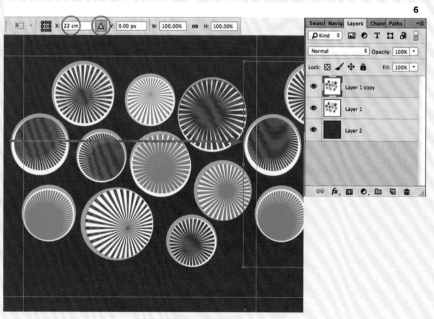

6

6.7

Make two further copies and move these by −8.6 inches (−22 centimeters), one copy in the direction of the x-axis and one in that of the y-axis.

Now you can judge how the repeat looks at this stage. **(fig. 7)**

6.8

Rearrange the motifs within the original repeat square as necessary for a spacing you think works well and make copies of the existing motifs to fill any extra space. Concentrate on adding motifs where needed to one horizontal side and one vertical side only of the original repeat. Later you will copy these motifs to the opposite sides to complete the repeat. Select a motif; use the move copy combination of the **option/alt and command/control** keys to create a copy as you move it. Use Free Transform to rotate the motifs for more variety. **(fig. 8)**

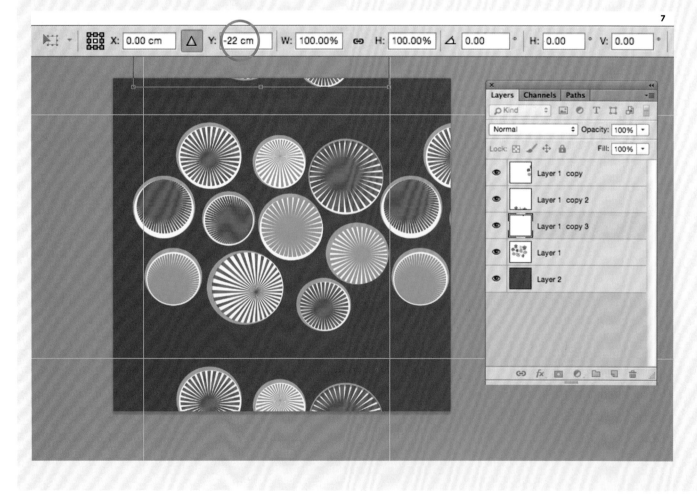

PROJECT SIX—
PHOTOSHOP:
REPEATS AND
COLORWAYS

PROJECT SEVEN —
COLOR THEORY
IN PRACTICE

PROJECT EIGHT—
PHOTOSHOP:
FILLS, TEXTURES,
AND LAYERS

PROJECT NINE—
ILLUSTRATOR:
PATHS TO FASHION

PROJECT TEN—
SIMPLE GEOMETRY
IN ILLUSTRATOR

PROJECT ELEVEN—
REPEAT PATTERNS
IN ILLUSTRATOR

CASE STUDY:
NADINE BUCHER

PROJECT TWELVE—
ILLUSTRATOR:
PHOTOSHOP AND
FILTERS

CASE STUDY:
TORD BOONTJE

6.9

After you have completed your arrangement of motifs the next stage is ensuring that you make copies of any new motifs that sit outside the repeat square. If you took the simplest option of deliberately keeping motifs away from the repeat square's edges then this awkward spacing will stand out in the final repeat and will compromise the design as a continuous allover repeat.

If you have not done any repeat work before then the need to account for the elements that cross the repeat square boundary may not be initially obvious. If part of an element leaves the square on the right it has to be carried over to the opposite side and come in from the left. The same is true for the top and bottom. This method of moving copies guarantees that everything will match up.

8
Concentrate on adding any new motifs only to these two sides of the repeat box.

8

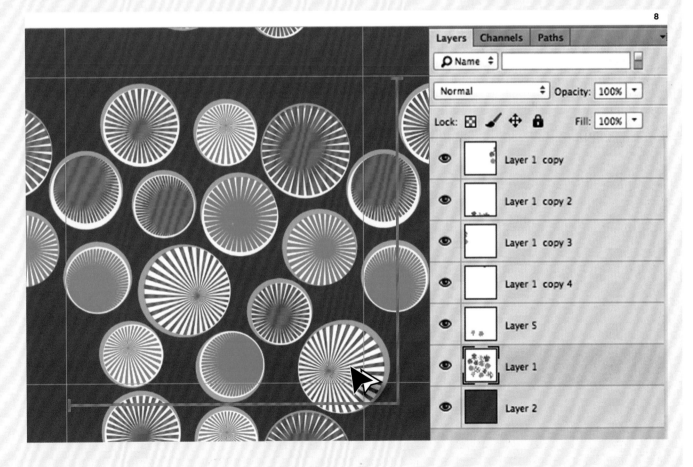

6.10

To move a copy of a motif you could use the **command/control + option/ alt + shift** combination of keys combined with the cursor to drag the copy horizontally or vertically while reading the distance from the Info window or from the little pixel position guide. However, an easier and more exact method is to select the motif, go **Edit → Copy, Edit → Paste Special → Paste in Place**. This ensures the copy is in the exact same position on a new layer. Then use Free Transform to move this copy exactly 8.6 inches (22 centimeters). Remember, use negative values to move to the left or upward. By moving any copy 8.6 inches (22 centimeters) around a repeat square of 8.6 inches (22 centimeters) everything is guaranteed to match up when the design is cropped.

Note that a motif may have to appear four times, as in the example here, if it crosses more than one guideline. **(fig. 9)**

Once your motif is on its own layer you can duplicate the layer and use Free Transform without needing to make a selection. You may end up with quite a few layers but that is fine and you will merge them together shortly. **(fig. 10)**

6.11

When you have made the necessary copies of the motifs select the fixed size rectangular marquee tool again. Bring it close to the guides and it will align itself. Go **Image → Crop** to crop the design to exactly 8.6 inches by 8.6 inches (22 centimeters by 22 centimeters).

6.12

Highlight all the layers except the background layer, the original Layer 2 in the Millefiori design. Merge all these layers (do not include the background layer, Layer 1) so that all the motifs sit on the same layer. This is important if you are going to use the Offset filter.

The Offset filter enables you to seamlessly rearrange the design within the square. If you apply this filter a few times and you see anything you think needs adjusting to improve the spacing you can select the motifs and move them easily, as they are not fixed to the background.

9

The shaded parts need to reoccur inside the repeat on the opposite sides to where they exit the repeat box. This keeps all elements complete.

9

Motif required to be copied 3 times

PROJECT SIX—
PHOTOSHOP:
REPEATS AND
COLORWAYS

PROJECT SEVEN —
COLOR THEORY
IN PRACTICE

PROJECT EIGHT—
PHOTOSHOP:
FILLS, TEXTURES,
AND LAYERS

PROJECT NINE—
ILLUSTRATOR:
PATHS TO FASHION

PROJECT TEN—
SIMPLE GEOMETRY
IN ILLUSTRATOR

PROJECT ELEVEN—
REPEAT PATTERNS
IN ILLUSTRATOR

CASE STUDY:
NADINE BUCHER

PROJECT TWELVE—
ILLUSTRATOR:
PHOTOSHOP AND
FILTERS

CASE STUDY:
TORD BOONTJE

6.13

Go **Filter → Other → Offset**. In the Offset Filter window enter a suitable offset in both the vertical and horizontal input boxes (make sure both Preview and Wrap Around are on) to see the design shift around within the repeat square. If you find you have only a partial element then there was not an equivalent copy on the other side of the box. You can easily remedy this by noting which motif was incomplete and then going back to a previous history state in the History window or using the step backward undo of **command/control + option/alt + Z** to go back to before you cropped the design. Make the correction and then crop again.

6.14

When you're satisfied, save the whole design as a pattern fill. **Edit → Define Pattern…** to save the design as a pattern fill. Create a new larger document, at least A3 size. With that the active document, go **Edit → Fill**. In the Fill dialog window that opens select Pattern for the contents of the fill. In the Pattern Options section click on the Pattern Picker drop-down menu and find your pattern in the list. It should be the last tile in the list. Select your pattern then go back in the Fill main window to exit the Pattern Picker window. Make sure Blending Mode is normal and all other options are unticked. Click Okay to apply the fill. The pattern will run seamlessly across the document.

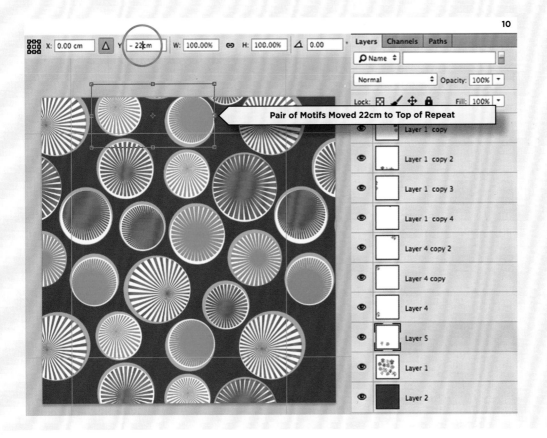

10

Pair of Motifs Moved 22cm to Top of Repeat

COLORWAYS

An easy method to create colorways for the design is to convert the color mode of the design to indexed colors and create new color tables. Indexed Color mode produces 8-bit image files with only 256 colors or less. When converting to indexed color, Photoshop builds a color lookup table (CLUT) that stores and indexes the colors in the image. It is an ideal method for converting a design to have exact color library colors such as those in a PANTONE® range.

1. Go **Image → Mode → Indexed Color...** (If your image is not RGB mode to begin with, for example it is CMYK, you will first have to convert it to RGB.)

In the Indexed Color window there are a number of settings that determine the way the image is converted into Indexed Color. With Palette Options a number of palette types are available. For the Perceptual, Selective, and Adaptive options, you can choose using a local palette based on the current image's colors. Select the number of colors you want the design to

be reduced to. In the color settings have None Forced, no Transparency (Transparency unticked) and in the options have None selected for Matte. Unless you are using the Exact color table option, the color table may not contain specific colors used in the image.

The final option in the window to examine is Dither. To simulate extra colors to those in the color table, you can dither the colors. Dithering mixes the pixels of the available colors to simulate additional colors. If your artwork does not have flat colors you can choose a dither option from the menu and enter a percentage value for the dither amount. No dither, or None in the options, gives a flat, crisp-edged version and this should be selected here as most appropriate for the design Millefiori. Select Local Adaptive as the palette type and five as the number of colors. Notice that after conversion your screen may display the design slightly differently at various magnifications. Because of the restriction on colors Photoshop can no longer soften any edges. **(fig. 11)**

11

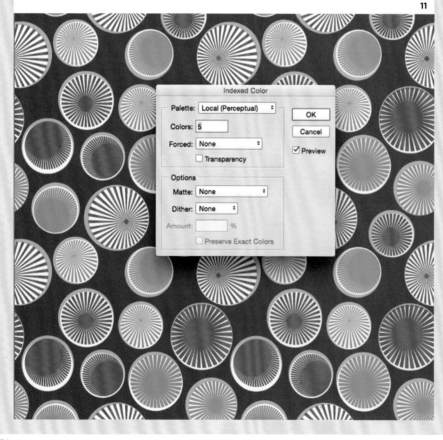

PROJECT SIX—
PHOTOSHOP:
REPEATS AND
COLORWAYS

PROJECT SEVEN —
COLOR THEORY
IN PRACTICE

PROJECT EIGHT—
PHOTOSHOP:
FILLS, TEXTURES,
AND LAYERS

PROJECT NINE—
ILLUSTRATOR:
PATHS TO FASHION

PROJECT TEN—
SIMPLE GEOMETRY
IN ILLUSTRATOR

PROJECT ELEVEN—
REPEAT PATTERNS
IN ILLUSTRATOR

CASE STUDY:
NADINE BUCHER

PROJECT TWELVE—
ILLUSTRATOR:
PHOTOSHOP AND
FILTERS

CASE STUDY:
TORD BOONTJE

2. You can edit colors in the color table to produce additional colorways. Choose **Image → Mode → Color Table**. This opens up the color table displaying the actual colors in the indexed color image.

To change a color, click the color and choose a new color with the color picker that opens. As well as the color picker to change the colors, color libraries can be accessed for specific colors. If the Adobe Color Picker is selected under Photoshop Preferences then access to the PANTONE for Graphics will be available. If the Apple Color Picker is selected under Photoshop Preferences then access is available to PANTONE for Fashion and Home colors if they have been installed. To change a range of colors together, drag in the color table to select the range of colors you want to change. In the color picker, choose the first color you want in the range and click Okay. When the color picker re-displays, choose the last color you want in the range and click Okay. The colors you selected in the Color Picker replace the start and end colors in the range you selected in the Color Table and Photoshop finds appropriate colors for the in-between ones. Click Okay in the Color Table dialog box to accept and apply these new colors to the image. **(fig. 12)**

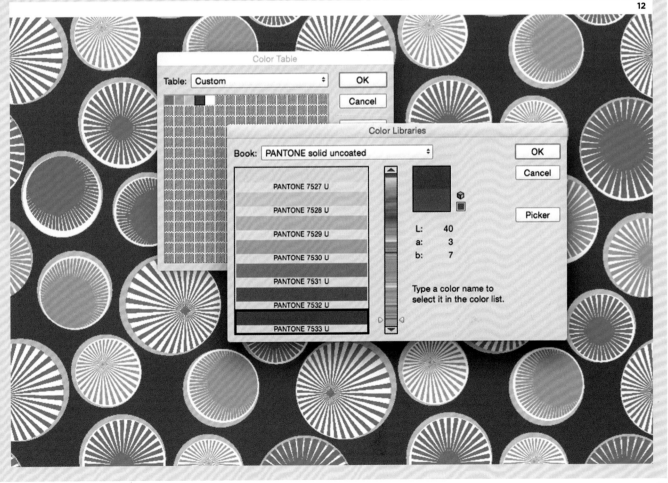

12

ADVANCED USE

You may find the order of the colors that Photoshop chooses for the Color Table difficult for easy managing of your colorways. For example you might want the colors ordered to run from dark to light or for them to be grouped together by color groups. When Photoshop creates the index color reduction it determines the order of the colors, but there are two ways round this and they allow you to control the sequence of the colors in the Color Table. Neither method is instant but if you want to reorder the colors you can decide which method suits you.

Method One—Reduction to a Custom Palette

With the Color Table window open you can sample a second set of the index image's colors in a new row after the current one.

1. Click a blank box and it will switch to black and the Color Picker window opens. Sample a color from the image. Choose the color you want to be first in the new sequence. Click Okay on the Color Picker window to return to the Color Table window and click on the next empty color box. Select your next color and continue this process until you have the new set of colors in the order you want. **(fig. 13)**

2. Now untick Preview in the Color Table window, as it will be distracting in the next process. Holding down the **command/control** key click on the first color in the old sequence. It is removed. Click on the next color until only your new set remains. Save this set of colors now as a new Color Table file.

3. Cancel the Color Table window to exit. You don't want to use the new colors yet.

4. Convert the image back to an RGB image with Color Mode. Then immediately go to Image Mode again to convert the image to indexed color. When the Index Color window opens select Custom as the palette. When the Color Table window opens select your recently saved, reordered Color Table as the color table to use for the conversion. **(fig. 14)**

5. Click Okay to select the color table, click Okay to close the Indexed Color window. The design is now converted again to the same colors but with the order changed. If you want your colors in a particular order it makes sense to do this process before embarking on creating colorways.

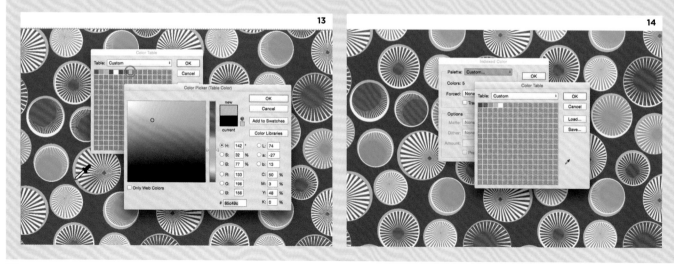

13

14

PROJECT SIX—
PHOTOSHOP:
REPEATS AND
COLORWAYS

PROJECT SEVEN —
COLOR THEORY
IN PRACTICE

PROJECT EIGHT—
PHOTOSHOP:
FILLS, TEXTURES,
AND LAYERS

PROJECT NINE—
ILLUSTRATOR:
PATHS TO FASHION

PROJECT TEN—
SIMPLE GEOMETRY
IN ILLUSTRATOR

PROJECT ELEVEN—
REPEAT PATTERNS
IN ILLUSTRATOR

CASE STUDY:
NADINE BUCHER

PROJECT TWELVE—
ILLUSTRATOR:
PHOTOSHOP AND
FILTERS

CASE STUDY:
TORD BOONTJE

Method Two—Paste into an Awaiting Palette

1. Make a duplicate of your RGB design. **Image → Duplicate**. Change this duplicate design to indexed color. Choose any one of the Local settings and two as the number of colors, as this gives you the minimum cleaning up work in the next stage. These settings are only important in so far as they allow the conversion to an Indexed Color image.

2. Select the resulting indexed image and delete it. You should now have a blank indexed color document. Place the original RGB design next to the blank Indexed Color document. Open the Color Table for the Indexed Color document. Start sampling colors from the original RGB design into the boxes in the order you want in the Color Table. Click on a box in the Color Table and then, with the Eyedropper tool, double click on a color in the design document to sample that color. **(fig. 15)**

3. When you have your colors in the order you want them click Okay and close the window. Now switch to the RGB image and use Select All and then Copy. Switch to the Indexed Color document and Paste. The image is converted into the colors as it arrives and in the order of colors you specified.

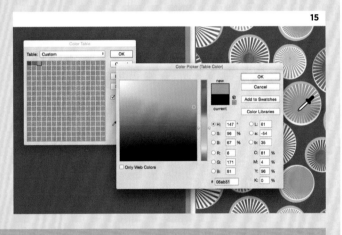

15

PROJECT REVIEW

REVIEW
You should be able to put your design into a step repeat, making adjustments as necessary to the design elements to eliminate any awkwardness that may appear when the design is in repeat. You should have some insight into good practice in repeat work and understand the need to consider it a process of evaluation and adjustment.

PRACTICE
Look at existing fabrics, wall coverings, and even architecture for interesting arrangements and repetitions of elements. Try to analyze what makes the arrangements work. Looking analytically at successful repeat work helps develop your intuitive awareness of good design layout and balance. Put at least one more design into step repeat and evaluate and correct the layout of elements where necessary. Reduce the colors to a manageable number with the indexed color method and create and save at least three varied colorways.

PROJECT SEVEN—
COLOR THEORY IN PRACTICE

7

Confidence with color is essential to textile and fashion design. Color is perceived before shape and texture so it carries great weight in the success of your work.

Everybody has personal inclinations toward certain color combinations, but the designer works with material intended for a wider audience so the colors need to have appeal beyond the designer's personal taste. Design with color is a combination of intuition, system, and experience. It is not realistic to think of it as a science with strict rationale, as frequently the ostensible rules are broken by a great design.

Photoshop and Illustrator provide excellent tools for manipulating color. They allow you to see the elements that define a specific color, see how colors interact, and allow you to refine your color treatment of a design. In this project you will see some of the possible arrangements of colors following color harmony systems. Illustrator has a powerful Color Guide tool to help the designer in this area. Note that color adjustment on screen can be seriously undermined if the output is to a printer with a narrow color gamut or to one that is not correctly calibrated.

PROJECT SIX—
PHOTOSHOP:
REPEATS AND
COLORWAYS

PROJECT SEVEN —
COLOR THEORY
IN PRACTICE

PROJECT EIGHT—
PHOTOSHOP:
FILLS, TEXTURES,
AND LAYERS

PROJECT NINE—
ILLUSTRATOR:
PATHS TO FASHION

PROJECT TEN—
SIMPLE GEOMETRY
IN ILLUSTRATOR

PROJECT ELEVEN—
REPEAT PATTERNS
IN ILLUSTRATOR

CASE STUDY:
NADINE BUCHER

PROJECT TWELVE—
ILLUSTRATOR:
PHOTOSHOP AND
FILTERS

CASE STUDY:
TORD BOONTJE

79

As a general rule, a commercial design is offered in at least three variations: a warm color scheme, a cool color scheme, and a neutral color scheme. It is more economical to show a design in a number of color variations than to show a number of single designs in one colorway only. It is also not economical to have the colorways too similar either, as the intention is to offer a choice that is as wide and clear as possible. This is different from the earlier stage of design development where small variations on an original scheme may be developed for consideration and refinement. Manipulation of specified colors in a color story may be required in order make them work in the actual context of a design. There is no precise formula, but a systematic approach is very important and builds understanding and confidence.

COLOR THEORY IN PRACTICE

In this project you will:
- Look at some established ways of creating balanced color combinations and at some of the principles of creating professional colorways.
- Examine Photoshop and Illustrator's tools for recoloring and making colorways.

Outcome
You should be able to create colorways of your artwork in both Photoshop and Illustrator and match them to specific swatch colors.

Aim
To practice the techniques and tools for precise recoloring.

As a general rule, a commercial design is offered in at least three variations: a warm color scheme, a cool color scheme, and a neutral color scheme.

Perceivable color in reality is represented more accurately by a complex three-dimensional model, but the color wheel provides a simplified practical aid.

16a
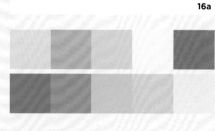

16b
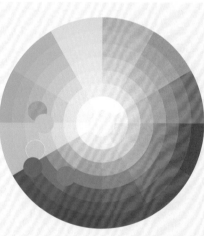

16a
Monochromatic color palette or schemes, the blue chips ordered dark to light. Colors are harmonious because they are tones, shades, and tints of a specific *hue*.

17a

17b

17a
Analogous color palette or scheme created using colors that are close to each other on the color wheel. Colors are harmonious because they have similar levels of purity of color or *chroma*.

18a

18b
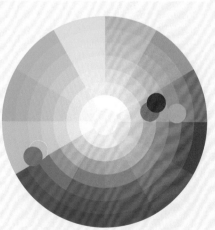

18a
Complementary color palette or scheme created using colors that are from opposite sides of the color wheel. Colors directly opposite are the most striking schemes and may need to be separated by white, black, or gray to avoid too dramatic a contrast.

PROJECT SIX—
PHOTOSHOP:
REPEATS AND
COLORWAYS

**PROJECT SEVEN —
COLOR THEORY
IN PRACTICE**

PROJECT EIGHT—
PHOTOSHOP:
FILLS, TEXTURES,
AND LAYERS

PROJECT NINE—
ILLUSTRATOR:
PATHS TO FASHION

PROJECT TEN—
SIMPLE GEOMETRY
IN ILLUSTRATOR

PROJECT ELEVEN—
REPEAT PATTERNS
IN ILLUSTRATOR

CASE STUDY:
NADINE BUCHER

PROJECT TWELVE—
ILLUSTRATOR:
PHOTOSHOP AND
FILTERS

CASE STUDY:
TORD BOONTJE

19a

19b

19a
Split complementary color palette or scheme.
In this scheme colors on either side of the hue
opposite the base hue are used.

20a

20b

20a
Triadic color palette or scheme. Triadic schemes
are made up of hues spaced around the color
wheel. This is a diverse color scheme and if
the colors have some uniform value such as
saturation it can prevent the scheme from
becoming too frenetic.

If you are required to recolor an
existing design to new colors then
these new colors should maintain
the same relationships between
themselves as did the original
colors, and so should any colorways.
Otherwise you are altering the
essential nature of the design. The
exception to this is if you do intend
to remake the design.

For recoloring you can move
the hues of the colors around the
color wheel in Photoshop to create
the colorway. If you have specific
colors from a client's palette or
key forecasted colors to match to
you can then substitute these for
the approximate colors that the
manipulation through **Image →
Adjustments → Hues/Saturation**
gives you. In Illustrator you need to
access the color wheel edit feature
of recolor artwork. Remember to link
all the colors.

21

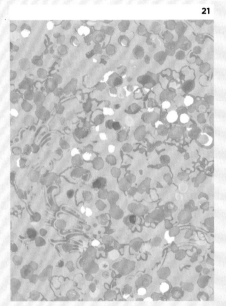

21
Monochromatic color scheme

22

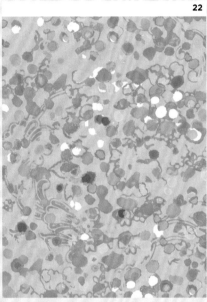

22
Analogous color scheme

23

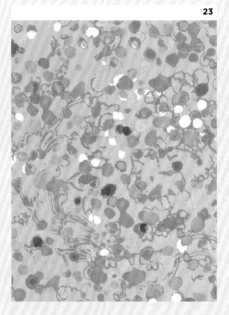

23
Complementary color scheme

24

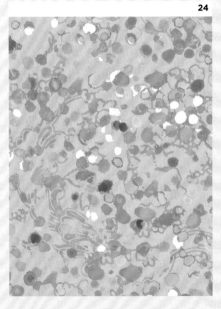

24
Split complementary color scheme

25

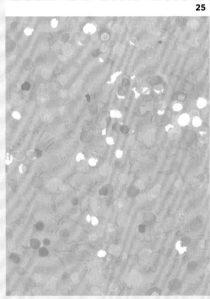

25
Triadic color scheme

21–25
Here are examples of a design colored following the five schemes. Note that these are not five colorways, but they show five different possible harmonic relationships between colors in a design.

PROJECT SIX—
PHOTOSHOP:
REPEATS AND
COLORWAYS

**PROJECT SEVEN —
COLOR THEORY
IN PRACTICE**

PROJECT EIGHT—
PHOTOSHOP:
FILLS, TEXTURES,
AND LAYERS

PROJECT NINE—
ILLUSTRATOR:
PATHS TO FASHION

PROJECT TEN—
SIMPLE GEOMETRY
IN ILLUSTRATOR

PROJECT ELEVEN—
REPEAT PATTERNS
IN ILLUSTRATOR

CASE STUDY:
NADINE BUCHER

PROJECT TWELVE—
ILLUSTRATOR:
PHOTOSHOP AND
FILTERS

CASE STUDY:
TORD BOONTJE

Photoshop

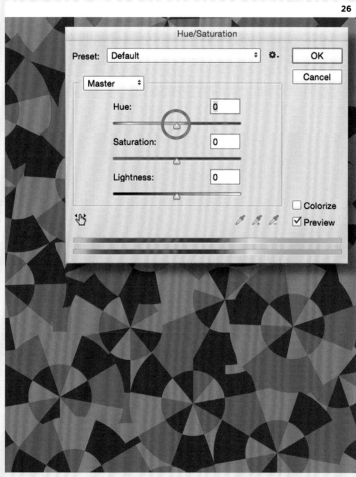

26

27

PANTONE®
18-5128

28

26
Hue adjustment slider in Photoshop

27
Select color to replace. Have desired color
as foreground color and then fill selection.

28
Cool colorway

Use some of your own artwork to
practice these recoloring techniques.

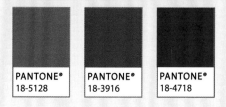

PANTONE®
18-5128

PANTONE®
18-3916

PANTONE®
18-4718

7.1

In Photoshop, use **Image →
Adjustments → Hue/Saturation** (or
an adjustment layer) to move the hue
of the colors in the design around
the color wheel to get the desired
colorway. Select the individual color
and match it more specifically to
a color swatch; if the color is solid
replace it with a fill of the swatch
color. Use a selection and edit fill or
bucket fill to introduce the new color.

29

30

29
Neutral colorway

| PANTONE®
15-6410 | PANTONE®
15-3802 | PANTONE®
14-0002 |

30
Hot colorway

| PANTONE®
19-3217 | PANTONE®
19-2431 | PANTONE®
16-1054 |

PROJECT SIX—
PHOTOSHOP:
REPEATS AND
COLORWAYS

**PROJECT SEVEN —
COLOR THEORY
IN PRACTICE**

PROJECT EIGHT—
PHOTOSHOP:
FILLS, TEXTURES,
AND LAYERS

PROJECT NINE—
ILLUSTRATOR:
PATHS TO FASHION

PROJECT TEN—
SIMPLE GEOMETRY
IN ILLUSTRATOR

PROJECT ELEVEN—
REPEAT PATTERNS
IN ILLUSTRATOR

CASE STUDY:
NADINE BUCHER

PROJECT TWELVE—
ILLUSTRATOR:
PHOTOSHOP AND
FILTERS

CASE STUDY:
TORD BOONTJE

7.2

If the color is tonal, you can use **Adjustments → Replace Color** and use the Eyedropper and Add To Sample Eyedropper to collect up all the tones of the individual color for replacing. You can open a color library from the Color Picker window to find a standard color reference. Tones of this color will be applied to the current selected color and its tones.

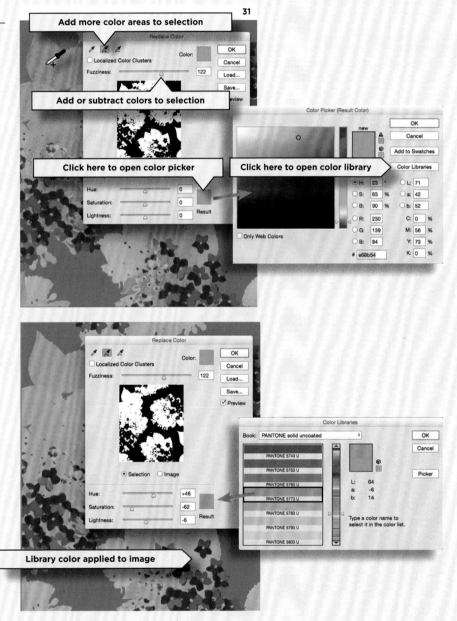

31
Changing tonal colors in a design

Creating colorways
in Illustrator

7.3

To create colorways of a design in Illustrator you can use **Edit → Edit Colors → Recolor Artwork** or go straight to the Recolor button (in earlier versions of Illustrator this was Live Color) that appears in the header Toolbar if an object is selected. There are many options in the very useful Recolor tool and investigating some of its possibilities is a good investment of time.
If you are unfamiliar with Illustrator you can return to this section after you have completed some of the introductory Illustrator projects.

7.4

If you have already created color groups in the swatches window these can be used to create colorways, and further colors are always accessible within the Recolor window itself.
To create your colorways you could first make duplicates of your artwork on the artboard and with one of these copies active open up the Recolor window and change the colors to make the new colorway. If your design is in repeat and exists as a swatch in the swatches palette in repeat then if you recolor an object filled with this swatch a new repeat swatch is created in the new colorway. Each recoloring of the repeat generates a new repeat swatch when you okay the changes in the Recolor window. Both methods for creating colorways are very useful.

Recolor Artwork window using Assign
You can use some of the color Harmony Rules **(fig. 32, 1)** to aid your recoloring. Click on the drop-down menu to access possible variations. If you click on a color group **(fig. 32, 2)** in the right-hand panel these colors will be used to recolor the artwork. Ensure that Recolor Art box is ticked **(fig. 32, 3)**. If you do not like the order in which Illustrator arranges the new colors from the color group to replace the current colors then you can drag colors to the correct position for substitution **(fig. 32, 4)**.

You can switch to Edit view for a different way of recoloring and move the colors around the color wheel with their relative positions remaining intact as long as the lock button is on.

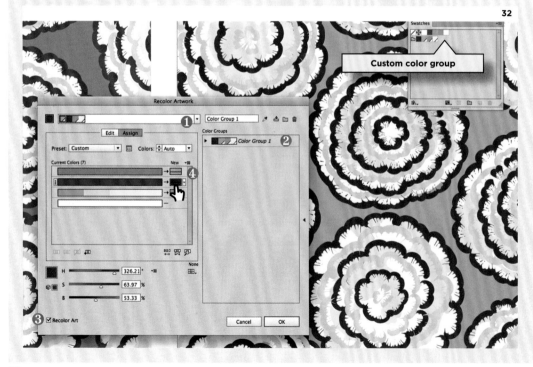

Custom color group

32

PROJECT SIX—
PHOTOSHOP:
REPEATS AND
COLORWAYS

PROJECT SEVEN —
COLOR THEORY
IN PRACTICE

PROJECT EIGHT—
PHOTOSHOP:
FILLS, TEXTURES,
AND LAYERS

PROJECT NINE—
ILLUSTRATOR:
PATHS TO FASHION

PROJECT TEN—
SIMPLE GEOMETRY
IN ILLUSTRATOR

PROJECT ELEVEN—
REPEAT PATTERNS
IN ILLUSTRATOR

CASE STUDY:
NADINE BUCHER

PROJECT TWELVE—
ILLUSTRATOR:
PHOTOSHOP AND
FILTERS

CASE STUDY:
TORD BOONTJE

7.5

Recolor Artwork window using Edit.
Click on the Edit button **(fig. 33, 1)**.
To confine colors to a swatch library,
click the Limits The Color Scheme
To Colors In A Swatch Library button
(fig. 33, 2) and choose a library
from the list.

If the color bars are showing, click
the Color Wheel icon **(fig. 33, 3)**
to display the color wheel instead.
Drag the base color marker (the
largest, double-ringed color marker
(fig. 33, 4)) around the wheel to set
the base color you want. Moving this
and only this will help you keep your
colorways consistent. Clicking on
the Link Harmony Colors button
(fig. 33, 5) ensures that the individual
colors retain their relative positions
to each other while you move the
base color marker. You can save the
new colors as a color group and this
set of colors can be used to create a
matching colorway in another design.
If you click on the new color group
button **(fig. 33, 6)** the colors are
saved in the swatches palette.

PROJECT REVIEW

REVIEW
You should have some understanding of an ordered approach
to creating colorways and to sympathetic recoloring of your
own artwork. Photoshop and Illustrator offer great freedom
in altering color and some structured thinking enables the
generation of compelling and professional colorways. As color
is so important in the reception of your work, use of specific
forecasted colors helps keeps it relevant.

PRACTICE
Look at existing fabrics, wall coverings, garments, and even
paintings for colors that work strongly together and try to
analyze what makes the combinations work. Looking seriously
at successful color helps develop your intuitive awareness.
Create a series of colorways for spring/summer and autumn/
winter for your own designs.

33

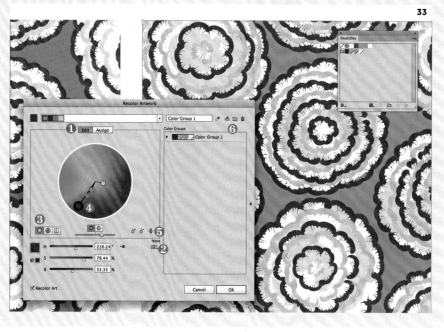

PROJECT EIGHT—PHOTOSHOP:
FILLS, TEXTURES, AND LAYERS

Photoshop is first and foremost an image-based application and at times there can be very little practical distinction between what might be classed an image, texture, or brush stroke. The application is so flexible that images can furnish material to be used in varied creative ways. Using selection tools, elements can be plucked from one image and introduced into another, forming diverse textural effects. Blending Modes allow complex and attractive interrelationships to be fashioned between layers. However, because collage is so easy in Photoshop and because layer after layer of texture and nuance can easily be built up, the designer has to guard against overloading the artwork, losing both individuality and an economy of expression and instead producing a cluttered, generic Photoshop image.

34

PHOTOSHOP: FILLS, TEXTURES, AND LAYERS

In this project you will:

• Look at various ways of introducing pattern and texture into a Photoshop design.
• Four methods will be examined and the benefits of the less automatic process will be indicated.
• Use the specific areas of a garment sketch to explore color and pattern.
• Selections will enable you to use masks, an extremely powerful tool in Photoshop.
• Use Layer Comps to switch between colorways.
• Some attitudes toward the purpose of design drawing will be explored.

Outcome

You should create a number of ideas for print combinations having tested these by experimenting within the garment shape. This context draws attention to how scale and proportion can greatly change the character of a design.

Aim

To practice developing designs through manipulation in Photoshop, see how selection tools create masks and how masks enable the imagination to explore composition, and see how printed textiles might be used in varied ways in a garment.

Project files are available at
www.bloomsbury.com/hume-textile-design

In this project you will explore pattern and texture within a garment sketch, but you could explore the same ideas within the shape of a snowboard, sneaker, bag, sofa, or any other context where you would be creating surface pattern ideas.

A note here about garment drawing: The intention of a professional drawing is to convey either an initial mood and general character of a design or, later, the more specific styling details of the design and possibly additional construction guidance. Too much detail invested in the hair, lipstick, and so on, of the croquis figure is potentially distracting and not essential to the message of the drawing. You should judge whether the detail in the drawing compared to the design itself is demanding more visual attention than it deserves. If you apply colored and patterned borders to a design sketch viewers cannot avoid including those in their visual reception of the design. If the client doesn't like that patterned border and it accompanies a number of designs then its effect will mar the reception of all the garment designs. A presentation of your design will be stronger by avoiding anything that does not support and reinforce the essential message of the design. Presentation meetings are often time pressured, and quick comprehension of the essentials of a design proposal is therefore always important.

Invest time in practicing drawing. Excessive reliance on photographs locks you into the composition of the specific photographs. Elaborate drawings can be counterproductive; too much detail in anything other than the garments is a potential distraction.

8.1

Open the document Ines_model. This is a sketch that has been prepared for you. It has been scanned from a pen drawing and separate layers have been made for individual garment pieces. In a design of your own there might only be a single area you intend to apply pattern to, but in the example here there are possibilities offered by the specific design of the garment.

In the document Ines_model there are layers for the body, yoke, and fishtail sections of the dress. Click the visibility for the layers off and on so that you can see where these garment parts are. There is a layer for the outline drawing and one for some coloring up of the figure.

8.2

You will introduce pattern fills into the garment shapes. Any image can be used as a pattern fill but images that repeat without awkward joins are preferable. Like many operations in Photoshop there are a number of different ways to introduce a pattern and the different methods have varying attractions. Begin by opening the file Texture01 and define the whole of this document as a pattern fill. Then you will use Bucket fill for the first method.

PROJECT SIX—
PHOTOSHOP:
REPEATS AND
COLORWAYS

PROJECT SEVEN —
COLOR THEORY
IN PRACTICE

**PROJECT EIGHT—
PHOTOSHOP:
FILLS, TEXTURES,
AND LAYERS**

PROJECT NINE—
ILLUSTRATOR:
PATHS TO FASHION

PROJECT TEN—
SIMPLE GEOMETRY
IN ILLUSTRATOR

PROJECT ELEVEN—
REPEAT PATTERNS
IN ILLUSTRATOR

CASE STUDY:
NADINE BUCHER

PROJECT TWELVE—
ILLUSTRATOR:
PHOTOSHOP AND
FILTERS

CASE STUDY:
TORD BOONTJE

8.3

Make Body Layer the active layer. Select the Paint Bucket fill tool. **(fig. 35)**

From the Paint Bucket tool options select Pattern as the source of the fill rather than foreground color and click on the Pattern Picker to select the new pattern you just saved. (It will be the last one.) **(fig. 36)**

Have the Tolerances for the tool set at about 11. Have Opacity as 100 percent.

Click inside the dress with the Paint Bucket tool. The dress is then filled with the pattern. The bucket fill method is simple but it has severe limitations. If the scale of the pattern is not correct in the garment you cannot rescale it. You cannot adjust or control where the pattern falls within the shape. You can however adjust the color of the pattern once in place.

TIP

Low tolerances ensure that similar colors are not also filled by the bucket flood fill. If you have All Layers ticked then Photoshop uses dissimilar colors as the boundaries on all layers. If Contiguous is ticked then there has to be an unbroken connection between the color you initially click and colors similar to it. With Contiguous off they only need to be similar and need not be connected; the fill will find them wherever they are in the document. In the document Ines_model example, with Contiguous ticked then only the front panel of the taupe body is filled. With Contiguous off the small strip of the back panel is also filled.

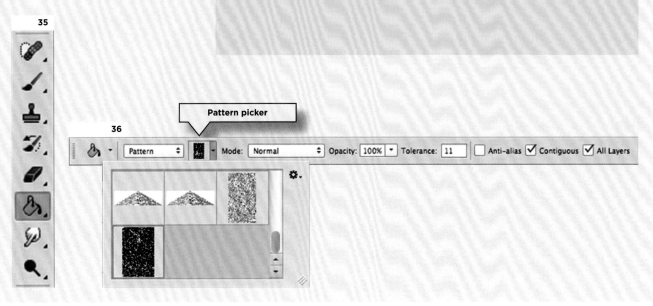

35

36

Pattern picker

Pattern   Mode: Normal   Opacity: 100%   Tolerance: 11   Anti-alias ☑ Contiguous ☑ All Layers

8.4

Now for method two. Use **command/control + Z** to undo the previous fill. Double click to the right of the name of the body layer in the Layer window, in the active layer's highlighted area, to launch the Layer Style window. In the window, double click beside the word Pattern Overlay to open the pattern overlay options and access the pattern picker. From the picker select again your new pattern by double clicking on it. This time you are able to adjust the scale of the pattern to be inserted and, as this is an effect, you will be able to reopen this window and change the pattern scale at any time. If you reduce the pattern scale Photoshop will generate more repeats to fill the space. You cannot alter the color of the pattern fill directly but you can add a Color Overlay in Layer Styles

that will alter its appearance. This though is a very limited way to adjust color. Again with this method you cannot transform the pattern apart from its scale. **(fig. 37)**

Method three uses masks. Using masks is similar to the method of controlling images that is common in Illustrator where clipping masks are used to clip artwork to the specific shape of the mask. Masks in Photoshop were introduced in the stripe and weave project, Project 5, as a method to control what was revealed and what was not on individual layers.

You will create a layer for the pattern fill and use a mask to make only a section of it visible. The shape of this section can easily be taken from the garment drawing.

8.5

Use **command/control + Z** to undo the previous fill. Holding down the **command/control** key click on the thumbnail for the body layer to create a selection from that layer's contents (the dress body). **(fig. 38)**

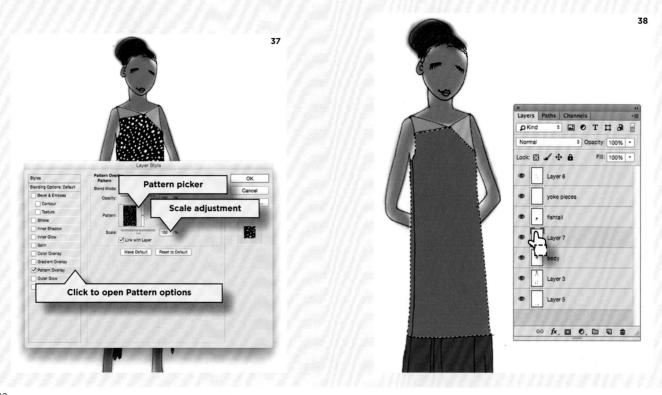

37

38

92

PROJECT SIX—
PHOTOSHOP:
REPEATS AND
COLORWAYS

PROJECT SEVEN —
COLOR THEORY
IN PRACTICE

**PROJECT EIGHT—
PHOTOSHOP:
FILLS, TEXTURES,
AND LAYERS**

PROJECT NINE—
ILLUSTRATOR:
PATHS TO FASHION

PROJECT TEN—
SIMPLE GEOMETRY
IN ILLUSTRATOR

PROJECT ELEVEN—
REPEAT PATTERNS
IN ILLUSTRATOR

CASE STUDY:
NADINE BUCHER

PROJECT TWELVE—
ILLUSTRATOR:
PHOTOSHOP AND
FILTERS

CASE STUDY:
TORD BOONTJE

8.6

Go → **Layer** → **New Fill Layer** → **Pattern**. Just click Okay in the first dialog window that opens. In the second window that opens you can select your pattern; the most recent pattern is offered by default. Okay the Pattern Fill window to exit. **(fig. 39)**

You can change the scale of the pattern at any time by clicking on the pattern fill thumbnail in the Layer window. You can break the link between the pattern and mask to enable you to reposition the pattern itself relative to the mask shape. As mentioned elsewhere in the book, don't allow Adobe's use of the term "mask" to confuse you, as the selection actually defines the area that is not masked and therefore is visible. Creating a mask to define a pattern area has advantages over

using a layer as the source of a clipping path to define the pattern area. By double clicking on the mask thumbnail you have options, such as how soft, or feathered, its edge is, to change the mask properties. You can also edit the mask shape with drawing tools in the Channels window. However, with this method of pattern filling no transformation tools, such as Rotate, are available to alter the pattern in situ. This can prove to be inconvenient and does restrict your freedom to try out options in the garment shape and experiment more as a designer.

The suggested method, the next one—method four, is less automatic but it gives the most flexibility for all pattern and texture fills and so is the best method to become familiar with.

8.7

Delete the Pattern Fill Layer. Create a new layer with **command/control + shift + N** or click the New Layer button in the Layers window. As before, the new layer should be created above the active layer, the body layer. The new layer is now the active layer. Go → **Edit** → **Fill...** and select the same pattern as previously selected for the fill. (Have Scripted Patterns unticked.) The pattern now fills the entire layer.

8.8

Hold **command/control** and click on the thumbnail for the body layer to create a selection of that layer's contents. Check that your new layer is still the active, target layer (highlighted) and click the New Layer Mask button in the Layers panel to create a mask that reveals the selection. **(fig. 40)**

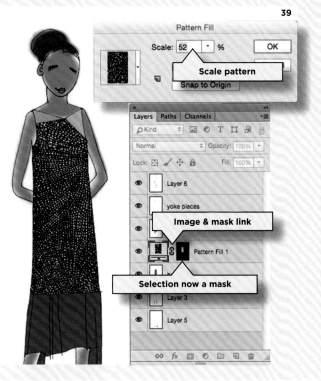

39

Pattern Fill

Scale: 52 %   OK

Scale pattern

Snap to Origin

Layer 6

yoke pieces

Image & mask link

Pattern Fill 1

Selection now a mask

Layer 3

Layer 5

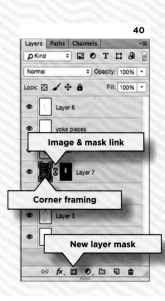

40

Layer 6

yoke pieces

Image & mask link

Layer 7

Corner framing

Layer 3

New layer mask

8.9

As done before in Project Five, make the image the active element of the masked layer. It is the image and not the mask that you want to edit at the moment. (Refresh yourself by consulting the stripe and weave project again.) Break the link between the image and mask by clicking on the chain symbol. This allows the elements to be transformed separately.

Check that the layer image is the active element (four corners framed) and zoom out so the whole document is visible. **Command/ control + T** to bring up the Free Transform box. Select a corner of the box, hold down shift to keep the proportions constant, and then you can shrink or enlarge the pattern in situ. You can also use all the other aspects of the Free Transform tool to rotate, flip, skew, and even warp to change the pattern fill. **(fig. 41)**

With the pattern fill in the form of a masked layer it is as easy as with any other layer to change the color of the pattern. If you want to change the color of a pattern that is black (this is true for white as well) with the Hue Adjustment window then you first need to switch the method to colorize and move the lightness and saturation settings away from zero. Then it is as easy as changing any color. **(fig. 42)**

Now for the additional parts of the garment.

8.10

Create a new layer and fill this layer entirely with the pattern. Select a different part of the garment and use that to create a mask for the pattern. In this second area rescale the pattern to a different scale from that you used previously.

You can introduce more texture into your design by introducing different images or patterns on additional layers and experimenting with the ways the layers interact using transparency and blending mode settings.

41

42

PROJECT SIX—
PHOTOSHOP:
REPEATS AND
COLORWAYS

PROJECT SEVEN —
COLOR THEORY
IN PRACTICE

**PROJECT EIGHT—
PHOTOSHOP:
FILLS, TEXTURES,
AND LAYERS**

PROJECT NINE—
ILLUSTRATOR:
PATHS TO FASHION

PROJECT TEN—
SIMPLE GEOMETRY
IN ILLUSTRATOR

PROJECT ELEVEN—
REPEAT PATTERNS
IN ILLUSTRATOR

CASE STUDY:
NADINE BUCHER

PROJECT TWELVE—
ILLUSTRATOR:
PHOTOSHOP AND
FILTERS

CASE STUDY:
TORD BOONTJE

8.11

Go → File → Place... Embedded... and select the document Swirl from the project folder. Then click Place and the file is introduced on a fresh layer in your Ines_model document. The cross box indicates that you can change the size and position of the placed image before committing. When happy, click the tick box in the transform options bar or press **return/ enter**. Use a selection from the body garment piece to create a mask for the swirl. With the new swirl layer the active layer, from the Layer Blending Mode drop-down menu select a different blending mode and see how this affects the look of the layer. The blending modes of a layer determine how its pixels blend with pixels on underlying layers in the image.

A variety of special effects are possible with blending modes and the result is dependent on the particular pixels of the active layer blending with pixels on layers below. The outcome in each case is determined by the pixels in your specific image so it is good to experiment and start learning from the result. The precise actions of the blending modes are described in support literature on the Adobe site but the literature may not help you as much as practical experience with your own work. **(fig. 43)**

Double clicking on a layer in the Layer window launches the Layer Style window. Blending modes are accessible here too and you saw previously in this project that there are tools for changing the

appearance of a layer contents by a style such as Color Overlay. There are additional tools for manipulating how the pixels on the layer interact with layers below using the knockout sliders. Knockout settings let you specify what range of material on underlying layers punches through or what range of material drops out of the active layer.

You first introduced a black and white pattern to give interest to the design, then the blue colored swirl, which added color and tone variation to the spot pattern. Now, by introducing a full color image even more textural possibilities can be explored. You will also practice adding selections to create a new combined selection and subsequent mask.

43

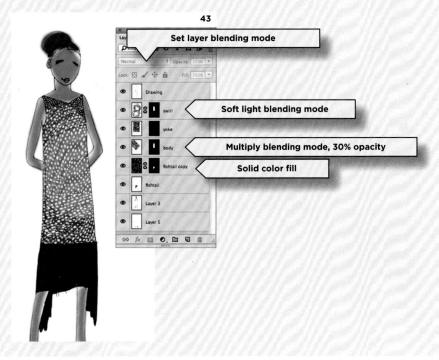

Set layer blending mode

Soft light blending mode

Multiply blending mode, 30% opacity

Solid color fill

8.12

Using the Place Embedded command place the paint_texture image within your document and above the current layers. You will create a mask for this image that will be all the garment pieces combined. To create a selection from a layer's image contents hold down the **command/control** key and click on the layer's image thumbnail. Similarly, to create a selection from a layer's mask hold down the **command/control** key and click on the mask thumbnail. To add a new selection to the current selection hold down the **shift** key, so now you can select the mask for the fishtail and then, one stage at a time, add,

holding down the **shift** key, the other garment section masks. Make the Paint_Texture layer active and click on the Add Layer Mask button to apply the selection as a mask.
(fig. 44)

Use blending modes to explore ways of applying texture from the new image. Overlay and Multiply are definitely ones to consider. Explore how the order of the layers may also create different effects. You could also experiment with bringing in an image of your own, masking it, and combining it with some of the textures you have already added.

Color Variations Using Layer Comps
It is easy to manipulate the colors of a number of layers together when you combine them as a group. You can record the colors of this group with a layer comp, alter the colors, and then create a second layer comp, effectively creating colorways. You don't then need to save the color variations as separate documents, layer comps allows you to switch easily between them in the same document. If you haven't guessed, "comp" is short for composition. To group layers, first select multiple layers in the Layers window, then either go **Layer → Group Layers** or hold down the **option/alt** key and drag the layers onto the folder icon at the bottom of the Layers window to create a group of the selected layers.

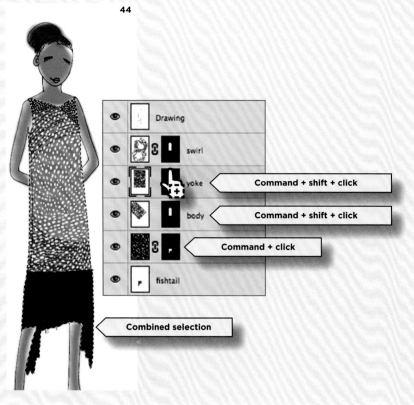

44

Drawing

swirl

yoke — Command + shift + click

body — Command + shift + click

Command + click

fishtail

Combined selection

96

8.13

In your design, select the layers on which you want to manipulate the color and make them into a group. The grouped layers disappear inside a little folder thumbnail but they can still be edited individually by expanding the group.

The colors, as they currently are, will be the first variation. Record these colors by creating the first layer comp. A layer comp is a snapshot of the state of the layers, recording their positions, whether layers are visible, and the appearance of individual layers, whether a layer style is applied, and the nature of the layer's blending mode. Including adjustment layers in the layer comp allows for very easy switching between color variations.

8.14

Open the Layer Comp window, click on the New Layer Comp button to record the current state of the layers. Make sure the Apply Visibility, Position, and Appearance to Layers tick boxes are ticked. Name this comp Version 1. **(fig. 45)**

8.15

Check that the Group layer is still highlighted and go **Layers →
New Adjustment Layer → Hue/
Saturation...** Tick the Use Previous Layer to Create Clipping Mask box. This label may not be clear but what it does is link the adjustment layer you are creating to the single layer, or in this case the group, and to

only adjust the colors of that layer or group. You would not want to change the color of all the layers in the document at the same time, including the color of the drawing outlines and the model's body for example. Before clicking okay to exit the New Adjustment Layer window you might want to give this Adjustment layer a useful title to help differentiate it from the next Adjustment layer. Look for the small Hue/Saturation window and adjust the hue slider to get the desired colors. **(fig. 46)**

Click on the New Layer Comp button to record this color variation as Version 2.

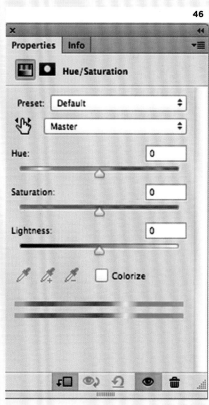

46

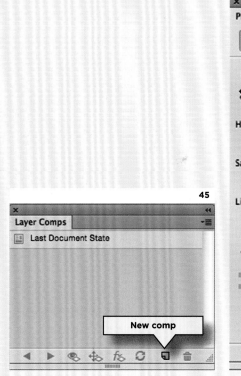

45

New comp

8.16

Make the current adjustment layer invisible (because this adjustment layer is associated with the second comp) and go **Layers → New Adjustment Layer → Hue/Saturation** to create a new adjustment layer for a new colorway. Adjust the colors as desired and then record this version as a third layer comp. If you use the forward and back buttons on the Layer Comp window you can move backward and forward between your color variations. **(fig. 47-49)**

50-51
Designer Samantha Fynes draws first on paper until she is happy with the design, and then scans in those designs to start working in Photoshop. She takes "as much as I can from the pencil drawing in the form of shape, whereas most of the detail takes place in Photoshop using brushes, patterns, layers etc."

PROJECT SIX—
PHOTOSHOP:
REPEATS AND
COLORWAYS

PROJECT SEVEN —
COLOR THEORY
IN PRACTICE

**PROJECT EIGHT—
PHOTOSHOP:
FILLS, TEXTURES,
AND LAYERS**

PROJECT NINE—
ILLUSTRATOR:
PATHS TO FASHION

PROJECT TEN—
SIMPLE GEOMETRY
IN ILLUSTRATOR

PROJECT ELEVEN—
REPEAT PATTERNS
IN ILLUSTRATOR

CASE STUDY:
NADINE BUCHER

PROJECT TWELVE—
ILLUSTRATOR:
PHOTOSHOP AND
FILTERS

CASE STUDY:
TORD BOONTJE

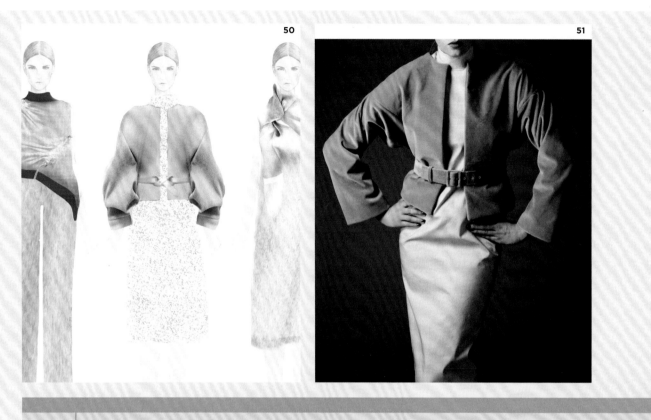

PROJECT REVIEW

REVIEW

You should feel confident using masks for controlling pattern and texture fills. You should be gaining experience with the powerful collage effects that are possible with blending modes. Layer comps should now enable you to create a number of colorways within the same document for a complex design.

PRACTICE

Using your own images, identify some of the separate elements in the images suitable for different pattern fills and then place these elements on individual layers in a document. Whether you have drawn garments or sketched objects their shape and contours can be emphasized or deconstructed using pattern fills. Explore some of the effects gained with both blending modes and the knockout sliders. Create masks to control the placement of your patterns and motifs and explore transforming the pattern or texture fill within the masks.

PROJECT NINE—ILLUSTRATOR: PATHS TO FASHION

Adobe's Illustrator is the most common application chosen for fashion design. Fashion designers like the crispness, detail, and precision available in the application. Without a need for photorealism, very accurate representations can be made of garments. Diverse individuals and companies use Illustrator. Naturally the style of drawings varies among creators, but the use of Illustrator drawings is widespread across the whole industry. Drawings are produced to develop the design of both individual garments and of whole ranges. In meetings they act as proposals for specific garments and allow for discussion and evaluation. Illustrator drawings can provide detailed guidance for making samples and they can be the print-ready artwork for any garment graphics and pattern design.

Hand drawing is still the way that designs are created, but progressively more of that drawing is digital. Pauline Ainslie, Unit Leader Fashion Coordinator at C&A Europe says, "I think within my (fifty strong) team of garment designers there are maybe 30 percent who rough sketch the range before translating it into CAD, these do however tend to be the older designers, most people now feel confident to design straight into Illustrator."

PROJECT SIX— PHOTOSHOP: REPEATS AND COLORWAYS

PROJECT SEVEN — COLOR THEORY IN PRACTICE

PROJECT EIGHT— PHOTOSHOP: FILLS, TEXTURES, AND LAYERS

PROJECT NINE— ILLUSTRATOR: PATHS TO FASHION

PROJECT TEN— SIMPLE GEOMETRY IN ILLUSTRATOR

PROJECT ELEVEN— REPEAT PATTERNS IN ILLUSTRATOR

CASE STUDY: NADINE BUCHER

PROJECT TWELVE— ILLUSTRATOR: PHOTOSHOP AND FILTERS

CASE STUDY: TORD BOONTJE

There are excellent tools in Illustrator for converting pencil sketches into vector drawings, but if you don't develop confidence with Illustrator's own drawing tools then editing your design may give you problems. Illustrator is as smoothly designed as Photoshop, and working in the application is easy once you understand how the tools work. Earlier in this book the differences between vector and bitmap were explained. Illustrator allows you to access the power of vectors and to use processes that are not available in Photoshop.

Illustrator is also popular for textile design and it is often combined with Photoshop in a natural working method, switching between the two as the particular task dictates.

Previous Photoshop projects introduced Layers, Selections, Masks, Paths, and Custom Brushes. These projects also introduced what are key aspects of working in Illustrator. Drawing and manipulating Paths, as practiced in Project Four, is very good preparation for Illustrator, where drawing is about objects composed of anchor points and their connecting paths. Like Photoshop, fills and masks are used to display patterns and in Illustrator custom brushes are particularly useful to create garment details like stitching, ruching, and zipper fastenings.

ILLUSTRATOR: PATHS TO FASHION

In this project you will:
- Learn how objects are defined in Illustrator, manipulate an anchor point, precisely scale a geometric shape.
- Do precise repeated transformations, create a pattern brush and apply it to an object, change fills and strokes on objects, and use Isolation Mode to drill down into the sublayers of an object and edit them individually.

Outcome
You should have a flower with a number of petals exactly distributed around the center. The center should have a pattern resembling disc florets of a daisylike flower. The petals and center should be suitably colored.

Aim
To practice drawing, selection, and modification techniques in Illustrator. To understand the fill and stroke attributes of any object. To understand how the selection tools are used to adjust the points on a path or define an object. To create a complex object from scratch that uses some of the opportunities of working in vectors in Illustrator. To introduce the particular way of drawing in Illustrator that can enable the making of precise designs for textiles, fashion, and graphics.

WORKING IN ILLUSTRATOR

In Illustrator there are many processes available that can help with efficiency. When duplication of elements is required, as often happens in design, Illustrator provides excellent tools for easily achieving this task. For example, if you require a number of petals equally arranged round the center of a flower, Illustrator will allow you to distribute these perfectly, whatever the number, as you will see in this project. In garment design it is common practice to draw only one half of the garment and then flip a copy to complete the design. (You may recall you had some preparation for this when drawing the leaf in Project Two.)

As another example, a path that defines a seam edge can be offset to give a perfectly placed stitch line. In Illustrator all elements in the design are separate objects by default. This allows the individual belt loops on a drawing to be altered easily without changing any other part of the trouser design or, if wanted, all the loops to be changed together if defined as a group.

Good practice in Illustrator is to organize your design logically. Objects should have the minimum number of anchor points needed, they should have complete outlines, or paths, and they should be composed of obvious shapes. For example, in a garment drawing of a T-shirt, it is natural that the body and sleeves should be complete objects, as should any collar and cuffs. A colleague might work on your drawing at a later stage so it is important that the structure is clear and easy to edit.

There is a popular style of flat drawing where the outline of the garment has a thicker line than internal lines. In that case there would be a composite outline made from all the elements of the drawing that have an outer edge. Stitching and trims should be on a separate layer, above, so that any changes to the body fabric do not conceal them. If you want to introduce some shadows for a more three-dimensional effect they, too, should have their own layer and have some transparency so they change to reflect whatever the underlying colors are.

The first stage to confidence in Illustrator is becoming familiar with how objects are composed and the use of selection tools. **(fig. 52)** In Illustrator objects are defined by anchor points and the connecting paths between them. Exactly like the paths you drew in Project Four in Photoshop, the paths in Illustrator can be straight or curved and the anchor points have control arms that allow those curves to be adjusted at any time. Using Paths in Photoshop is very good preparation for Illustrator, as the system is identical.

In Illustrator you have the same two selection tool pointers: the Selection tool, for easy selection of whole objects, and the Direct Selection tool, for selection of elements of an object such as individual points or individual connecting paths. Again, the same shortcuts with selections apply in Illustrator; the shift key allows you to select multiple instances of whatever you want.

52

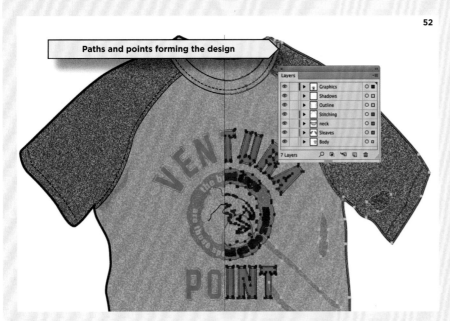

Paths and points forming the design

52
Remember that the color of the user interface in the examples has been chosen as light gray for clarity and that you can change this from the default in the application preferences.

PROJECT SIX—
PHOTOSHOP:
REPEATS AND
COLORWAYS

PROJECT SEVEN —
COLOR THEORY
IN PRACTICE

PROJECT EIGHT—
PHOTOSHOP:
FILLS, TEXTURES,
AND LAYERS

**PROJECT NINE—
ILLUSTRATOR:
PATHS TO FASHION**

PROJECT TEN—
SIMPLE GEOMETRY
IN ILLUSTRATOR

PROJECT ELEVEN—
REPEAT PATTERNS
IN ILLUSTRATOR

CASE STUDY:
NADINE BUCHER

PROJECT TWELVE—
ILLUSTRATOR:
PHOTOSHOP AND
FILTERS

CASE STUDY:
TORD BOONTJE

Preset objects are defined by points and paths at the outset. The Ellipse tool, for example, creates ellipses with four anchor points and curved paths connecting these. With drawing tools like the Pen or Pencil you create points by clicking the mouse (or digital pen) and depending on whether you simply click or click, hold, and drag you will get straight paths directly between points or curved paths connecting the points.

Fill and Stroke

The big distinction between Illustrator and Photoshop, because the former is a vector application, is that points and paths—not colored pixels—define the image objects. Any object has two aspects: its fill, the color or pattern within the boundaries of its paths, and its stroke, which is the color, thickness, and pattern applied to the paths. Objects can have no fill, which still counts as a fill, and no stroke, which

counts as a stroke; these are the object's attributes. When an object is selected and active, with the paths and points displayed in the layer highlight color, refer to the Fill and Stroke display in the Toolbar (also known as the Tool Panel) to see the object's attributes. Sometimes an object has an unwanted white stroke, but is not apparent because the underlying document is also white. So keeping an eye on the fill and stroke attributes is important.

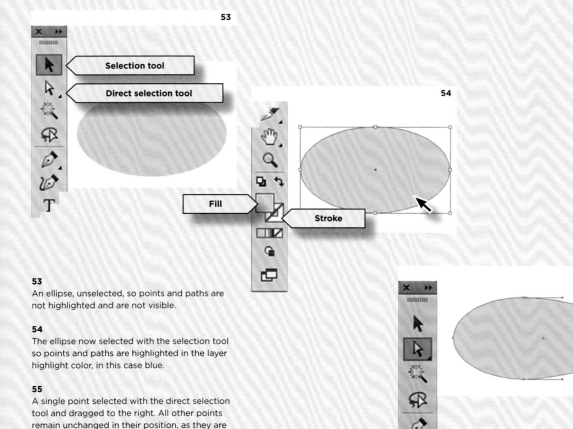

53

Selection tool

Direct selection tool

54

Fill

Stroke

55

53
An ellipse, unselected, so points and paths are not highlighted and are not visible.

54
The ellipse now selected with the selection tool so points and paths are highlighted in the layer highlight color, in this case blue.

55
A single point selected with the direct selection tool and dragged to the right. All other points remain unchanged in their position, as they are not selected (shown as tiny unfilled squares rather than the filled square indicating a selected and active point). The paths between an active point and a static unselected point adjust to accommodate the transformation.

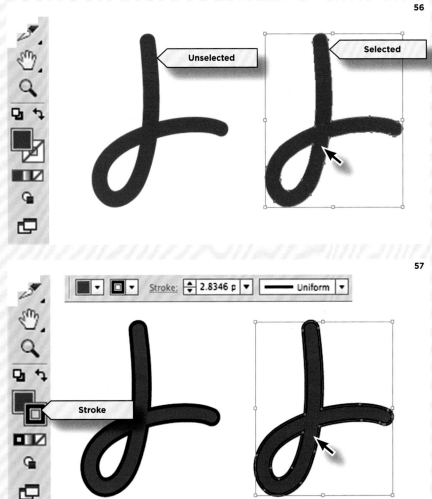

56

56
An object created freehand with the Blob brush. Note the points that have been created by Illustrator to define the shape. Points are placed only where the path makes a strong change in direction. If you use the Pen tool to draw an object you should follow the same principle as in Photoshop, the least amount of points to define a shape is best to give maximum control.

57

57
The object now has a stroke applied. In the Toolbar the stroke of the current selected object is shown in the hollow square. A red through line indicates no stroke. To choose whether to change the stroke or fill, use the X key to bring either to the front. Color can be changed in many ways in Illustrator, but the fill or stroke has to be selected first in either the Toolbar or the Object Options bar (Control Panel) in the applications header.

Note that in this example 1 mm was typed in the Stroke Thickness (called "weight" in Illustrator) option. This was applied to the object by Illustrator and shows in the header converted to a value in points, as points are the current stroke unit. Illustrator accepts your figure whatever the units you enter. This is an excellent feature, as you are more likely to think in inches or millimeters than points or picas. At times you may be mixing figures in imperial with metric and Illustrator has no problem with this. You can change default units in the application preferences.

PROJECT SIX—
PHOTOSHOP:
REPEATS AND
COLORWAYS

PROJECT SEVEN —
COLOR THEORY
IN PRACTICE

PROJECT EIGHT—
PHOTOSHOP:
FILLS, TEXTURES,
AND LAYERS

**PROJECT NINE—
ILLUSTRATOR:
PATHS TO FASHION**

PROJECT TEN—
SIMPLE GEOMETRY
IN ILLUSTRATOR

PROJECT ELEVEN—
REPEAT PATTERNS
IN ILLUSTRATOR

CASE STUDY:
NADINE BUCHER

PROJECT TWELVE—
ILLUSTRATOR:
PHOTOSHOP AND
FILTERS

CASE STUDY:
TORD BOONTJE

You will draw a single petal and from that build a flower as a means of learning some of Illustrator's powerful transformation tools.

9.1

Launch Illustrator if it is not already open. If you change your units to millimeters in Preferences your figures will match those shown in the screenshots, but both metric and imperial equivalent measurements are given in the project text. Unless you find the dark interface essential to work with, change it to the more neutral Light Brightness (gray) display in Preferences. Your interface will then match the screenshots shown in this book. Go ➔ **File** ➔ **New** and select Print as the Profile and A4 as the document size, and Portrait as the Orientation. The color mode may be RGB or CMYK. It is an option to change under the advanced drop-down menu within the New Document window, but is available to change at any time after in File drop down ➔ **Color Mode**.

9.2

Illustrator has many workspace options where the windows are arranged to aid a particular task. You can also save your own favorite window combinations and positions as a workspace. Under the Window menu go **Workspace** ➔ **Painting**. If it is already ticked then you have it already selected as the current workspace layout. Open one additional window, the Info window.

Click **command/control + R** to bring up the rulers. Select the Direct Selection tool. Exactly as in in Photoshop, draw out of the rulers a horizontal and then a vertical guide roughly to cross in the center of the document. The guideline becomes a nonprinting blue when you release. These guides enable you to organize your layout.

9.3

Select the Ellipse drawing tool. The default Rectangle tool may be the tool displayed, so hold down on the tool icon to display the other tools and select Ellipse. **(fig. 58)**

58

Rectangle Tool	(M)
Rounded Rectangle Tool	
Ellipse Tool	(L)
Polygon Tool	
Star Tool	
Flare Tool	

9.4

Hold down the **option/alt** key and click the ellipse tool once at the crossing point of the guides. Release the **option/alt** key when the ellipse window opens. In the value boxes type either 0.5 inches for the width and 1.3 inches for the height or 13 millemeters for the width and 33 millimeters for the height. Regardless of the general units set in preferences, Illustrator will accept either type of units in the input boxes. (The figures are only significant in relation to the project and to enable you to create the same images as the screenshots.) Using the **option/alt** key enables you to position your object precisely and to easily specify exact dimensions. **(fig. 59)**

By default the ellipse will have a white fill and a black stroke. Press **shift + x** to swap the two colors around. You now have a black fill and a white stroke. Stroke should be uppermost of the two in the Toolbar. Click on the very small red strike-through at the bottom of the Toolbar to change the stroke to none. Or better still, use the shortcut "/" (backslash) on your keyboard for none. **(fig. 60)**

9.5

There are two methods of moving things in Illustrator. One, a more hands on way using the Info window, and one using figures entered in various transformation boxes. Both are good. You will use the second method more in the next project. Here you are going to do most things manually.

The Ellipse tool should still be the active tool. Now as part of developing a professional and highly efficient way of working use the **command/control** key to switch the tool temporarily to the direct selection tool. Click inside the ellipse (keep the **command/control** key down all the time) and start dragging it up the document. Hold down the shift key as well to constrain the movement to exactly vertical. If you originally clicked the ellipse tool

exactly on the crossing of the guides then the center of the ellipse should move up the vertical guide. Look at the Info window and see that the figure for distance, D, is increasing. Stop when you get to 2.5 inches (64 millimeters). You may have noted that the height figure was a negative one; like Photoshop there are negative as well as positive values for direction. Release the shift key. **(fig. 61)**

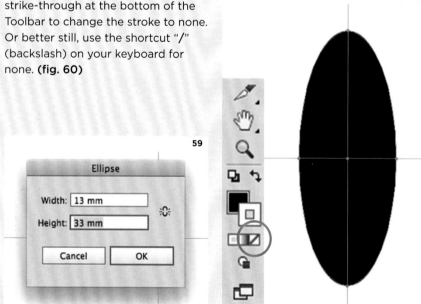

59

Ellipse

Width: 13 mm

Height: 33 mm

Cancel   OK

60

61

Navigator ◇ Info

X: 116.593 mm   W: 0 mm
Y: 22.006 mm   H: -64.601 mm

D: 64.601 mm   △: 90°

TIP

A note here about flowers. A number of people draw flower petals in Illustrator without seeming to have noticed that petals in reality are not regular ellipses. It is actually very easy to make a better, more informed and accurate petal shape. And this you are going to do in the exercise. Knowing the tools is all well and good but you need to keep looking at the world and at your work with a discriminating eye.

PROJECT SIX—
PHOTOSHOP:
REPEATS AND
COLORWAYS

PROJECT SEVEN —
COLOR THEORY
IN PRACTICE

PROJECT EIGHT—
PHOTOSHOP:
FILLS, TEXTURES,
AND LAYERS

**PROJECT NINE—
ILLUSTRATOR:
PATHS TO FASHION**

PROJECT TEN—
SIMPLE GEOMETRY
IN ILLUSTRATOR

PROJECT ELEVEN—
REPEAT PATTERNS
IN ILLUSTRATOR

CASE STUDY:
NADINE BUCHER

PROJECT TWELVE—
ILLUSTRATOR:
PHOTOSHOP AND
FILTERS

CASE STUDY:
TORD BOONTJE

9.6

You should still be holding down the **command/control** key to switch from the Ellipse tool to this one. Click the Direct Selection tool on the single anchor point at the base of the ellipse and start dragging that point down the document. Hold down the shift key to constrain the movement exactly vertical. Read off the distance from the Info window. Stop when you reach a distance of 1.3 inches or 33 millimeters. (If you are struggling with the key combinations then you can switch to the Direct Selection tool itself.) **(fig. 62)**

9.7

Double click with the Direct Selection tool inside your stretched ellipse to select the whole object (the four anchor point should be solid). Click on the rotate tool in the Toolbar to select it. Hold down the **option/ alt** key and click on the point, as before, where the two guidelines cross. This establishes the point of rotation. By default it would be at the center point of the object itself but you want it to rotate about a point outside the object. **(fig. 63)**

Enter the degree of rotation in the window that opens. Now you will have noticed that Illustrator and Photoshop accept the units you enter in the value boxes even if they differ from the default. Well, next you will see a truly clever aspect of the value input boxes that helps the designer even more. To get a number of petals

to run around evenly in a circle, 360 (degrees) needs to be divided by the number of petals chosen and the outcome of this is the amount to rotate the first petal. For a flower with six petals that would be $360 \div 6 = 60$, so 60 degrees of rotation for the first petal and all the subsequent ones. In Illustrator you don't even need to do the mathematics in your head, or on a calculator for trickier equations, for example, when the numbers don't divide so evenly into 360. In the value box in the Rotate window enter "360/" followed by the number of petals you want, in the example in this project—19. The backslash acts as a divide cue for Illustrator. Click the copy button rather than okay to keep the original in position and prepare for the next stage. **(fig. 64)**

62

63

Rotate tool

64

Rotate

Rotate

Angle: 360/19

Options: ☑ Transform Objects ☐ Transform Patterns

☑ Preview

Copy   Cancel   OK

9.8

Now for one of the processes that is so easy to achieve in Illustrator and so much harder elsewhere. All the transformation processes in Illustrator allow for you to repeat the exact transformation just done with a simple shortcut, **command/control + D**. Because you selected copy in the Rotate window, copying is included in the repetition. Note that the copy you made is now the selected or active object. Press **command/control + D** together and a fresh copy is made, rotated around the original center of rotation you specified at the start and by the same number of degrees as before (18.95˚, which is, in fact, 360 ÷ 19). Click **command/control + D** again to produce a further petal and continue clicking until all the petals are completed around the circle. **(fig. 65)**

9.9

Now to create the parts of the center of the flower. Select the Ellipse tool to draw a circle. Make sure that the fill is black with no stroke. Use the **option/alt** key, as before, and click anywhere beside the petals in the document to open the ellipse window and enter dimensions 0.12 inches by 0.12 inches or 3 millimeters by 3 millimeters in the value boxes.

9.10

Have the Brushes window visible. With the Selection tool drag the circle you have drawn into the Brushes window. A new Brush Options window opens; select the Pattern Brush radio button. **(fig. 66)**

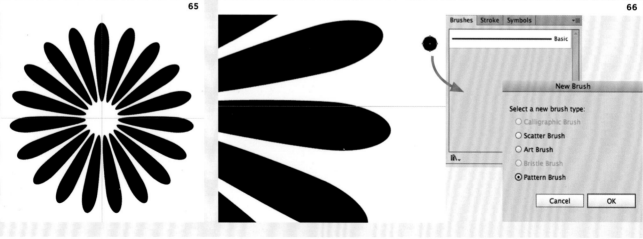

65

66

PROJECT SIX—
PHOTOSHOP:
REPEATS AND
COLORWAYS

PROJECT SEVEN —
COLOR THEORY
IN PRACTICE

PROJECT EIGHT—
PHOTOSHOP:
FILLS, TEXTURES,
AND LAYERS

**PROJECT NINE—
ILLUSTRATOR:
PATHS TO FASHION**

PROJECT TEN—
SIMPLE GEOMETRY
IN ILLUSTRATOR

PROJECT ELEVEN—
REPEAT PATTERNS
IN ILLUSTRATOR

CASE STUDY:
NADINE BUCHER

PROJECT TWELVE—
ILLUSTRATOR:
PHOTOSHOP AND
FILTERS

CASE STUDY:
TORD BOONTJE

9.11

In the Pattern Brush Options window that opens adjust the spacing of the brush to 30 percent and the Colorization method to Tints. Changing Colorization to Tints rather than None allows the brush to be given a color other than the original black. You can leave the other options as is and click okay. **(fig. 67)**

9.12

Select the Polar Grid tool. It is the tool at the bottom of the drop-down menu where, by default, Line Segment tool is displayed. Polar Grid tool is a convenient tool for drawing concentric circles. Hold down the **option/alt** key and click with the Polar Grid tool at the crossing of the guidelines in the center of the flower. **(fig. 68)**

9.13

In the Polar Grid Options window that opens enter 1.18 inches or 30 millimeters as the dimensions for width and height, five as the number of concentric dividers, and none as the number of radial dividers. Click okay. A set of concentric circles appears within the center of the flower. **(fig. 69)**

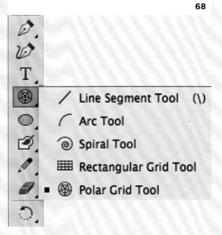

68

/ Line Segment Tool   (\)

⌒ Arc Tool

◎ Spiral Tool

▦ Rectangular Grid Tool

◉ Polar Grid Tool

69

Polar Grid Tool Options

Default Size

Width: 30 mm

Height: 30 mm

Concentric Dividers

Number: 5

Skew: ——————●—————— 0%
In   Out

Radial Dividers

Number: 0

Skew: ———————●——— 0%
Bottom   Top

☐ Create Compound Path From Ellipses

☐ Fill Grid

Cancel   OK

67

Pattern Brush Options

Options

Name: Pattern Brush 3

Scale: Fixed ▾   100%   100%

Spacing 30%

Flip

☐ Flip Along

☐ Flip Across

Fit

◉ Stretch to fit

○ Add space to fit

○ Approximate path

Colorization

Method Tints ▾   ♀

Key Color:

Cancel   OK

Experiment with various combinations of spacing and size to get a version of a flower center that you are happy with. **(fig. 70)**

In the document you can delete the circle that was originally used to make your brush but if you consider the arrangement of the center of your particular flower requires one single circle in the dead center you can use the single circle for that. Select the Direct Selection tool, click within the circle, and drag to the crossing of the guidelines in the center of the flower. The transformation box that appears around the circle has a control point at each corner. If you select one of these you can resize the circle on the fly by pulling the corner outwards or inwards. If you hold down the shift key at the same time the scaling will be exactly in proportion, so the circle will remain a circle. If you hold down the **option/alt** key, the scale will take place from the center and that is usually the ideal situation.

Hold down both keys together as you start adjusting the size of the circle to fit with the other circles proportionally. **Shift** and **option/ alt** act as modifying keys on all transformation tools so they are very useful aids to learn and to employ.

If you find the resizing a little jerky that may be because there is a snap-to-guides action taking place. The easiest remedy is to hide the guides. The shortcut is **command/control +**; which hides the guides; the same command will reveal them. **(fig. 71)**

With the flower shape finished you can now change the colors. A useful selection technique is **Select → Same Fill Color**. You have only to select one object and, using this command, Illustrator searches out and makes active all the other objects of the same fill. This kind of selection technique is useful if you have group of designs in a document, for example, pattern ideas or garment styles, and you need to modify an attribute across all of them. For example, if the client has specified a different ecru to be used, all instances of the ecru can be changed together. With the command Select Same there are a number of other attributes that can be helpful used as the selection mode.

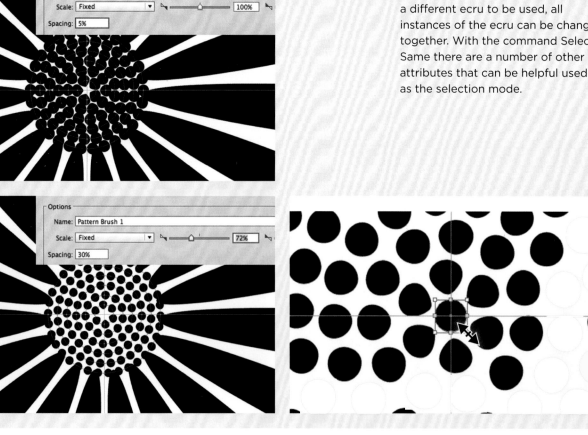

70

71

PROJECT SIX—
PHOTOSHOP:
REPEATS AND
COLORWAYS

PROJECT SEVEN —
COLOR THEORY
IN PRACTICE

PROJECT EIGHT—
PHOTOSHOP:
FILLS, TEXTURES,
AND LAYERS

**PROJECT NINE—
ILLUSTRATOR:
PATHS TO FASHION**

PROJECT TEN—
SIMPLE GEOMETRY
IN ILLUSTRATOR

PROJECT ELEVEN—
REPEAT PATTERNS
IN ILLUSTRATOR

CASE STUDY:
NADINE BUCHER

PROJECT TWELVE—
ILLUSTRATOR:
PHOTOSHOP AND
FILTERS

CASE STUDY:
TORD BOONTJE

9.14

Immediately go to the brush window and click once on your new brush. This will apply the brush to the current selection, which is the active object, the set of concentric circles you have just created. See now that your brush is applied to the polar grid.

9.15

Double click on your brush in the Brushes window. This opens up the Brush Options window again and allows you to make adjustments to the spacing and size of the brush tip and see how it looks in the design. You might have guessed that, as in Photoshop, there are many different ways to change color. A second method is to select a specific color swatch in the Swatches window for either the fill or the stroke. There are a number of basic swatches by default in Illustrator. You can load more from Swatch libraries via the window drop-down menu. You can also store your own colors in the swatch window. **(fig. 72)**

9.16

Select one petal with the Selection Tool. Go **Select → Same → Fill Color**. All petals are then selected and not the polar grid, as Illustrator knows this doesn't have any black fill. It only has the pattern brush, which is a stroke. The single circle in the middle of the polar grid pattern will also be selected with the petals because that also has the same black fill. You don't want this circle included so you can practice removing it from a selection. To subtract an object from a selection, hold down the shift key and click on the selected object with the Selection tool. Shift will add the object to the selection or subtract it if it is already selected.

9.17

Ensure that fill is foremost in the Toolbar (use the **X** key to bring it forward if need be). Double click on the Fill icon to open the Color Picker window. Select a suitable color to change the fill color of all the petals. **(fig. 73)**

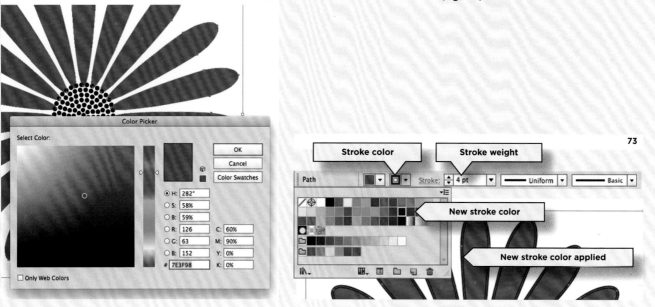

72

73

9.18

With the petals still selected go to the Control Panel, above the document and in the application header. For the current selected object or objects the fill and stroke are displayed and the weight and style of stroke. The menu arrow alongside the Fill and Path options accesses the current swatch content. Selecting a swatch will immediately apply it to the selected object.

9.19

Having colored the petals you can now adjust the colors in the center of the flower. Changing the fill for the polar grid will apply color to its divider rings. Changing the stroke will apply color to the circles of the pattern brush (because you specified Tints in the brush options) that are acting as a stroke on the rings. Using Isolation Mode you can even recolor the individual divider rings and their circles.

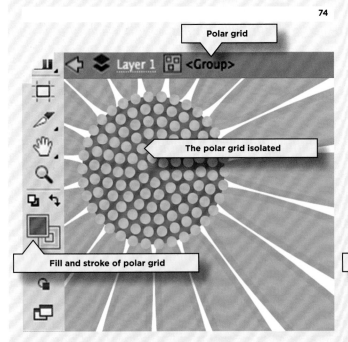

74

Polar grid

Layer 1 <Group>

The polar grid isolated

Fill and stroke of polar grid

75

Single divider isolated

Layer 1 <Group> <Group>

Fill and stroke of single divider

74
Double clicking on the polar grid has taken it into Isolation Mode. The rest of the flower is hidden or dimmed.

75
Double clicking on a single divider has further isolated its fill, and stroke can then be changed separately.

PROJECT SIX—
PHOTOSHOP:
REPEATS AND
COLORWAYS

PROJECT SEVEN —
COLOR THEORY
IN PRACTICE

PROJECT EIGHT—
PHOTOSHOP:
FILLS, TEXTURES,
AND LAYERS

**PROJECT NINE—
ILLUSTRATOR:
PATHS TO FASHION**

PROJECT TEN—
SIMPLE GEOMETRY
IN ILLUSTRATOR

PROJECT ELEVEN—
REPEAT PATTERNS
IN ILLUSTRATOR

CASE STUDY:
NADINE BUCHER

PROJECT TWELVE—
ILLUSTRATOR:
PHOTOSHOP AND
FILTERS

CASE STUDY:
TORD BOONTJE

Isolation Mode

If you double click on an object you can enter Isolation Mode. When this happens it frequently confuses beginners. It is, though, a very useful way of drilling down into the elements that make up your design and altering the specific one you want. However, students often find it tricky at the start.

When you activate Isolation Mode all objects in your document, other than the one you double clicked on, are dimmed and automatically become locked in order that only the objects selected in isolation mode are affected by any edits you make. The isolated object's name and location (sometimes referred to as "bread crumbs") appear in the special (gray colored) isolation mode border at the top of the document. The Layers window displays only the artwork contained in the isolated group.

When you exit isolation mode, the other layers and groups reappear in the Layers window. To exit Isolation Mode instantly you can press the escape key. You can also exit in stages by clicking the Back One Level button in the isolation mode border. This acts somewhat like a Show the Previous page button in a browser. In isolation mode you can drill down a number of levels so you might want to go back only one level. If so, use the Back One Level button to progress back up to the surface, level by level.

PROJECT REVIEW

REVIEW
You should have gained confidence in creating vector objects and seeing how easily they are manipulated. You should be able to transform objects by two methods: directly by moving anchor points and through entering new values in transformation options windows.

PRACTICE
Rotate is only one of the transformation tools. Explore the possibilities of transforming and duplicating an object or group of objects using other transformation tools. Select the tools from either the Toolbar or from under Transform in the Object menu.

PROJECT TEN—SIMPLE GEOMETRY IN ILLUSTRATOR

10

A strong reason for designing with Adobe Illustrator is the ability to generate designs that require precise geometry, which is very easy to achieve in Illustrator.

As you gain confidence in the application it is good to start adopting some of the efficiencies in work practice that come with digital design. The computer is so adept at making perfect copies you can save a lot of time by creating a resource of elements you use frequently. In garment design, with a little time spent drawing a component such as a zipper pull, you need never draw it again. Illustrator allows you to use these "symbols" as originally drawn, or to quickly customize them as need be.

With a busy work schedule it is easy to make small mistakes when working by eye. The precision inherent in Illustrator helps you avoid the frustration at the output stage when tiny misalignments in your work suddenly become apparent. Let Illustrator do more of the work, ensuring objects match up without a single pixel gap. Most designers don't want to work too much with numbers and Illustrator is very ready to make precision painless.

PROJECT SIX—
PHOTOSHOP:
REPEATS AND
COLORWAYS

PROJECT SEVEN —
COLOR THEORY
IN PRACTICE

PROJECT EIGHT—
PHOTOSHOP:
FILLS, TEXTURES,
AND LAYERS

PROJECT NINE—
ILLUSTRATOR:
PATHS TO FASHION

PROJECT TEN—
SIMPLE GEOMETRY
IN ILLUSTRATOR

PROJECT ELEVEN—
REPEAT PATTERNS
IN ILLUSTRATOR

CASE STUDY:
NADINE BUCHER

PROJECT TWELVE—
ILLUSTRATOR:
PHOTOSHOP AND
FILTERS

CASE STUDY:
TORD BOONTJE

SIMPLE GEOMETRY IN ILLUSTRATOR

In this project you will

- Use transformation tools to move, copy, reflect, and shear objects in Illustrator.
- Use the Divide Objects Below command as a simple alternative to the Shapebuilder tool.
- Learn to move objects from one layer to another, an important technique for organizing your design.
- Practice keeping note of the stroke and fill of objects.
- Reduce the complexity of a design by using symbols to replace multiple copies and learn of their significance in an efficient workflow. Offset path will enable you to create well-shaped concentric paths inside or outside an existing object.

Outcome

You should have created a precise pattern with simple geometric shapes and perfectly aligned elements. You should learn that reducing unnecessary complexity in objects and in working methods, where possible, both simplifies and speeds up working within Illustrator and aids sharing files with colleagues, saving and outputting to devices

Aim

To practice drawing and modification techniques in Illustrator. To be confident with the fill and stroke attributes of any object. To create a pattern from simple objects from scratch that uses some of the opportunities for working in vectors. To gain some good practice in Illustrator that can enable fast and efficient working.

10.1

Go **File → New**, name the document Geometric Design, select the document profile as Print, the size as A4.

10.2

Click **command/control + R** to display the rulers. Drag out a horizontal guideline and a vertical guideline to form a cross in the approximate middle of the document.

10.3

Select a suitable fill color, use the guide if you want to match the colors of the example precisely. Colors are introduced in the project in the order left to right. You can use the color window to create new colors precisely. Note that none of the objects have stroke in this project. **(fig. 76)**

10.4

If matching the colors from the guide, use the Color Picker or Color window to create a fill color with values cyan 12 magenta 0 yellow 60 black 0. Select the Rectangle tool (keyboard shortcut "M"), hold down the **option/alt** key, and click on the crossing point of the guides. In the window that opens, enter 2.83 inches or 72 millemeters in both input boxes to create a square. **(fig. 77)**

10.5

Change the fill color for the ellipse to a darker tone of the color used in the square (or to match that in the illustration precisely cyan 15 magenta 0 yellow 75 black 25). Select the Ellipse tool, keyboard shortcut "L." By default, Rectangle tool is the one displayed in the shape tool position in the Toolbar. Pressing down on the Rectangle tool icon displays the other tool options.

TIP | The rectangle is constructed from four anchor points only. Any additional points are Illustrator's means of displaying modification options. If you select the Direct Selection tool, only the four points are displayed. If the Selection tool is selected, the bounding box handles are displayed, and if the object has corners, the live corner widgets are displayed. For the novice this can make the object appear more complex than it is. The bounding box handles allow you to pick up a side or corner and alter the shape of the object freehand. The corner widgets allow you options on the existing corner shape. For now corner widgets are not needed so, for simplicity, you can turn off Show Corner Widget in the View menu.

76

C=12 M=0 Y= 60 K=0	C=15 M=0 Y= 75 K=25	C=16 M=0 Y= 80 K=0	C=8 M=0 Y= 40 K=0	C=10 M=0 Y= 50 K=50

77

Rectangle

Options
Width: 72 mm
Height: 72 mm

OK
Cancel

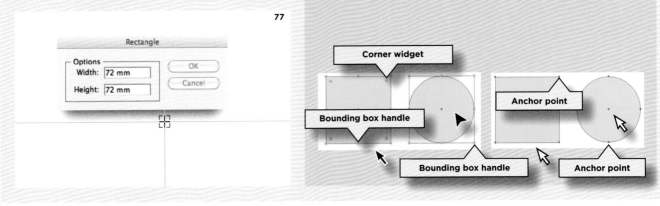

Corner widget

Bounding box handle

Anchor point

Bounding box handle

Anchor point

PROJECT SIX—
PHOTOSHOP:
REPEATS AND
COLORWAYS

PROJECT SEVEN —
COLOR THEORY
IN PRACTICE

PROJECT EIGHT—
PHOTOSHOP:
FILLS, TEXTURES,
AND LAYERS

PROJECT NINE—
ILLUSTRATOR:
PATHS TO FASHION

**PROJECT TEN—
SIMPLE GEOMETRY
IN ILLUSTRATOR**

PROJECT ELEVEN—
REPEAT PATTERNS
IN ILLUSTRATOR

CASE STUDY:
NADINE BUCHER

PROJECT TWELVE—
ILLUSTRATOR:
PHOTOSHOP AND
FILTERS

CASE STUDY:
TORD BOONTJE

A small triangle at the lower, right corner of a tool icon indicates the presence of hidden tools. Hold down the **option/alt** key and again click on the crossing point of the guides done previously. Enter 2.83 inches or 72 millimeters in both input boxes of the window to place a 2.83-inch, 72-millimeter diameter circle exactly over the square. **(fig. 78)**

10.6

Deselect the circle by clicking in a blank area of the document with the Selection tool. Select the next tone of green in the guide for the color fill. If using your own colors, the Color Guide can be useful for accessing tones. At the crossing of the guidelines, create a new rectangle with a width of 0.62 inches or 16 millimeter and a height of 1.4 inches or 36 millimeters. Move this rectangle so that its right-hand side lines up with the vertical guide and the bottom of the rectangle aligns with the horizontal guide.

10.7

Select the Shear tool; this is in the set with the Scale tool. Click once on the center crossing point of the guidelines. This moves the axis or point of transformation for the rectangle from its center to the bottom right-hand corner. Now put the cursor inside the rectangle and drag the rectangle to the left to shear it so the top left corner matches that of the square. **(fig. 79–81)**

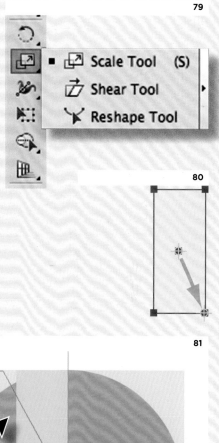

79

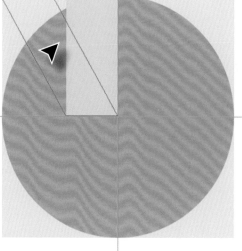

80

81

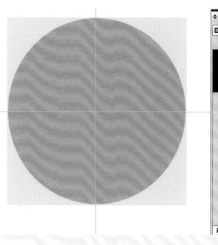

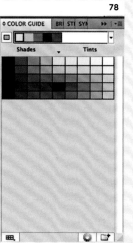

78

10.8

Make sure you do not deselect the sheared rectangle. Select the Reflect tool, the shortcut is the letter "**O**" key. **(fig. 82)**

Hold down the **option/alt** key and click on the horizontal guideline to set this as the point of transformation. Select the radio button for the horizontal axis if not selected. Click Copy rather than Okay. **(fig. 83)**

10.9

Go to the Layer window, from the options drop-down menu select New Layer. Click Okay in the Layer options dialog box to create a new layer. With the Selection tool select the two sheared rectangles that make the chevron. Note the highlight color they have when selected. Go to the Layer window. Look for the little colored square that indicates the selected artwork. Each layer has a specific highlight color for selected

objects. Click on the square with the mouse or digital pen and push this square up to the new layer. This action moves the selected artwork from Layer 1 to Layer 2. This is the method for changing the location of artwork in the layer structure in Illustrator. Lock Layer 2 by clicking in the space next to the eye, and click on the eye to make the layer invisible. Click on Layer 1 in the Layer window to make it active. **(fig. 84)**

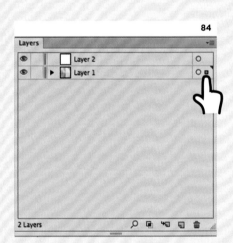

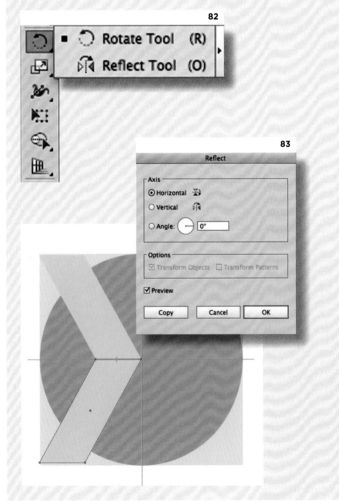

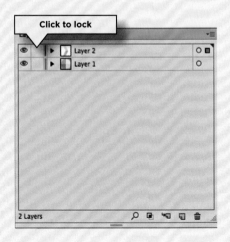

PROJECT SIX—
PHOTOSHOP:
REPEATS AND
COLORWAYS

PROJECT SEVEN —
COLOR THEORY
IN PRACTICE

PROJECT EIGHT—
PHOTOSHOP:
FILLS, TEXTURES,
AND LAYERS

PROJECT NINE—
ILLUSTRATOR:
PATHS TO FASHION

**PROJECT TEN—
SIMPLE GEOMETRY
IN ILLUSTRATOR**

PROJECT ELEVEN—
REPEAT PATTERNS
IN ILLUSTRATOR

CASE STUDY:
NADINE BUCHER

PROJECT TWELVE—
ILLUSTRATOR:
PHOTOSHOP AND
FILTERS

CASE STUDY:
TORD BOONTJE

10.10

Select the Line Segment tool (shortcut is the "\" key), and draw a vertical line along the guideline bisecting the rectangle and square and extending a little beyond them. Stroke and fill color are unimportant, but do not click elsewhere after drawing the line to deselect it. **(fig. 85)**

10.11

Go **Object → Path → Divide Objects Below**. The selected, active line is then used as a cutting line to split all objects underneath it. The line itself disappears. Repeat this dividing process now with a horizontal line this time drawn through the center of the square and circle. After the command Divide Objects Below you should have four circle segments sitting on top of four small squares. **(fig. 86)**

10.12

Unlock and make Layer 2 visible. Now add more tones to all of the different areas, again you can use the color guide for more tones. **(fig. 87)**

10.13

Select all elements then go **Object → Transform → Move...** Enter 2.83 inches or 72 millimeters for the horizontal move distance and zero for the vertical move distance. Click Copy, not Okay. **(fig. 88)**

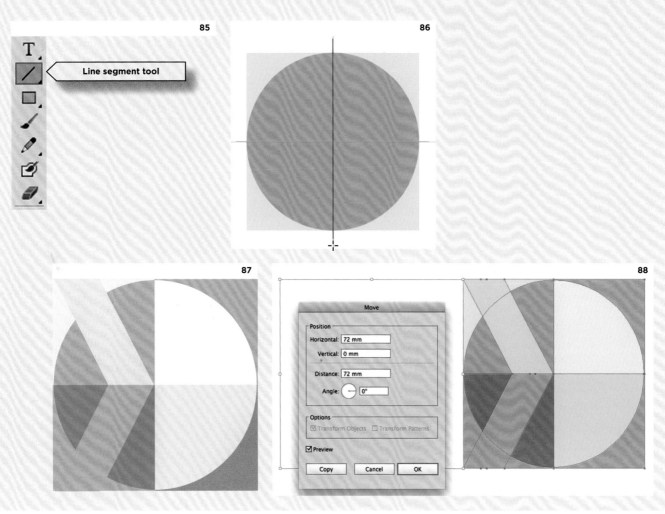

10.14

To create further copies click **command/control + D** to repeat the transformation and copy. Each **command/control + D** creates a further copy beyond the last.

10.15

Select all the copies and then go **Object → Transform → Move**. This time enter zero for the horizontal distance and 2.83 inches or 72 millimeters for the vertical; click Copy, not Okay. Create a further copy using **command/control + D** to repeat the transformation and copy.

10.16

To make the pattern more dynamic by changing the position of the motifs in alternate rows take the selection tool and drag over the second row, selecting all the elements. Go **Object → Transform → Reflect…** Select Vertical as the axis of reflection; click Okay. Once more go **Object → Transform → Reflect**, and this time select Horizontal as the axis for reflection. This should give you a pattern like the one shown here. **(fig. 89)**

89

ADVANCED USE—SYMBOLS

In the pattern shown here there are nine separate copies of the same motif and these can be counted as duplicates in Illustrator even if some are mirrored. Following the principle that keeping things simple is the best practice, all of those separate motifs could actually be replaced by one symbol. At the moment the design is composed of only a small number of elements, but if your motif was complex and copied a number of times Illustrator could spend some time processing the file when sending it to a printer. If you wanted to adjust the motif in some way then you would have to change all the individual motifs. Using Symbols to replace multiple items can be very efficient.

A symbol is an object that can be reused in a document; you add instances of the symbol multiple times without adding any more complexity to the artwork. Each symbol instance is linked to the symbol in the Symbols window. Using symbols can save you time and greatly reduce file size. They have been very popular in practices where drawing requires many repeated standard elements, such as mapmaking, but they also make a lot of sense for fashion.

Symbols and symbol libraries offer an efficient way to organize objects that are frequently used in drawing. For example, a patch pocket can be a symbol used multiple times in a selection of garment drawings and, should the stitch detailing change, then the single symbol is edited and all instances are updated to match the edit.

Although symbol instances are linked to the master symbol you do have freedom to move, scale, rotate, shear, reflect, or warp individual symbol instances like other objects and without breaking the link to the master symbol. You can also perform operations from the Transparency, Appearance, and Graphic Styles windows and effects from the Effect menu on individuals without breaking the link.

You can replace all the symbol instances in the document with new artwork in one operation by using the selected artwork to redefine the symbol in the Symbols window. There is also the flexibility to break the link between a single instance and the master symbol in order that the individual object can be adjusted separately.

Creating a Symbol
1. Open the Symbols window, shortcut **command/control + shift + F11**. Select one complete motif from your artboard and drag this into the Symbols window. A dialog box opens and Illustrator asks you to select the symbol type as movie clip or graphic. However the window also tells you that unless you are going to be using flash it doesn't actually matter either way so just click Okay.

The original motif stays on the artboard, but is now defined as an instance of the symbol and any copies that you make will be instances as well. If you don't want the original artwork to become an instance, press shift as you create the new symbol. And, if you want to skip the New Symbol dialog box when you create a new symbol, press **option/alt** and click on the New Symbol button at the bottom of the Symbols window.

2. Your symbol on the artboard should still be selected. Use **Transform → Move** and **command/control + D** to create a pattern of instances following the method used earlier and use Reflect to change the direction of some of them.

3. Now you will edit an instance and see all other instances of the symbol change too. Double click on one of the instances. A warning window opens to tell you that all instances will be edited. Click Okay in this window. **(fig. 90)**

4. A version of the Isolation Mode window opens allowing you to edit the symbol. Now use a very useful, simple command in Illustrator—the Offset Path command. You can make a copy of an object set off from the selected object by a specified distance. Negative values are used to place the new object path inside the original. As the object gets smaller the angles between anchor points adjust to keep the paths as parallel to the original as possible. This is very useful when drawing inset paths within shapes like garment pieces and is a much better technique than scaling because it creates a more proportionate copy.

Click on one of the light green quarter circles to select it. Go **Object → Offset Path...** and enter –0.11 inches or –3 millimeters as the distance.

5. With the Eyedropper tool, sample the color of the vertical opposite quarter circle. Because the offset shape is active it will assume this color. Hold down the **command/control** key to switch to the selection tool and click on the opposite light green quarter circle. Go **Object → Offset Path...** and enter –0.11 inches or –3 millimeters **(fig. 91)**

Releasing the **command/key** the tool should revert to the Eyedropper. Sample the outside color of the opposite quarter circle. Use the escape key to exit the Symbol Editing window. Note that all symbol instances are updated. **(fig. 92)**

91

New Symbol 8

Offset Path

Offset: -3 mm
Joins: Miter
Miter limit: 4
☐ Preview   Cancel   OK

90

Adobe Illustrator

You are about to edit the Symbol definition. Any edits to the symbol will be applied to all its instances. Do you want to continue?

☐ Don't Show Again   Cancel   OK

PROJECT SIX—
PHOTOSHOP:
REPEATS AND
COLORWAYS

PROJECT SEVEN —
COLOR THEORY
IN PRACTICE

PROJECT EIGHT—
PHOTOSHOP:
FILLS, TEXTURES,
AND LAYERS

PROJECT NINE—
ILLUSTRATOR:
PATHS TO FASHION

**PROJECT TEN—
SIMPLE GEOMETRY
IN ILLUSTRATOR**

PROJECT ELEVEN—
REPEAT PATTERNS
IN ILLUSTRATOR

CASE STUDY:
NADINE BUCHER

PROJECT TWELVE—
ILLUSTRATOR:
PHOTOSHOP AND
FILTERS

CASE STUDY:
TORD BOONTJE

As mentioned earlier, both symbols and offset paths are very useful when drawing for fashion. Offset paths are the ideal way to create stitch lines that follow the outlines of garment pieces and are much easier than scaling a copy of an outline when shapes are not symmetrical. A gallery of frequently used objects can be made once, stored as symbols, and then replicated many times with the freedom to alter them all together at any time, or to break the link and adjust a single instance, or to make a global change when, for example, the button has been replaced by a snap fastener in all raincoat designs. **(fig. 93)**

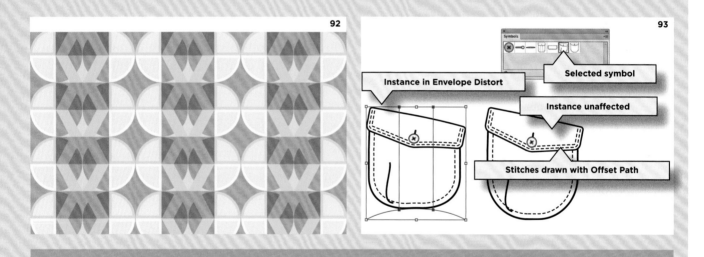

92

93

Selected symbol

Instance in Envelope Distort

Instance unaffected

Stitches drawn with Offset Path

Symbols

PROJECT REVIEW

REVIEW
You should have two patterns that precisely line up. One of multiple copies of your geometric pattern and one by contrast composed of instances of a single symbol. You have seen how using transform commands ensures that your work will be precisely placed or precisely transformed. You have seen that the offset path command is an ideal tool for quick and precise generation of concentric objects, whatever the shape.

PRACTICE
Create some geometric or similarly precise objects, define these as symbols, and use these in creating patterns or components in some garment sketches.

PROJECT ELEVEN—REPEAT PATTERNS IN ILLUSTRATOR

11

With the release of Illustrator CS6, and subsequently CC, came a dramatic increase in the possibilities for repeat work. The old method for creating a repeat fill swatch was replaced with a much more powerful and flexible tool that enables working live in repeats. More tiling options, beyond the standard step, are now available, including half drop. And the design itself can be worked on while displayed in repeat, the edits applied instantly to the repeat copies. So Illustrator CC currently has an advantage over Photoshop in that you are able to switch between the forms of repeating, edit the motifs themselves, and see copies update in repeat. The dramatic or subtle adjustments needed to refine the repeating of your design are now so much easier to do in real time. However, along with the extra freedom to improve your work comes the requirement to master another tool. The layout is similar to Isolation Mode so familiarity with that provides preparation for this excellent tool.

The target with the repeating in this project is to have a continuous flow of motifs without any spaces between. You can choose to use your own motif rather than the supplied petals file but ensure your design has elements that allow for overlapping. You do not want elements simply floating in isolation, as this will not enable you to practice with the editing tools in Pattern Options.

PROJECT SIX—
PHOTOSHOP:
REPEATS AND
COLORWAYS

PROJECT SEVEN —
COLOR THEORY
IN PRACTICE

PROJECT EIGHT—
PHOTOSHOP:
FILLS, TEXTURES,
AND LAYERS

PROJECT NINE—
ILLUSTRATOR:
PATHS TO FASHION

PROJECT TEN—
SIMPLE GEOMETRY
IN ILLUSTRATOR

**PROJECT ELEVEN—
REPEAT PATTERNS
IN ILLUSTRATOR**

CASE STUDY:
NADINE BUCHER

PROJECT TWELVE—
ILLUSTRATOR:
PHOTOSHOP AND
FILTERS

CASE STUDY:
TORD BOONTJE

REPEAT PATTERNS IN ILLUSTRATOR

In this project you will:
- Practice the Pattern tool in Illustrator.
- Put a group of connecting motifs into half-drop repeat and look at ways of adjusting the space—either adding or subtracting as necessary.
- Consider removing material from the motif or adding material to make the repeat successful visually.
- Note the difference between the editable original motif and all the uneditable copies.
- Add and subtract material, editing while in repeat mode.

Outcome
You should create a design that has a successful repeat with no sharp design lines to spoil the flow. You should have this saved as a swatch and apply it to a rectangle equivalent to an A4 document

Aim
To practice using the Pattern Repeat tool in preparation for solving the specific visual requirements of putting your own designs into repeat.

Project files are available at
www.bloomsbury.com/hume-textile-design

11.1

Open the file named Petals. Use **command/control + A** to select all; that is the five-petal motif. **(fig. 94)**

94

11.2

Go to **Object → Pattern → Make** and click Okay in the window that opens to inform you that a new swatch has been added to the swatches palette. This swatch is your motif in repeat. The repeat is always editable but, as will be explained later, you have to be cautious not to overwrite a pattern you are happy with. Note the window that opens displaying the petals repeated is very similar to the Isolation Mode window. **(fig. 95)**

11.3

The selected motif automatically goes into the default repeat. In the Pattern Options window select Brick by Column, as the tile type and Brick Offset should be 1/2 for the equivalent of a half-drop.

11.4

By default, the repeat or tile size is the perimeter of the artwork. This can be adjusted by activating the Pattern Tile tool at the top left of the Pattern Options window and adjusting the bounding box manually, or by entering new figures into the width and height boxes. Adjust the width and height of the repeat

95

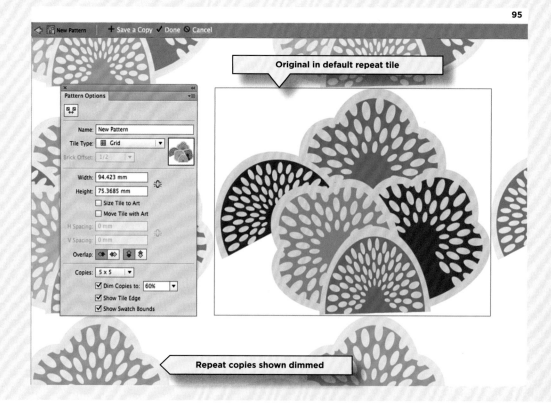

Original in default repeat tile

Repeat copies shown dimmed

to reduce the space between the motifs and, if using your own motifs, experiment with the Overlap options to see which is most appropriate for your design. The Dim Copies setting allows you to distinguish easily between the editable original and the copies. The amount of dimming can be changed as has been done in the illustrated example to make the difference even more obvious.
All the parts of the original motif are editable so you can use the Select and Direct Selection tools to adjust the elements in order to make them work better in repeat. The repeat automatically adjusts to accept the changes. **(fig. 96)**

With the petal motif the ideal arrangement for the overlap is for left and top sides to be in front and a repeat square of 2.2 inches or 56 millimeters. Evaluating the way the design now appears in this repeat layout it makes sense to connect things up smoothly by merging the two blue petal motifs into one. By stretching out the smaller it can be made to line up with the position of the larger. Some additional editing will need to be done. In Pattern Options you are able to do this fine-tuning of repeats. **(fig. 97)**

Transformation tools, such as Rotate, and various drawing tools can be used to create any new material that you need to connect up repeating elements.

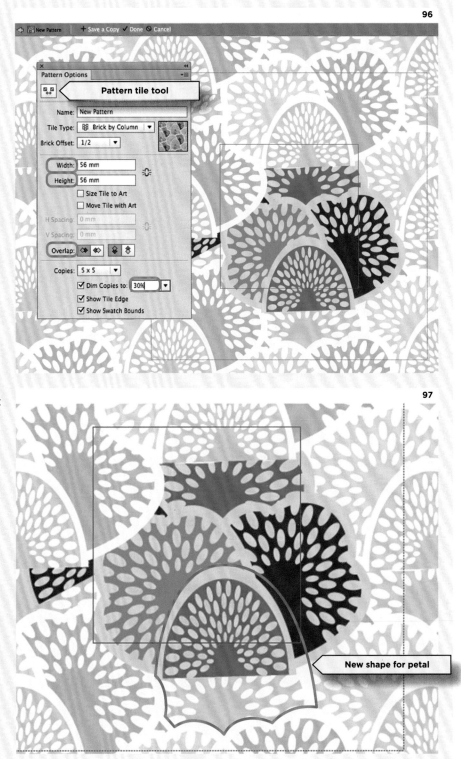

96

97

New shape for petal

11.5

Use the Selection tool to resize and move the entire smaller blue petal so that it lines up with the larger. As you add or change an element in the original (indicated by a blue bounding box) copies appear or change in the repeat tiles. **(fig. 98)**

Now the spots in the two blue petals need to be adjusted so that they align correctly.

11.6

First switch to the larger petal at the top of the repeat tile and remove or adjust there the spots that do not match the arrangement of the smaller petal (in the faded-out copy). Use the Direct Selection tool to pick the spots and then the delete key to remove them. Make sure you click inside the spots to select them rather than clicking on their individual anchor points. Your experience adjusting paths with the Direct Selection tool and with the pen tool should enable you to edit objects

here where necessary. Remember not to use the Selection tool (the black arrow); it will select the whole petal, as it is a group, and you cannot use isolation mode here in pattern mode. **(fig. 99)**

This exercise provides some practice in selecting and adjusting small elements within a larger group. In Illustrator elements are often grouped for convenience, but you will still need to be able to adjust them as individual elements at any time. For example, elements of a pocket may be grouped together as part of a garment design and you may need to amend the details of the fastening. You will then have to select the fastening details from within the group, hence the need for both the Selection and the Direct Selection tools.

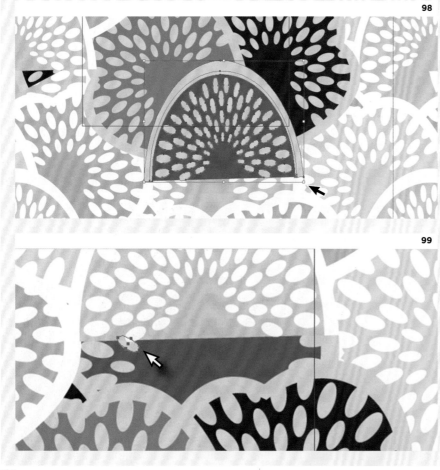

98

99

PROJECT SIX—
PHOTOSHOP:
REPEATS AND
COLORWAYS

PROJECT SEVEN –
COLOR THEORY
IN PRACTICE

PROJECT EIGHT—
PHOTOSHOP:
FILLS, TEXTURES,
AND LAYERS

PROJECT NINE—
ILLUSTRATOR:
PATHS TO FASHION

PROJECT TEN—
SIMPLE GEOMETRY
IN ILLUSTRATOR

**PROJECT ELEVEN—
REPEAT PATTERNS
IN ILLUSTRATOR**

CASE STUDY:
NADINE BUCHER

PROJECT TWELVE—
ILLUSTRATOR:
PHOTOSHOP AND
FILTERS

CASE STUDY:
TORD BOONTJE

11.7

Now you will make copies of some of the existing spots in the smaller petal at the bottom of the repeat rectangle. This will complete the pattern of spots. Move to the bottom of the repeat rectangle where the smaller blue petal is undimmed and therefore editable. On the right-hand side of the petal shape click with the Direct Selection tool inside one of the spots you wish to copy. Then holding down the shift key click, one by one, on the other spots to select the seven shown in figure 100. Make sure you select the whole of each spot by clicking inside the spot and not near the edge. Four solid anchor points indicate that the whole spot is selected. If one anchor point is hollow then click inside the spot one more time to completely select all anchor points. Zoom in as necessary. **(fig. 100)**

11.8

Select the Rotate tool. Click once with the Rotate tool to set the center of rotation as the center of the pattern of spots. Click and hold dragging the mouse or digital pen clockwise. As you start dragging, hold down the **option/alt** key so that a copy is created along with the rotation. Release the mouse or digital pen and then the **option/alt** key when the new spots are in the correct position, that is, they have the same spacing as the existing spots. **(fig. 101)**

Repeat this procedure for the left-hand side.

The pattern is now almost finished, but there is a little more fine-tuning to be made in order for the pattern to connect up smoothly. In figure 102 you can see there are two spots in the undimmed section that are part of another petal that needs removing. Leave the rest of the petal because it is contributing the blue background to the lower section of the petal.

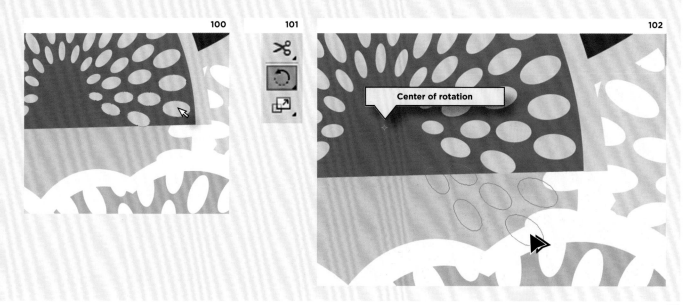

100

101

102

Center of rotation

11.9

Select the Direct Selection tool, press the A key—the shortcut to select this tool. Move to the top of the repeat square where the spots to be removed are undimmed and editable. Click within one of these spots and the whole petal edge should be selected. Use the delete key to get rid of this petal edge. **(fig. 103)**

The fragment showing of another petal is now redundant in this particular arrangement so you should remove it completely.

11.10

Select the Selection tool, as you want to select the whole group, and click once on the visible section. Then use the delete key to remove the whole petal. **(fig. 104)**

You might want to evaluate how your design looks repeated outside of the Pattern Options window.

11.11

Click the word Done in the Pattern Options window header. The window closes and a pattern swatch is placed in the Swatches window. Check that Fill is uppermost in the Toolbar (click "**X**" otherwise). With the Rectangle tool draw out a rectangle to cover half of the artboard, the equivalent to an A4 document. It is filled with your repeat pattern. You now have a pattern swatch in Illustrator that could be printed out as a design or used as a fill in a garment drawing.

There is though something that could do with further refinement in this repeat pattern. Notice that the brown petal is partially covered in alternate columns. You could change the order of the overlap or the order of the petals themselves but it won't go away. To fix this introduces you to a truly advanced but very useful way of working in Illustrator. **(fig. 105)**

103

104

PROJECT SIX—
PHOTOSHOP:
REPEATS AND
COLORWAYS

PROJECT SEVEN —
COLOR THEORY
IN PRACTICE

PROJECT EIGHT—
PHOTOSHOP:
FILLS, TEXTURES,
AND LAYERS

PROJECT NINE—
ILLUSTRATOR:
PATHS TO FASHION

PROJECT TEN—
SIMPLE GEOMETRY
IN ILLUSTRATOR

**PROJECT ELEVEN—
REPEAT PATTERNS
IN ILLUSTRATOR**

CASE STUDY:
NADINE BUCHER

PROJECT TWELVE—
ILLUSTRATOR:
PHOTOSHOP AND
FILTERS

CASE STUDY:
TORD BOONTJE

TIP | **Exiting the Window**

There are three ways to exit the widow—Save a Copy, Done, and Cancel. Done accepts the changes. You should be aware that using the escape key also exits the window but it is the equivalent of Done, so your changes will be applied to the original, which may reasonably not be what you expect from escape. If you want to keep the original version, for example you have created a new color arrangement while in the Pattern Options window, then you should use Save a Copy. A new pattern swatch is then created. Then click Cancel to leave the original unaltered; otherwise that gets changed too.

Illustrator produces a warning box at this stage to highlight what might happen, but there is no denying that it is easy to be caught out. For variations of a pattern, the safest option is to make a copy of the swatch before entering Pattern Options and then double click on that duplicate swatch to launch the Pattern Options window and then edit that version.

You will make a copy of part of the brown petal from the original motif and place it into the pattern swatch you just created. This illustrates how flexible the patterns can be, allowing for elements to be added or removed at any time. You will also be introduced to a very useful application of the Live Paint tool. Live Paint is often used following Live Trace on a scanned drawing but it has other uses too. A Live Paint group is quite a different way of working to that done traditionally in Illustrator. You can work on the elements of a group without any regard to the layers or stacking order.

All objects in a Live Paint group are treated as parts of the same flat surface. Many of the conventional ways of working in Illustrator can be completely disregarded when working in a Live Paint group, for example, single paths can be assigned different strokes and weights at varying places along their length. There are interesting implications for fashion drawing that will be explored later. In this project you will use the technique to cut a section out of a petal and bring it into the pattern swatch.

105

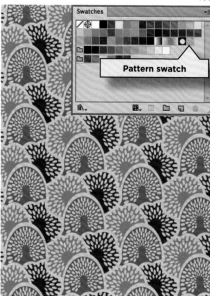

Pattern swatch

11.12

With the Selection tool select the brown petal on the right-hand side of the original motif, and holding the **option/alt** key and the **command/control** key drag a copy out and to the side. With the Pen tool draw a line that bisects the petal in the manner shown in the illustration. **(fig. 106)**

11.13

With the Selection tool drag a box to include the petal and line so that both are selected. Go **Object → Live Paint → Make**, or use the shortcut **command/control + option/alt + X** to define the selection as a Live Paint group. Note the special box around the group. Press **shift + L** to select the Live Paint Selection tool. As the tool hovers over elements of the Live Paint group they become highlighted in red. With the Live Paint Selection tool click on an individual object to select it or click and drag over multiple objects to select in one go and then click the delete key to remove. Delete all the elements below the line you drew. For clipping a complex object this live paint method is much easier than the "traditional" one of using a path and the Divide Objects Below command. **(fig. 107)**

11.14

Check that there are no invisible objects that need to be deleted by moving the tool around to see if they are highlighted by the Live Paint Selection tool. Switch to the Selection tool and select the group by clicking on it. When you have finished editing the petal as a Live Paint group it is important that you "expand" the Live Paint group, changing the components of the group back to ordinary paths and objects, before adding the petal to the pattern swatch. If you don't do this Illustrator will have serious processing problems from the demands of a Live Paint group within the Pattern Options window. **(fig. 108)**

11.15

Go **→ Object → Live Paint → Expand**. Then use **command/control + C** to copy the expanded result. Click outside the group to deselect (otherwise the next stage can apply the pattern swatch to active objects). Double click on your pattern swatch in the Swatches window to launch the Pattern Options window.

11.16

With the Pattern Options window open, click **command/control + V** to paste. With the Selection tool, line up your clipped petal with the brown petal that is currently covered in the repeat (lower left side). It should fit exactly, as it is a perfect copy of part of the same petal. Note in your design the repeats show that all brown petals are now complete. **(fig. 109)**

107

106

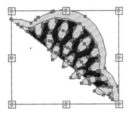

108

PROJECT SIX—
PHOTOSHOP:
REPEATS AND
COLORWAYS

PROJECT SEVEN —
COLOR THEORY
IN PRACTICE

PROJECT EIGHT—
PHOTOSHOP:
FILLS, TEXTURES,
AND LAYERS

PROJECT NINE—
ILLUSTRATOR:
PATHS TO FASHION

PROJECT TEN—
SIMPLE GEOMETRY
IN ILLUSTRATOR

**PROJECT ELEVEN—
REPEAT PATTERNS
IN ILLUSTRATOR**

CASE STUDY:
NADINE BUCHER

PROJECT TWELVE—
ILLUSTRATOR:
PHOTOSHOP AND
FILTERS

CASE STUDY:
TORD BOONTJE

11.17

Click Done in the window header to save the modified version and exit. Note that the rectangle you previously filled with the pattern swatch has updated automatically and now contains the improved repeat pattern. Illustrator allows you to create a complex repeat and gives you the flexibility to make changes and additions at any time.

109

11.18

To create colorways of your design select the A4 rectangle filled with the pattern. Click the Recolor Artwork button in the application header. (See Project Seven for a detailed explanation of this tool.) Adjust the colors as desired. When you okay the results a new pattern swatch with the new colors is placed in the Swatches window. The rectangle now shows the new swatch as the fill but the original swatch is still preserved in the Swatches window. Each new color version can be preserved as pattern swatches with the document.

PROJECT REVIEW

REVIEW

This project introduced you to the flexibility of repeat work in Illustrator. The importance of the Selection and Direct Selection tools for different tasks was highlighted. The possibilities for fast editing with the Live Paint group were examined. The emphasis of the project was on evolving a satisfying repeat pattern through evaluation and editing. Creating a repeat is not a single-stage process and editing live in repeat is a great advantage and aids the development of your skill.

PRACTICE

With arrangements of your own motifs explore the possibilities offered by some of the other tiling patterns in Pattern Options. Look for a good flow between elements and a strong and even balance with no conspicuous design lines. Use Recolor Artwork to create some colorways that follow the principles of warm, cool, and neutral.

CASE STUDY: NADINE BUCHER

Nadine Bucher works in a number of design disciplines including interiors, product design, and lately textiles. For her fashion textile collections she created a range of fabrics to be woven and printed in her native Switzerland. Admirably, Nadine wanted to support local industries that are under great pressure from competing overseas manufacturers. But finding Swiss companies inclined to supply a modest, independent enterprise was not straightforward. She succeeded however and her fabrics now retail in sophisticated Swiss boutiques.

Apparent in her work is an interest both in structure and the built environment and in nature and organic materials. Nadine is inspired by varied sources and for her the concept for a new design initially begins in a fairly abstract form. She says "it starts first in my head, with a vision in my mind. I add forms and contours together, develop a topic, see the colors." There is a playing with the ideas, giving them the freedom to flow and come together and when they begin to coalesce the design development moves to the computer.

She works in Photoshop and Illustrator; drawing shapes by hand with the geometric and line tools. She explores variations in scale and layout with transformation tools such as Reflect. When various potential designs start taking shape she prints them out onto paper, "and then I cut out shapes for what the fabric

may be used for. This can be a skirt or a blouse or a scarf. This is the best method for me to see if the pattern is working or not. Sometimes I change the size of a pattern as many as seven times. There is a lot of balancing to consider if I design a fabric for a skirt or for a scarf. And then I start with the color—usually 10 to 20 different color options. I hang the best outcomes on a wall in my atelier and I look at them over several days until I select the best." Designs get evaluated at this stage and some are discarded when they look less successful in context than they did in the computer. "I love graphic patterns. Sometimes one single pattern is very nice on its own, but the space between the elements when multiplied it is not nice. Then I have to decide what to do with this pattern. Mostly I suspend it from the evaluation process."

110

111

112

PROJECT SIX—
PHOTOSHOP:
REPEATS AND
COLORWAYS

PROJECT SEVEN —
COLOR THEORY
IN PRACTICE

PROJECT EIGHT—
PHOTOSHOP:
FILLS, TEXTURES,
AND LAYERS

PROJECT NINE—
ILLUSTRATOR:
PATHS TO FASHION

PROJECT TEN—
SIMPLE GEOMETRY
IN ILLUSTRATOR

PROJECT ELEVEN—
REPEAT PATTERNS
IN ILLUSTRATOR

CASE STUDY:
NADINE BUCHER

PROJECT TWELVE—
ILLUSTRATOR:
PHOTOSHOP AND
FILTERS

CASE STUDY:
TORD BOONTJE

Next the fine adjustment of successful designs takes place, fitting them and their repeat to the exact dimensions of the fabric. "The most difficult part for me is to find a suitable and agreeable repeat. I work with the whole width of the chosen fabric, normally 140 cm or 160 cm, and I draw out a repeat to fit an exact number of times within it. Most recently with the architectural collection motifs it was very difficult because the motifs slid every row a few millimeters. It took 5 or 8 rows before the motif corresponded again to the beginning.

Weaving and printing fabrics in Switzerland is very difficult. First of all the high manufacturing costs, but more difficult still is to find a factory which will produce just 100 or 200 meters of fabric. And in Switzerland only a limited number of companies remain. But when you produce in your own country the appreciation of the customers is very high. They are willing to pay more for a scarf made in Switzerland than one made in Vietnam. At the moment we have a lot of new shops that sell only products made in Switzerland and so it is not bad timing for my products.

Selling out my first scarf collection encouraged me to do the second. This maybe sounds very easy, but the whole process, all the different decisions, the high manufacturing costs means it is not always easy. The next time people may not like my fabrics and then what? It needs a lot of time and good nerves and luck! But for me it is a big honor to produce my own fabrics, and have shops selling them."

"Next time people may not like my fabrics and then what? It needs a lot of time and good nerves and luck! But for me it is a big honor to produce my own fabrics, and have shops selling them."

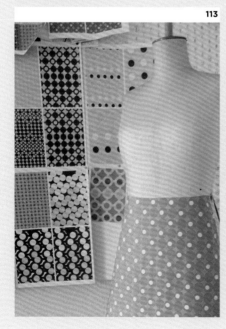

113

114

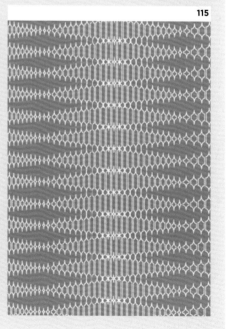

115

PROJECT TWELVE—ILLUSTRATOR: PHOTOSHOP AND FILTERS

12

INTRODUCING FILTERS

Photoshop and Illustrator contrast with traditional media in their extreme predictability. Whereas this is normally to your advantage sometimes as a designer you might want some unexpected variation in the results. This is where Filters and Effects can come to your aid. With Filters and Effects you still have to think as a designer and use your individual creativity. Otherwise, an off-the-peg filter used artlessly can make your work look exactly like someone else's who has used the same filter.

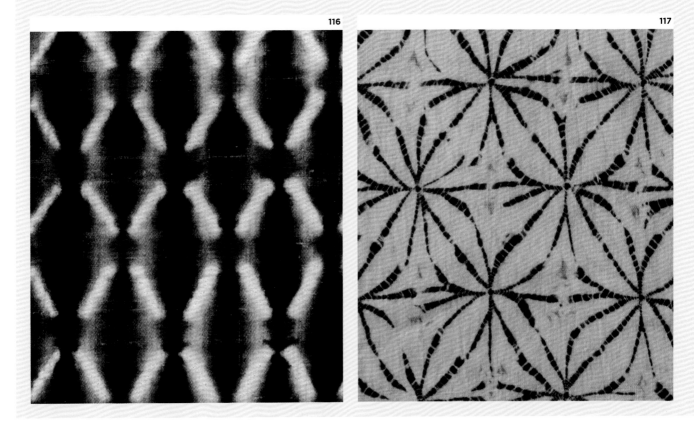

116

117

PROJECT SIX—
PHOTOSHOP:
REPEATS AND
COLORWAYS

PROJECT SEVEN —
COLOR THEORY
IN PRACTICE

PROJECT EIGHT—
PHOTOSHOP:
FILLS, TEXTURES,
AND LAYERS

PROJECT NINE—
ILLUSTRATOR:
PATHS TO FASHION

PROJECT TEN—
SIMPLE GEOMETRY
IN ILLUSTRATOR

PROJECT ELEVEN—
REPEAT PATTERNS
IN ILLUSTRATOR

CASE STUDY:
NADINE BUCHER

**PROJECT TWELVE—
ILLUSTRATOR:
PHOTOSHOP AND
FILTERS**

CASE STUDY:
TORD BOONTJE

ILLUSTRATOR: PHOTOSHOP AND FILTERS

In this project you will:
- Look at ways of creating naturalistic effects like dip dyeing and wax and Shibori resists.
- Look at how motifs created in Illustrator can be brought into Photoshop and put into repeat.
- Explore how filters can be applied to the designs and how the designs can then be presented in garment outlines.

Outcome

You should create designs that have the quality associated with wet processes in textiles but be able to do these with freedom in Photoshop.

Aim

To practice integrating Photoshop Filters with the creative process of design development.

*Shibori is a traditional Japanese textile dye technique. Fabric is twisted, folded, and stitched to limit the access of the dye when dipped in a vat, usually of indigo blue.

Project files are available at www.bloomsbury.com/hume-textile-design

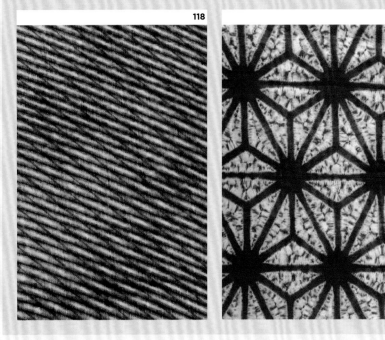

118

119

120

12.1

Start by creating a motif in Illustrator. You will use the technique of Pattern Brush. In Illustrator create an A4 document. You will need to select the Ellipse tool, one of the shape tools. By default, Rectangle tool is the one displayed in that position in the Toolbar. Press down the Rectangle tool icon to display the other tool options. A small triangle at the lower right corner of a tool icon indicates the presence of hidden tools. You can use the keyboard shortcut "**L**" to select the Ellipse tool. **(fig. 121)**

12.2

For a precise ellipse hold down the **alt/option** key and click somewhere near the center of the document with the Ellipse tool. Enter 5.4 millimeters for the width and 9.5 millimeters for the height. **(fig. 122)**

12.3

Zoom in to the **ellipse—command/ control + spacebar** or **command/ control + plus** key—so you can more clearly see what is happening. With the ellipse still selected, Go to **Object → Path → Offset Path (shift + command/control + O)**, enter –0.7 as the value, and repeat to have four concentric ellipses in total. **(fig. 123)**

121

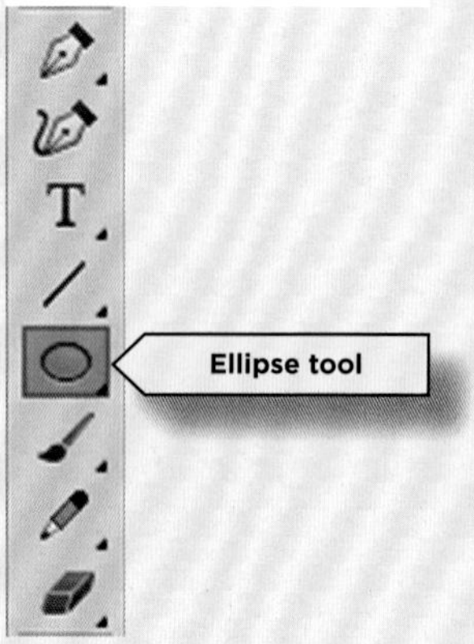

Ellipse tool

122

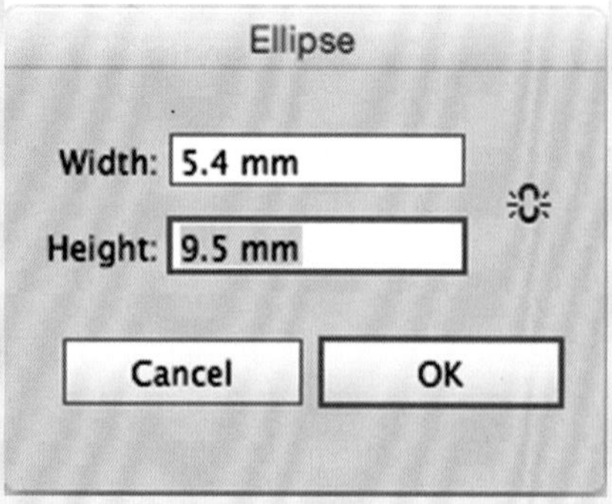

Ellipse

Width: 5.4 mm

Height: 9.5 mm

Cancel   OK

TIP If your default general units are other than millimeters Illustrator will convert your entry immediately into those default units, for example points, but it will still be the equivalent value of the millimeters. To change your general units default to millimeters, go to the user preferences in Illustrator.

PROJECT SIX—
PHOTOSHOP:
REPEATS AND
COLORWAYS

PROJECT SEVEN —
COLOR THEORY
IN PRACTICE

PROJECT EIGHT—
PHOTOSHOP:
FILLS, TEXTURES,
AND LAYERS

PROJECT NINE—
ILLUSTRATOR:
PATHS TO FASHION

PROJECT TEN—
SIMPLE GEOMETRY
IN ILLUSTRATOR

PROJECT ELEVEN—
REPEAT PATTERNS
IN ILLUSTRATOR

CASE STUDY:
NADINE BUCHER

**PROJECT TWELVE—
ILLUSTRATOR:
PHOTOSHOP AND
FILTERS**

CASE STUDY:
TORD BOONTJE

12.4

In the Toolbar ensure the fill is black with no stroke. The forward slash key, "/", is the shortcut for None so you can bring Stroke to the front with the **X** key and then click "/" to change the stroke to None. You will now draw a circle with the Ellipse tool. Hold down the **option/alt** key and click near the existing ellipses, enter 0.4 millimeter for both the height and the width.
(fig. 124)

You have created a little circle that you will use as the Pattern Brush. From the Windows menu open the Brushes window. Drag the circle you drew into the Brushes window. In the Dialog window that opens select Pattern Brush as the option.
(fig. 125)

In the Options window that opens next you need only change the spacing to 100 percent. Then click Okay to exit the Options window.
(fig. 126)

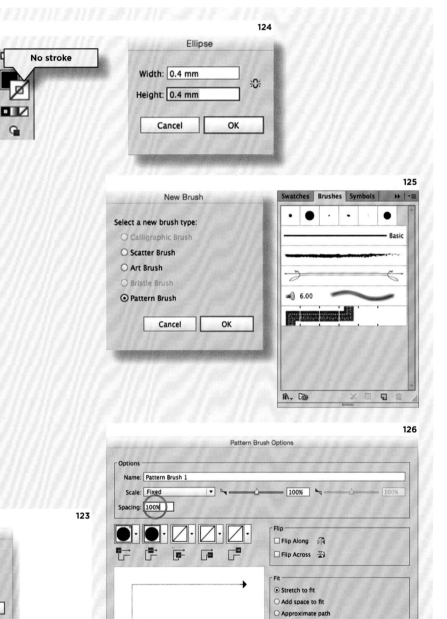

12.5

With the Selection tool drag a box around the ellipses you drew in order to select them. Click on your new brush in the Brushes palette to apply that brush to the ellipses. Because of the acuteness of the inner ellipses some of the circles get a little distorted even though Illustrator tries to help out with auto corner correction. Don't worry about these irregular shaped dots for this project, but note that you can use the control arms and the Direct Selection tool to adjust them. **(fig. 127)**

Drag a few copies of your original dot into the center of the ellipses to roughly fill in the gap. **(fig. 128)**

12.6

Drag the Selection tool across all the ellipses to select all—Go ➜ **Object** ➜ **Group** **(command/control + G).**

12.7

Select the Rotate tool. By default the center of the transformation (in this case the center of the rotation) is the center point of the object or group. Click to the left of the ellipse group and drag counterclockwise. Now hold down the **shift** key to constrain the rotation to 45 degree increments. Release the mouse or digital pen when you have rotated the ellipse group just 45 degrees counterclockwise. **(fig. 129)**

129

45°

TIP

Note that when you transform an object with a pattern brush applied sometimes Illustrator redraws the pattern brush slightly differently after the transformation. To avoid differences creeping in and if you are happy with the arrangement in your object then you can go **Object ➜ Expand Appearance** to lock the pattern in place.

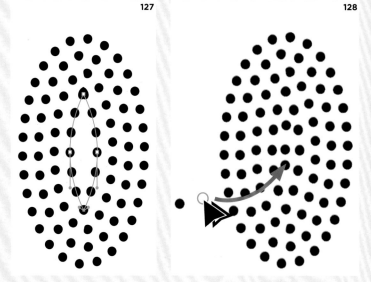

127

128

PROJECT SIX—
PHOTOSHOP:
REPEATS AND
COLORWAYS

PROJECT SEVEN —
COLOR THEORY
IN PRACTICE

PROJECT EIGHT—
PHOTOSHOP:
FILLS, TEXTURES,
AND LAYERS

PROJECT NINE—
ILLUSTRATOR:
PATHS TO FASHION

PROJECT TEN—
SIMPLE GEOMETRY
IN ILLUSTRATOR

PROJECT ELEVEN—
REPEAT PATTERNS
IN ILLUSTRATOR

CASE STUDY:
NADINE BUCHER

**PROJECT TWELVE—
ILLUSTRATOR:
PHOTOSHOP AND
FILTERS**

CASE STUDY:
TORD BOONTJE

12.8

From the vertical ruler draw out a vertical guideline very close to the right edge of the ellipse group. Then select the Reflect tool (keyboard shortcut "**O**"); this is the tool for mirroring and is in the same group as the Rotate tool. **(fig. 130)**

Check that the ellipse group is still selected, then hold down the **option/ alt** key and click on the vertical guideline. This action determines where the axis of reflection, or the mirroring plane, will be. A little crosshair target is placed in position as a reference point.

In the Reflect dialog window select Vertical as the mirroring plane or, as described by Illustrator, the axis of reflection. Note there is a difference between the way mirroring is described in Photoshop and Illustrator. In Photoshop flipping refers to the direction the object will be flipped, whereas in Illustrator the mirror rather than the object is referred to. Do not click on okay, but instead click on copy to leave the original in place and create a mirrored copy. **(fig. 131)**

12.9

Draw out a horizontal guideline from the ruler and place it just below the two ellipse groups. Select the original and the copy of the ellipse group. Select the Reflect tool and while holding down the **option/alt** key click on the horizontal guide above the ellipse groups. **(fig. 132)**

130

TIP | Remember: guidelines are pulled out of rulers with any tool. Use **command/control + R** to display rulers.

131

132

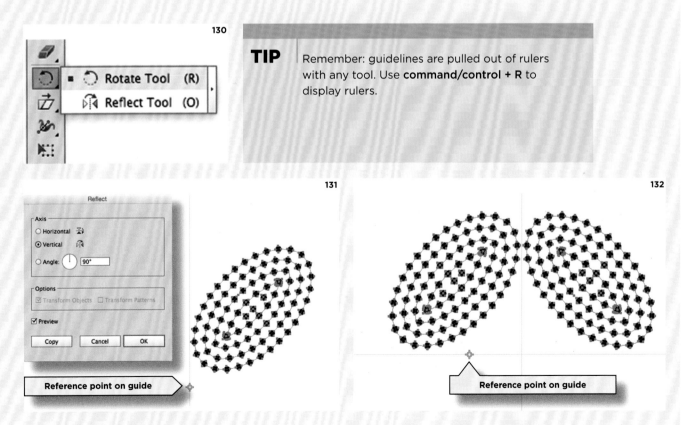

12.10

If Photoshop is not running launch it now, as you are going to copy the ellipse motif directly from Illustrator into Photoshop. It is common practice while designing to move between the two applications and the applications are designed to facilitate this.

In Illustrator, with the Selection tool, drag over all four copies of the ellipse group, then go ➔ **Edit** ➔ **Copy** (shortcut **command/control + C**). Switch to Photoshop, create a new A4 document, with color mode RGB and resolution 300 ppi. To match the sizes given with this project ensure that the Ruler in Photoshop displays pixels as the units so that the info window will display pixels too. From the Windows menu select Info. From that window's options menu select Panel Options. In the options window that opens change the units for the mouse coordinates to pixels. **(fig. 133)**

12.11

Go ➔ **Edit** ➔ **Paste** (shortcut **command/control + V**). Of the options presented in the pop-up window select Pixels, which is the simplest version of pasting. The motif from Illustrator has been held in the computer's memory and now will be converted from a vector to a raster image (as that was the option you selected).

You now need to determine the size that the pasted element will be in Photoshop and the application will make the translation to raster image at that size. It is important to choose an adequate size to avoid pixilation problems later. You can either drag out the bounding box while holding down the shift key to keep it in proportion and read off the figures either from the little feedback box or from the Info window until the height or width reaches 870 pixels, or, alternatively, you can enter 870 into the height and width text boxes in

the transformation options bar that has appeared as part of the pasting sequence. Double click or press return to commit the pasting at the specified size. **(fig. 134)**

12.12

Now carrying on in Photoshop, from the Rulers draw guidelines up to each side of the motif. This helps in making the selection as close as possible to the motif. Under the View menu have Snap to Guides on. Draw a selection box very close around the pasted motif. If you use a different means of selection you may have to flatten the design. Make sure the new layer (generated by pasting) is active. Go ➔ **Edit** ➔ **Define Pattern**. Choose a name or leave Photoshop to assign it. Make sure you deselect the motif. **(fig. 135)**

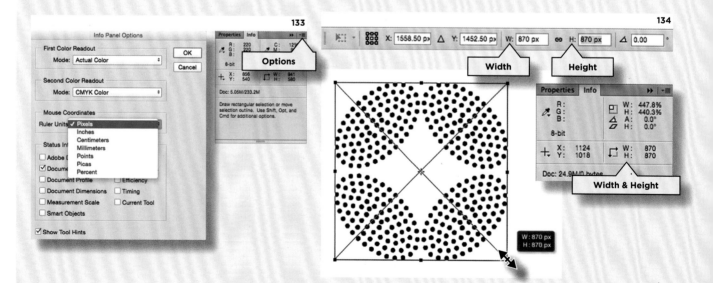

12.13

Create a new layer. Hide the guides— **command/control + ;** (semicolon). Make Layer 1, the layer with the motif, invisible. With Layer 2 the active layer Go ➔ **Edit** ➔ **Fill**. Select Custom Pattern as the fill mode and select the new pattern from the pattern picker (it will be last in the list). Have all boxes unticked. Click Okay to exit. **(fig. 136)**

12.14

Use Magic Wand to select the white on the new layer. Have Contiguous unticked to ensure all of the white in the layer is selected. Click the delete key to delete all white.

12.15

Now fill the dots themselves with white. There are often many alternative ways to do a specific thing in Photoshop and in this case there are several ways to select the dots:

- With the selection still active, Go ➔ **Select** ➔ **Inverse** to select all the dots.
- Click on a black dot with the Magic Wand and Contiguous off to switch the selection to all black dots.
- Click on the layer icon to select everything on that layer (my preferred way). **(fig. 137)**

12.16

Now with the dots selected fill them with white. Here you can practice a few advanced shortcuts. Press the **D** key, which in Photoshop gets you back to the default black foreground and white background in the Toolbar; press the **X** key, which swaps them around so white is now the foreground color; press **option/ alt + delete** to fill with the current foreground color and the selected dots are filled with white. An even more impressive shortcut, if you can remember it, is **shift + option/ alt + delete**, which then fills while preserving transparency. This results in filling in color only where there are actual pixels present in the layer, so with this shortcut the dots need not even be selected as was done in Stage 15.

12.17

Create a new layer below the dot layer. Click on the foreground color in the Toolbar and select a rich blue, the one in the example was R 42 G 57 B 174. Fill the new layer with the blue, use the shortcut **option/alt + delete** again to fill the area with the foreground color.

135

Pattern Name

Name: Pattern

OK
Cancel

136

Fill

Contents: Pattern

OK
Cancel

Options
Custom Pattern:

Scrip

Pattern picker

Blending
Mode: Normal
Opacity: 100 %

Preserve Transparency

137

Layers | Paths | Channels

Kind

Normal | Opacity: 100%

Lock: | Fill: 100%

Layer 2

Layer 1

Background

12.18

Now merge the dots and blue layers in preparation for applying a filter to these combined layers. So that originals of the layers can be kept for possible later work create a merged copy. The following is a top tip: It is not displayed in the Layer options drop-down menu but if you hold down the **option/alt** key when clicking on Merge Layers a new separate merged layer will be created instead of merging the originals. The shortcut for this—based on merging visible layers—is **option/alt + shift + command/control + E**. When merging layers you can preselect them by shift clicking or by choosing visible layers as the selection method. **(fig. 138)**

12.19

You now want your background color to be the blue, R 42 G 57 B 174, so use the **X** key to swap it to the foreground position with white then swapping to the background position. Note that filters use the current foreground and background colors in determining their results. Go to Filters in and then down to

Filter Gallery in the drop-down menu. Go to the Sketch folder and click on Photocopy. This previews the Photocopy filter applied to the artwork. Set Detail to 11 and Darkness to 8. Now you will add a second filter. Go to the bottom of the Filter Gallery window and click on the New Effect Layer button. **(fig. 139)**

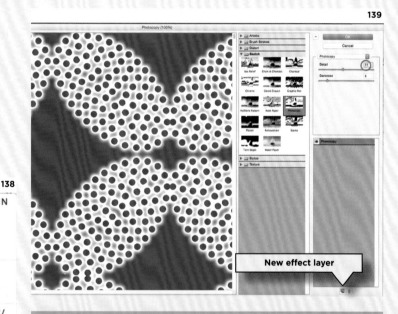

139

New effect layer

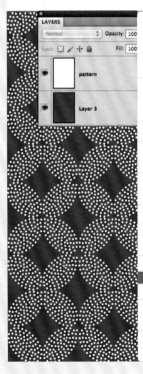

138

TIP

Appropriate Use of Filters

You have now created a convincing textile print. The next stage is to give the image some of the variation that could be found in a hand-dyed process. Filters can be used here but they have to be used judiciously in design work because they may appear to the beginner to give an exciting difference but in reality the same treatments are in every copy of Photoshop and may in effect give your work a generic quality.

PROJECT SIX—
PHOTOSHOP:
REPEATS AND
COLORWAYS

PROJECT SEVEN —
COLOR THEORY
IN PRACTICE

PROJECT EIGHT—
PHOTOSHOP:
FILLS, TEXTURES,
AND LAYERS

PROJECT NINE—
ILLUSTRATOR:
PATHS TO FASHION

PROJECT TEN—
SIMPLE GEOMETRY
IN ILLUSTRATOR

PROJECT ELEVEN—
REPEAT PATTERNS
IN ILLUSTRATOR

CASE STUDY:
NADINE BUCHER

**PROJECT TWELVE—
ILLUSTRATOR:
PHOTOSHOP AND
FILTERS**

CASE STUDY:
TORD BOONTJE

12.20

Now select Water Paper, which is in the same group as Photocopy, the Sketch group of filters. Choose Fiber Length as 22, Brightness as 30, and Contrast as 83. Click Okay.
(fig. 140)

12.21

The design has become a little dark so you will use levels to push the light tones toward white. Go → **Image** → **Adjustments** → **Levels**. Below the histogram drag the small white triangle from the right-hand edge toward the "foothills" of the mountain range that represents the tones in the image. **(fig. 141)**

TIP

A histogram is a photo adjustment tool that can be used on any sort of image. Tonal corrections can be made by adjusting the values of the extreme highlight and shadow pixels in the image, setting an overall tonal range for the image. This process is called "setting the highlights and shadows" or "setting the white and black points." Setting the white and black redistributes the midtone pixels proportionately. For further enhancement you might need to manually adjust the midtone value.

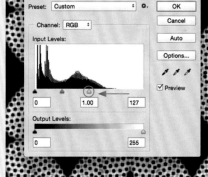

141

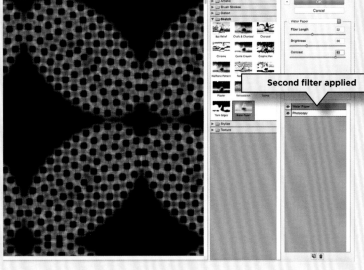

Second filter applied

140

12.22

Load the Swim Sketch file into Photoshop. Use the Magic Wand tool to select the area of swimsuit and the two-piece. (Remember to have Contiguous ticked and to use the shift key to add the separate garment areas to the selection.) On your pattern document use Select All and then copy all the pattern from that document, and use **Edit → Paste Special → Paste Into** to paste the pattern and generate a mask. You should be familiar now with this process and with the advantages of using masks. Select the image icon and resize and reposition the print to your liking. **(fig. 142)**

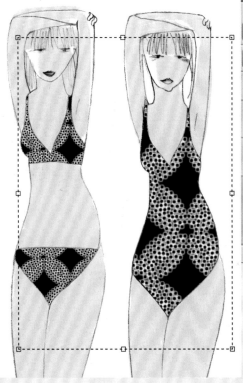

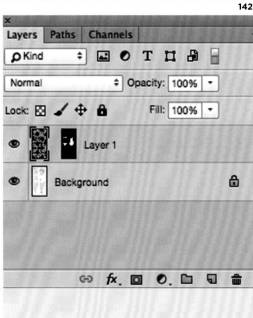

142

PROJECT SIX—
PHOTOSHOP:
REPEATS AND
COLORWAYS

PROJECT SEVEN —
COLOR THEORY
IN PRACTICE

PROJECT EIGHT—
PHOTOSHOP:
FILLS, TEXTURES,
AND LAYERS

PROJECT NINE—
ILLUSTRATOR:
PATHS TO FASHION

PROJECT TEN—
SIMPLE GEOMETRY
IN ILLUSTRATOR

PROJECT ELEVEN—
REPEAT PATTERNS
IN ILLUSTRATOR

CASE STUDY:
NADINE BUCHER

**PROJECT TWELVE—
ILLUSTRATOR:
PHOTOSHOP AND
FILTERS**

CASE STUDY:
TORD BOONTJE

PROJECT REVIEW

REVIEW
As stated at the beginning of this project filters can give work a generic quality when used without true relevance or sensitivity. However, with practice and imagination you can create varied and even organic effects, increasing your versatility in Photoshop. This project shows how work can be generated in one application where the ideal tools are, and then easily brought into a companion application to use the tools available there.

PRACTICE
Try further combinations of filters and designs to create other dye effects. Combine the output with further mark-making especially with the excellent Mixer Brush tool.

143

144

CASE STUDY: TORD BOONTJE

Tord Boontje was born in The Netherlands. Educated at the Eindhoven Design Academy and the Royal College of Art, he now runs his eponymous studio from London. The studio's approach is "that modernism does not mean minimalism, that contemporary does not forsake tradition, and that technology does not abandon people and senses." The emphasis on marrying modern attitudes to design with frequent reference to nature gives the studio's work a distinct and engaging character.

Tord Boontje has worked with numerous international companies, including Shiseido, Kvadrat, Alexander McQueen, Perrier-Jouët, Nanimarquina, Artecnica, Authentics, Swarovski, Moroso, and Habitat. The range of products created includes lighting, graphics, textiles, ceramics, and furniture.

Very comfortable with technology, Tord describes his introduction to computers in design as quite late. "As a student in Eindhoven I was given one project where we had to do a collage with flat areas of color and traditionally this was done with paper pieces all carefully glued together, and this was too fiddly for me. I went to the Phillips Design Office and instead used one of their computers to do the collage. The computer was so clunky—I had to type in all these commands by hand because there was no mouse. The printouts on photo paper where very small but I felt very positive about the outcome and glad that I didn't do anything traditional. And then I didn't work with computers at all for a long time.

Much later, after I graduated from the RCA, I started using the computer to do the designs for some shop fittings. I wanted to get some components laser cut in steel and for that the maker needed the .dxf file; they needed CAD files not paper designs. So then I started using 3D CAD programs for design work. I designed the Wednesday light and later the Garland light for Habitat in 3D. It wasn't until I had gone through the process and was talking to a graphic designer that this designer asked why I hadn't use Illustrator instead! It was much easier for this work than using such a massive tool as I was. So that's when I started learning Illustrator, arriving at that point from a very roundabout way.

I wasn't very good at drawing organic mesh forms on the computer. It was much easier to make square, flat things that I then cut out and assembled. Definitely that had an influence on how my work developed. Now I am very consciously using the very precise way in which Illustrator can draw to give character to these patterns that could otherwise look old fashioned if they were drawn by hand. But because they are computer drawings they immediately get something very sharp and modern to them. That is a very deliberate thing.

Most of the time a design starts with a hand drawing. This is actually a really important part, even though the end result is an Illustrator drawing that is used for production. It, in most cases, starts with a hand drawing scanned and then traced in Illustrator. For me, for sure, it is too difficult to create directly in Illustrator. The act of drawing freehand and the way that you make a lot of decisions without thinking—this is much more intuitive a process when done with paper and pen. Artwork is originated that way and then there is a whole stage of moving things around and refining in Illustrator. It can also happen that a drawing happens on several different pieces of paper that only come together later on the computer."

PROJECT SIX—
PHOTOSHOP:
REPEATS AND
COLORWAYS

PROJECT SEVEN —
COLOR THEORY
IN PRACTICE

PROJECT EIGHT—
PHOTOSHOP:
FILLS, TEXTURES,
AND LAYERS

PROJECT NINE—
ILLUSTRATOR:
PATHS TO FASHION

PROJECT TEN—
SIMPLE GEOMETRY
IN ILLUSTRATOR

PROJECT ELEVEN—
REPEAT PATTERNS
IN ILLUSTRATOR

CASE STUDY:
NADINE BUCHER

PROJECT TWELVE—
ILLUSTRATOR:
PHOTOSHOP AND
FILTERS

CASE STUDY:
TORD BOONTJE

Presentation

"I had to learn that not everyone can read technical drawings for designs, and the inability to look properly at drawings also goes further. That is why I think renderings are so successful in presentations. There is no other way of misinterpreting that drawing if the design has been translated into a single, photographic image. If the client is someone I have worked with for a long time then I will share the early sketches, hand drawings, etcetera. And if they are newer people that I am working with, in the case of bigger companies where you know a lot of people are involved with the decision making, then I need to be very precise in what I communicate.

With textiles I never present a textile pattern on fabric. I always present on paper. Very often I present the pattern with, for example, the suggestion that we could screen print it or that we could do this in digital printing. But it might be that I have screen printing in mind, when Kvadrat (a leading European manufacturer of design textiles) thinks no, we should do this as a jacquard. Or what I am thinking could be an upholstery fabric and they think in contrast that it could be a curtain fabric. At the early stage it is better to be more open minded

about things. They know so much more about textiles than I do. In a situation of working with someone who is really good at what they do then you need to leave space in the project for their input.

With textiles it is so significant seeing it realized in the character of the yarn. As an example, making a test piece of jacquard is quite an investment so it needs to be certain that things are interesting before they can commit to that. In this process I make the artwork as a computer drawing that then goes to the manufacturer. They leave the drawing alone as regards the composition and coloring and they do the mechanical translation for their machine to work on. There will be test blankets, with various colored yarn combinations, with a checkerboard grid of all these different color combinations, that is the best way of developing colors that are successful in the jacquard weave."

Design Development

"At the moment we are working on new patterns. They are very botanical; they reference the Arts and Crafts tradition, and are a series using clashes of plants and flowers. As an example, passion fruit and bramble—weird combinations. We test it for scale in Photoshop and see how the character changes completely with different usages of color.

We try what we think is interesting colorwise, but also at this stage how extreme you can make the differences in a pattern. Whether you stay more naturalistic with the colors or become very dramatic, say putting black behind it or shifting the color spectrum. Starting to understand the character of the design is important and this is linked to how you see the scale of the pattern."

145

145

Example of a booklet made by the studio for a presentation to clients of the new design story. In the meeting the presentation is on large size boards and the handmade booklet is left with the clients as an aide-mémoire.

146

146
"Pattern itself contains a certain atmosphere, a meaning, conveying on one hand something delicate with the leaves and on the other hand something quite aggressive with the barbs. The color is a tool for bringing out the character."

147
"For this collection the idea is about the garden. Whereas my previous patterns have been about the forest and about the wild fantasy, fairy tale, nature this is really about the city, living in the city where the plants become more sophisticated and form gardens and bouquets."

147

"In a meeting with the client the actual presentation is with A1 size paper printouts and then we leave these books with them as a memory. The story is presented completely open, with it not decided for example if designs could be print or could be embroidery. That also depends on what you might do with it, embroidery might not be durable enough for upholstery but the design itself could still be interesting for upholstery so you might think instead of laser engraving it onto a micro fabric. And that would give it a completely contemporary quality.

As part of this story we have done some designs for laser cutting that link to the world of the bees. We made some little models with a laser plotter. It's still in question how the textile would behave compared to paper and we would discuss with them how the fabric would work, their opinion on the type of textile."

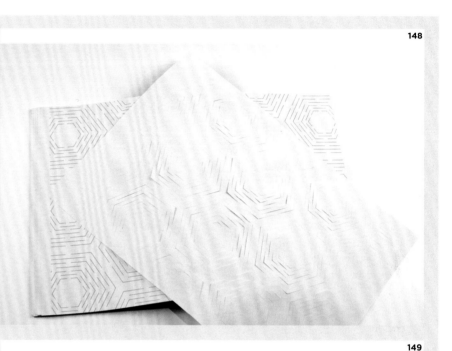

148

149

149
"With designs for furniture with a company such as Moroso generally even if we make renderings we still make the cardboard model. For me it is easier to see things than through rotating a model on the computer."

Experimentation

"Sometimes interesting accidents or coincidences do happen with the computer as happen in a workshop. In Photoshop there is a tool called color variations and you can see versions of things you might not expect. (Sadly, variations is an application plug-in that is no longer supported in Photoshop CC and CS6 T—RH). Things happen there you wouldn't necessarily think of. The shadow fabric (for Kvadrat) wasn't really an accident because we were very deliberately trying to recreate the feeling of a shadow. But messing around with the blur tool was the route to realizing this design. I think Photoshop is good for messing around with. Illustrator does not allow for accidents in the same way.

The idea of the shadow print was to make a curtain that looked as if there might be something on the other side of the window casting a shadow onto this curtain. That was an idea that actually came from watching the Hitchcock film Rebecca. From that idea a drawing had to be made that could be tested at different levels of scaling and blurring. A fine line drawing was first brought into Illustrator, refined, and then into Photoshop for the blurring.

150

151
Pages from the presentation booklet showing a possible scale for a garden print. Individual flowers painted on paper by Golnar Roshan were scanned and arranged in Photoshop for the design composition.

PROJECT SIX—
PHOTOSHOP:
REPEATS AND
COLORWAYS

PROJECT SEVEN —
COLOR THEORY
IN PRACTICE

PROJECT EIGHT—
PHOTOSHOP:
FILLS, TEXTURES,
AND LAYERS

PROJECT NINE—
ILLUSTRATOR:
PATHS TO FASHION

PROJECT TEN—
SIMPLE GEOMETRY
IN ILLUSTRATOR

PROJECT ELEVEN—
REPEAT PATTERNS
IN ILLUSTRATOR

CASE STUDY:
NADINE BUCHER

PROJECT TWELVE—
ILLUSTRATOR:
PHOTOSHOP AND
FILTERS

**CASE STUDY:
TORD BOONTJE**

Drawing was the way to do this rather than using a photograph as you have much more freedom and control with a drawing. You can play around and for example maybe add a little bird in the branches. You can play around with the composition. You don't necessarily want to have flowers that exist in reality; they can be more fanciful and more diverse. It's also about mixing things together, which drawing allows you to do, allows you to create anything you want."

Drawing

"The importance of drawing became something that I decided upon very early on when I became interested in the whole idea of decoration and ornamentation. I was spending a lot of time at the V & A museum and going round in Sweden looking at traditional folk craft.

In folk craft and the material in the V & A you do have a lot of repeat of pattern and ornament that reoccur. When I decided that I wanted to

do some pieces using ornaments I very deliberately chose not to make something that was traditional; it became a very conscious decision not to use existing ornament or artwork, to create everything myself. So drawing is the most straightforward tool to do that. Then I really started drawing and drawing became a much more important part of my approach. If I hadn't started drawing I think the work would have stayed too folksy or classical."

151

LEVEL THREE

This section builds on core techniques set out in earlier projects to tackle a series of advanced tasks. You will learn sophisticated techniques and practice working in both Photoshop and Illustrator at the level of a professional designer.

PROJECT THIRTEEN—ILLUSTRATOR: THE BLOB AND ART BRUSHES

13

The Blob Brush in Illustrator is a tool that lends itself to loose and expressive marks. It paints filled shapes, and these shapes can intersect and merge with other shapes of the same color. While that may not seem very spectacular, what Blob Brush actually offers is a very naturalistic and free-flowing pen tool in Illustrator. With a pressure sensitive pen and tablet the marks become very responsive. The Blob Brush has more of the look of a soft brush and ink than the actual Calligraphic Brush, which creates a varying stroked path with a ribbonlike quality. The Blob Brush can be set to calligraphic brush options and produce the same style of mark but as filled objects. The Blob Brush is an economical tool in that it creates marks with the minimum anchor points, even when there is a lot of variation in the tool.

Although the Blob Brush creates objects or shapes with a fill and no stroke, it actually takes the color for the fill counterintuitively from the stroke setting in the Toolbar. When drawing with the Blob Brush tool, new paths merge with the topmost path of an object encountered of the same color. If the new path touches more than one matching path on the same layer, then all of the intersecting paths are merged together. Blob Brush will also merge with paths

1

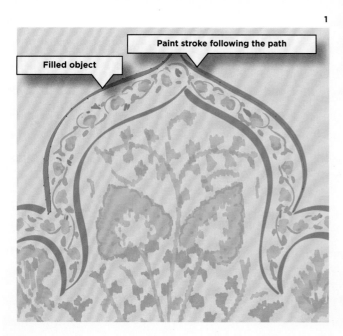

Paint stroke following the path

Filled object

1
Two different ways of creating visually similar objects. On the right, a stroked path drawn with the Paintbrush tool and on the left, a filled object drawn by the Blob Brush tool.

PROJECT
THIRTEEN—
ILLUSTRATOR:
THE BLOB AND
ART BRUSHES

PROJECT
FOURTEEN—
ILLUSTRATOR:
FLATS

PROJECT FIFTEEN—
ILLUSTRATOR: ALL
THE TRIMMINGS

PROJECT SIXTEEN—
ILLUSTRATOR:
LAYOUT

PROJECT
SEVENTEEN—
ILLUSTRATOR:
PRESENTATION

PROJECT
EIGHTEEN—
PHOTOSHOP:
PRESENTATION

CASE STUDY:
PRINTFRESH
STUDIO

CASE STUDY:
C&A DESIGNERS

created by other tools if those objects have no stroke and have the same fill as the Blob Brush. By double clicking on the tool button you can as usual access the options on the tool. Good results are often produced by a close fidelity setting for following your pen movements but a high variation in width setting based on pen pressure. Because Blob Brush can produce quite soft ink and paintlike marks without adding any extra colors it is well suited to textiles and fashion design.

With the Art Brush a graphic, or also an image in Illustrator CC, takes the shape of the stroke, scaling, bending, and stretching with the shape of the stroke gesture. By default the brush shape is stretched evenly along the length of the path and the excellent variant of the brush—the segmented Art Brush—enables a nonstretchable portion to be defined. This gives a lot of variation to the brush marks where you want it and without distortion in the elements where you don't.

Brushes that add colors or tones can make things more complicated for printing, requiring tonal separations or additional screens. So while the Bristle Brush can deliver interesting visual effects, a flat Art Brush with lots of fine, but single-tone, detail might be preferable.

ILLUSTRATOR: THE BLOB AND ART BRUSHES

In this project you will:
- Draw a section of a flower, creating some variations in your marks as you go.
- Use this to make an art brush to then draw the head of a flower.
- Add a stem to the flower, and in turn make this complete flower into an Art Brush.
- Then be able to quickly create an allover print design.

Outcome
You should have a flower brush that can be made to vary every time you draw with it. You should understand that this approach could be applied to every Art Brush to quickly create variations in your motifs and easily generate material for repeat patterns.

Aim
You should understand that brushes could be used to build further brushes. By controlling the variation to a segment of the brush multiples of a motif can be drawn, all with slight differences. This approach can be applied to any Art Brush to quickly create variations in your motifs.

2

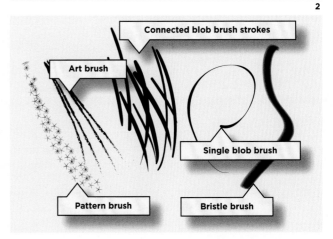

13.1

Create a new A4 document. Have print as the profile.

13.2

In recent versions of Illustrator CC the Blob Brush shares the Toolbar position with the Paintbrush, so hold down the icon for Paintbrush to reveal Blob Brush and drag down to select it (or use the shortcut **shift + B**). Now double click on the Blob Brush icon in the Toolbar. This opens the options window. If you don't have a pressure sensitive pen and tablet, such as a Wacom, then you will not have the advantage of the variation available in the Blob Brush. If you do have a pen and tablet, then from the first drop-down menu select Pressure so that the brush will react to pen pressure for greater expressiveness in your artwork. There are many way to adjust the brush and replicate some of the natural variation of nondigital media. **(fig. 3)**

13.3

Use the Blob Brush to draw something like an edge of one or two carnation-type petals (see the accompanying illustration fig. 10). Note that although you are creating filled shapes with the Blob Brush it takes its color, because it is a Brush tool, from the current stroke color. Make sure this is black. You can further refine your drawing with the eraser tool. Note that the top of the Wacom pen can be used to immediately access the eraser by turning the pen over and working with that end. **(fig. 4)**

13.4

Open the Brushes window if it is not already open. With the Selection tool drag the petal shape you have created into the brushes window. A New Brush window will open asking you to select which type of brush you will be creating. Select Art Brush. With an Art Brush, when you draw a path, the motif by default is stretched evenly along the length of the path. **(fig. 5)**

13.5

The only part of the options windows to worry about for now is the colorization section. You will also see the importance of drawing your original motif in black. Under Colorization Method select Tints. And click Okay the window to close. **(fig. 6)**

3

4

5

PROJECT THIRTEEN—ILLUSTRATOR: THE BLOB AND ART BRUSHES

PROJECT FOURTEEN—ILLUSTRATOR: FLATS

PROJECT FIFTEEN—ILLUSTRATOR: ALL THE TRIMMINGS

PROJECT SIXTEEN—ILLUSTRATOR: LAYOUT

PROJECT SEVENTEEN—ILLUSTRATOR: PRESENTATION

PROJECT EIGHTEEN—PHOTOSHOP: PRESENTATION

CASE STUDY: PRINTFRESH STUDIO

CASE STUDY: C&A DESIGNERS

13.6

You could now create the flower freehand but in this exercise you will create a set of concentric circles as guides. Create a new layer and make the original Layer 1 invisible. Select the Polar Grid tool; it is part of the Line Tool Set. Check that you still have Stroke set at black. **(fig. 7)**

13.7

Hold down the **option/alt** key and click in the approximate center of the document. In the Polar Grid Options window enter 120 mm for the width and height, five as the number of concentric dividers and zero the number of radial dividers. **(fig. 8)**

Note that if you have units other than millimeters displayed you can still type in 120 mm and Illustrator will accept this value and convert it to

be shown in the current units. As you saw in Project Nine the application is very good at accepting different units in the entry boxes and even doing the mathematics for you. Default units for a document can be changed under **File → Document Setup**.

13.8

The concentric rings will be a guide for your drawing of the petals. Lock this guide layer (Layer 2). Create a new third layer to draw your flower head on. **(fig. 9)**

Select the Paintbrush rather than the Blob Brush as the painting tool. From the Brushes window select the new Art Brush you created to be the brush tip. Select a new stroke color for the brush and then start drawing with the Paintbrush.

You can alternate two colors or create a multi-colored flower head. The length of the individual petals will depend on how long or short your painting gesture is. Follow the concentric paths and evenly place your petals. **(fig. 10)**

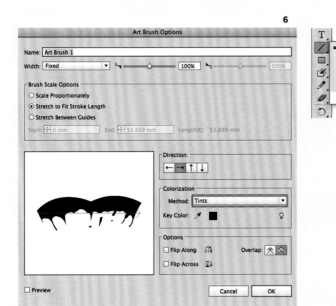

6

Art Brush Options

Name: Art Brush 1

Width: Fixed   100%   100%

Brush Scale Options
○ Scale Proportionally
◉ Stretch to Fit Stroke Length
○ Stretch Between Guides

Start: 0 mm   End: 53.889 mm   Length(X): 53.889 mm

Direction:
← → ↑ ↓

Colorization
Method: Tints
Key Color: ■

Options
☐ Flip Along   Overlap:
☐ Flip Across

☐ Preview   Cancel   OK

7

T
/ Line Segment Tool   (\)
⌒ Arc Tool
◎ Spiral Tool
▦ Rectangular Grid Tool
⊕ Polar Grid Tool

8

Polar Grid Tool Options

Default Size
Width: 120 mm
Height: 120 mm

Concentric Dividers
Number: 5
Skew: 0%
In   Out

Radial Dividers
Number: 0
Skew: 0%
Bottom   Top

☐ Create Compound Path From Ellipses
☐ Fill Grid

Cancel   OK

9

Click to toggle lock

👁 Layer 2   ○
👁 🔒 Layer 3   ○
Layer 1   ○

Click to toggle visibility

3 Layers

159

13.9

Finish the flower head and add a stem and some leaves using the Blob Brush. In Illustrator you can create a complete flower or any other complex motif and then define this as an Art Brush. The Art Brush distorts the artwork as you draw depending on your pen gestures. You can also restrict this distortion to only part of the brush; however, there will still be some degree of distortion in the rest of the motif to make it fit.

Drag the complete flower head, stem, and leaves as a group into the brushes window. Select Art Brush as the type of brush in the window that opens. In the Brush Options window that then opens Select the Stretch Between Guides Option and adjust the guides in the preview section by clicking and dragging. The art enclosed between the guides will stretch or contract to make the Art Brush fit the path length and art outside the guides will remain (relatively) unchanged. Exit the Brush Options window. Make the guide layer—Layer 2—invisible, as it is no longer needed. **(fig. 11)**

13.10

Create a new layer and make the layer with your original flower motif invisible. Create an allover pattern with the flower motif. You can open the Brush Options window by clicking on the brush in the brush window and change the size of the brush. To alter the size of individual Art Brush strokes rather than all that you have drawn have one or more paths selected and then click on the small Stroke Options button at the bottom of the Brushes window. Make the adjustment in that window; have preview on. **(fig. 12)**

You have created a pattern using just one drawn flower. It has distorted as you drew to create the impression of individual flowers. To further refine the design you can expand a drawn motif and tweak its shape to increase the individuality of the flowers. Use the Selection tool to select one or all the drawn motifs and go **Object → Expand Appearance.**

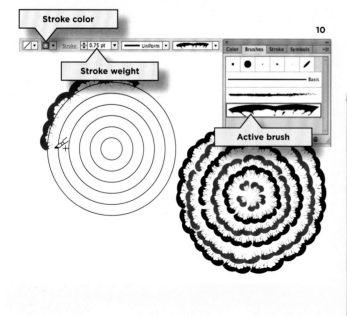

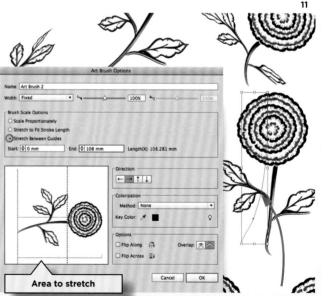

PROJECT THIRTEEN— ILLUSTRATOR: THE BLOB AND ART BRUSHES

PROJECT FOURTEEN— ILLUSTRATOR: FLATS

PROJECT FIFTEEN— ILLUSTRATOR: ALL THE TRIMMINGS

PROJECT SIXTEEN— ILLUSTRATOR: LAYOUT

PROJECT SEVENTEEN— ILLUSTRATOR: PRESENTATION

PROJECT EIGHTEEN— PHOTOSHOP: PRESENTATION

CASE STUDY: PRINTFRESH STUDIO

CASE STUDY: C&A DESIGNERS

13.11

Use the Free Transform tool to adjust individual expanded motifs. You do not need to click on the now available option buttons for the Free Transform tool in order to change to the tool variations. Instead you can switch more quickly using combinations of the modifier keys— **option/alt**, **shift**, and **command/ control**—as has always been the case. Hold down the command key (on Mac) or control key (on PC) with the Free Transform tool to adjust corners individually. **(fig. 13)**

PROJECT REVIEW

REVIEW
You should understand one of the ways Illustrator can automate the design process without loss of creative expression. Complex Brushes can be created that reflect subtle variation in your drawing gesture. And complex Brushes can assist in the speedy generation of variety in motifs.

PRACTICE
1. Reflecting on your own creative practice and interests, create an interesting motif; draw multiples of this motif by making it an art brush. From the results, select an appealing arrangement of the new brush marks and then create a new art brush from this.

2. Create three different designs using the same Art Brush but used very differently in each context. Note that to use the brush in a new document you will either have to save the brushes from the Brush window as an asset you can load into new documents or copy and paste an example of the brush between documents.

13

12

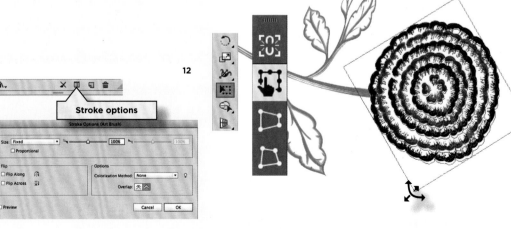

PROJECT FOURTEEN—ILLUSTRATOR: FLATS

14

A detailed realistic representation of a garment shown flat and without a figure is often, for obvious reasons, called a flat. This drawing, usually front view and back where necessary, allows accurate evaluation of the design's overall look and of its details. In the fast-paced environment of the design industry there may only be time for this type of fashion sketching and the flat will serve as a key guide to making up the initial garment sample. This form of design might also be called a technical drawing, CAD, or a spec and include supplementary written comments called callouts.

Describing style details precisely and succinctly in words can be difficult, so accurate visual rendering should take priority. Designs drawn digitally allow for accuracy and clarity, easy editing, and economic use of your time. Commonly used elements can be saved as individual files and reused in other designs. Brushes and symbols in Illustrator provide an excellent resource in this regard so they're often used in the projects in this book.

14 Helen Tran
Drawing garment flats, like any garment drawing, uses observation of real-world garments to inform the drawing of convincing original designs.

PROJECT
THIRTEEN—
ILLUSTRATOR:
THE BLOB AND
ART BRUSHES

PROJECT
FOURTEEN—
ILLUSTRATOR:
FLATS

PROJECT FIFTEEN—
ILLUSTRATOR: ALL
THE TRIMMINGS

PROJECT SIXTEEN—
ILLUSTRATOR:
LAYOUT

PROJECT
SEVENTEEN—
ILLUSTRATOR:
PRESENTATION

PROJECT
EIGHTEEN—
PHOTOSHOP:
PRESENTATION

CASE STUDY:
PRINTFRESH
STUDIO

CASE STUDY:
C&A DESIGNERS

Flats require accurate proportions. As an initial guide to the shape you could use a photo or a roughly similar garment; or start off by tracing your design on top of a body template you have previously established; or modify a previous digital drawing to build the new drawing. Both Illustrator and Photoshop allow you to display exactly scaled pattern designs and graphics in place in your garments' designs. Knowing what scale your designs are relative to the real world garment provides a guide for scaling down patterns and fabric scans. Note that while you need to know this scaling factor it is common practice for patterns, alongside details such as stitching and trims, to be shown slightly larger than they would be at the correct scale. The

scaling down gets tweaked as necessary so that the pattern or trims can be most easily read in the actual drawing. So it is important that the callouts or other text on the design specifies the actual size of elements such as buttons and buttonholes and the factory is given correct to scale artwork, labeled as such, for graphics and print designs.

Although clear communication of the precise details of a style is the priority with a flat, it is possible to enliven the drawing with some expression of movement and drape. A specific layer in Illustrator for shadows allows the shadows to be hidden when the design is sent off to the factory.

14

If you are currently drawing flats in pencil and in different thicknesses of fineliner pen then this process readily translates to the drawing of paths in Illustrator of various stroke thicknesses. In order to obtain the finished design in Illustrator the choice is whether to trace a scanned-in paper sketch or instead to draw the design from scratch in the application. Considering that you have been working with pencil and paper since a small child, in comparison, it is bound to feel more awkward in the beginning to use the tools in Illustrator.

A good way to quickly build your confidence is to forget about the designing and concentrate on drawing faithfully the shape and detail of existing garments around you. Hopefully, earlier projects in this book have built up your confidence with paths, stroke, fill, brushes, and objects in Illustrator; these are all the foundation you need to create the drawings you want in Illustrator. With practice what starts as deliberate and laborious becomes relaxed, intuitive, and fast.

The initial design might take a little time to create in Illustrator but once done, variations on the design are easily drawn and alternatives and refinements quickly explored. Getting ideas out of your head and quickly visualized allows them to be properly evaluated and allows for the creative process to flow.

ILLUSTRATOR: FLATS

In this project you will:
- Trace a sketch in Illustrator to create a professional looking fashion flat.
- Look at the advantages and disadvantages of Live Trace as a means of automatic tracing, and explore Live Paint as a technique to easily create and edit drawings by hand tracing.

Outcome

You should have a complete, fully colored and detailed garment drawing. You should have practiced making and editing symbols and seen the advantage of symbols for fashion drawing in Illustrator. You will have combined many of the techniques introduced in earlier projects.

Aim

To apply techniques from earlier projects: drawing with the pen tool, transforming and offsetting paths to create all the elements of a complex professional garment drawing. To practice drawing techniques that will allow you to draw designs from scratch in Illustrator.

Project files are available at
www.bloomsbury.com/hume-textile-design

PROJECT
THIRTEEN—
ILLUSTRATOR:
THE BLOB AND
ART BRUSHES

**PROJECT
FOURTEEN—
ILLUSTRATOR:
FLATS**

PROJECT FIFTEEN—
ILLUSTRATOR: ALL
THE TRIMMINGS

PROJECT SIXTEEN—
ILLUSTRATOR:
LAYOUT

PROJECT
SEVENTEEN—
ILLUSTRATOR:
PRESENTATION

PROJECT
EIGHTEEN—
PHOTOSHOP:
PRESENTATION

CASE STUDY:
PRINTFRESH
STUDIO

CASE STUDY:
C&A DESIGNERS

Bringing your pen or pencil sketches into Illustrator and converting them to vector art can make your sketches look crisper and more professional, but more importantly it gives you the opportunity to easily introduce color, patterns, and textures and to develop interesting variations from the initial design.

Image Trace is a very useful tool in Illustrator; it allows you to control the way the sketch is translated into vector artwork. It is a very convenient tool, but the resulting translated drawings can be much less flexible than if you did some of the tracing by hand in Illustrator. It is not possible for Image Trace to understand any connection between particular lines so all lines in the sketch become converted to discrete elements, frequently, very many elements. This is okay unless you want to start moving around components, for example pockets, and find the lines are not connected in the way you would choose yourself and that they have numerous unnecessary anchor points.

Organizing the Drawing

A good method to reduce the amount of editing is to break the development of the design down into separate stages. Draw the minimum on paper to establish the outline and components of the garment. Use Image Trace on the sketch to create vectors and then add the details that are made more effectively in Illustrator. Anything that involves repetition, such as the buttons, is best dealt with in Illustrator.

This exercise provides guidance in using Image Trace to bring your garment sketch into Illustrator. However, with the introduction of Live Paint really great tools became available for fashion drawing, offering opportunities to rethink the whole approach to drawing from scratch. So after this exercise in Live Trace, the serious emphasis in this project is familiarizing you with a very powerful Live Paint method that breaks the old rules of drawing flats in Illustrator. (You can go straight to this section if you want.)

Bringing your pen or pencil sketches into Illustrator and converting them to vector art can make your sketches look crisper and more professional, but more importantly it gives you the opportunity to easily introduce color, patterns, and textures and to develop interesting variations from the initial design.

Using Image Trace

14.1

Create a new A4 document. Go **File → Place** and find the coat_scan. tif. The coat_scan image is a sketch drawn with pen on paper and scanned in at 300 ppi; you can use an image of your own instead scanned at the same resolution.

The preferable method of bringing the image into Illustrator is using Place rather than just opening the image as a document. If you select the Link button in the Place window then, as the name implies, a linked version of the file will be placed in the document. Linking a placed image, rather than loading the actual image as a document, has the advantage of making the working document smaller in terms of memory and more manageable

to edit. The reason here for placing a linked image is to allow for easy adjustments to better control the Image Trace results.

If, when you attempt the image tracing, it seems necessary to adjust the original scan to get better results, for example to increase the contrast for stronger whites and blacks, then you can open the original image file in Photoshop, make the adjustment there, and then resave the file. Illustrator detects the changes and asks you if you would like to modify your linked file to update the changes and show the results in Illustrator. If you make any adjustments in Photoshop with adjustment layers then the changes to the data in the image are not permanent even if you save the file.

14.2

From the window menu select the Image Trace window to open it. In the Image Trace window look for the word "Advanced," indicating additional options, and click on the triangle to expand the window and show the options. Click Preview On at the bottom of the window. Of the presets, Sketched Art and Line Art are usually the most appropriate to use for outline artwork, but as indicated earlier, they are not perfect. **(fig. 15)**

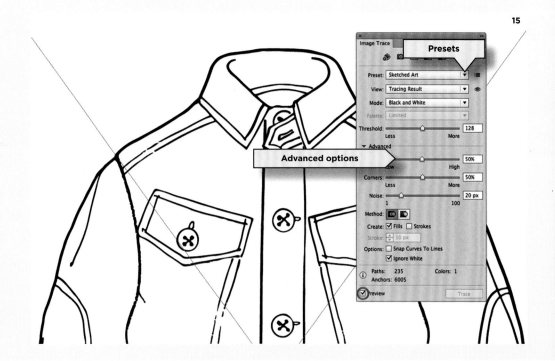

PROJECT
THIRTEEN—
ILLUSTRATOR:
THE BLOB AND
ART BRUSHES

PROJECT
FOURTEEN—
ILLUSTRATOR:
FLATS

PROJECT FIFTEEN—
ILLUSTRATOR: ALL
THE TRIMMINGS

PROJECT SIXTEEN—
ILLUSTRATOR:
LAYOUT

PROJECT
SEVENTEEN—
ILLUSTRATOR:
PRESENTATION

PROJECT
EIGHTEEN—
PHOTOSHOP:
PRESENTATION

CASE STUDY:
PRINTFRESH
STUDIO

CASE STUDY:
C&A DESIGNERS

14.3

Select the Sketched Art preset from the preset drop-down menu. These settings automatically ignore white in the image and restrict the conversion to black objects. The preview shows a crisp drawing. The original sketch lines are translated into filled regions and the edges of the original sketch lines become parallel paths. If you select **View → Outlines** then you can preview the paths revealed in cyan. Though parallel paths would make any editing of the design complicated. **(fig. 16)**

14.4

Keep the view as Outlines and change the preset to Line Art. With this method of translation stroked paths rather than filled regions are created. Image Trace now creates single paths, but areas of the sketch can disappear with the switch to this method. Increasing the pixel length of the strokes can improve matters, but parts may still be missing.

Single paths are better for editing, but note the very high number of anchor points that can be produced by the tracing. The results will be many small paths even with a long stroke length specified. You can reduce the number of paths generated by having a very low paths setting. However after making all possible adjustments to get the best outcome, you will have many more paths than you would have drawn yourself and paths that do not relate at all well to the content of the drawing. So editing this version will also not be very easy. **(fig. 17)**

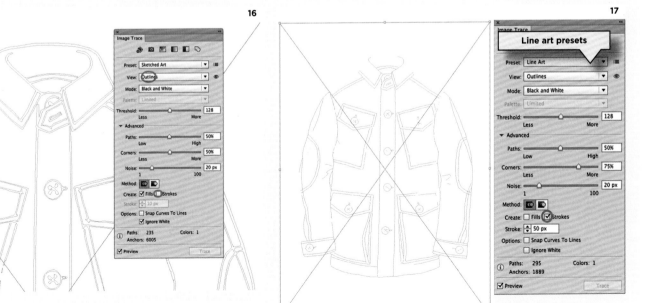

16

17

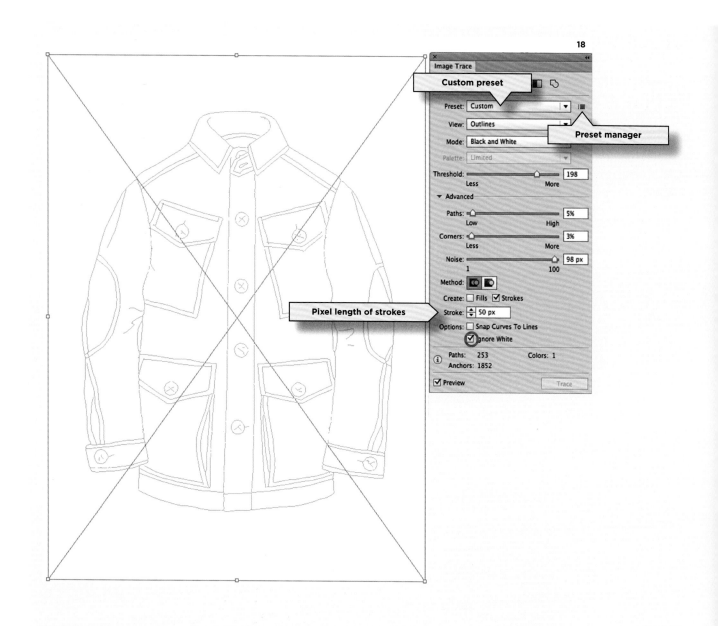

PROJECT
THIRTEEN—
ILLUSTRATOR:
THE BLOB AND
ART BRUSHES

PROJECT
FOURTEEN—
ILLUSTRATOR:
FLATS

PROJECT FIFTEEN—
ILLUSTRATOR: ALL
THE TRIMMINGS

PROJECT SIXTEEN—
ILLUSTRATOR:
LAYOUT

PROJECT
SEVENTEEN—
ILLUSTRATOR:
PRESENTATION

PROJECT
EIGHTEEN—
PHOTOSHOP:
PRESENTATION

CASE STUDY:
PRINTFRESH
STUDIO

CASE STUDY:
C&A DESIGNERS

Any modifications to the settings of an existing preset will change it to a custom preset. If you find a good combination of settings for your style of drawing, save it as a new preset using the Presets Manager button. Give it a useful name and you will see this personal preset appear as an option in the preset drop-down menu. **(fig. 18)**

The particular settings in the Image Trace window in the illustration capture most of the detail in the sketch and translate it into single paths. However, note in the image in the second illustration how many individual anchor points have been created (shown as the blue squares). Using **Object → Path → Simplify…** would reduce the points but distort the paths considerably, and manually reducing the anchor points would be slower than doing a complete manual tracing from the outset. **(fig. 19)**

Image Trace is a good method if you do not anticipate any editing of your design, which is not so common in the fashion business! Confidence with drawing directly within Illustrator can release you from any reliance on Image Trace to create your vector drawings. Manually tracing your own pencil sketch will build your confidence and allow you to practice the techniques used in drawing flats from scratch. **(fig. 3.18)**

Now we introduce a process that can be more free, dynamic, and controllable. One that will make you rethink the classic way of drawing flats.

19

Fast Tracing with Live Paint

This method involves manually tracing a sketch in Illustrator. You will use the pen tool and pencil tool to create paths with as few control points as needed. Previous projects should have made you feel comfortable with this style of drawing and with the reasons why drawings with the fewest anchor points are more easily edited. What is really cool about using Live Paint is that you don't have to worry about making lines end exactly where needed and can you be much looser in working than you can with the classic methods of flat drawing. With other methods you have to work very carefully to ensure there are no hidden overlaps of paths and that regions are butted up tightly. You might need to create copies of paths to trim sections. But complications in the classic ways of drawing flats will not be described at length because Live Paint breaks the old rules and offers an attractive alternative method.

14.5

To start the project you can use the placed scan from earlier by changing the view in the Image Trace window to Source and closing the Image Trace window to leave the original coat scan image unchanged. Or you can start fresh by deleting the current placed image and reloading a new linked copy. Remember to use Place when loading the image.

14.6

The scanned-in sketch acts as a guide to your new vector drawing. Double click on Layer 1 in the Layers window. Rename Layer 1 to original and click on the Template tick box. This locks the layer and dims the contents—ideal for manual tracing. However 30 percent is a better level of dimming for tracing so adjust the figure and click Okay to exit. Naming layers with their contents helps with navigating your documents and sharing them with others. **(fig. 20)**

14.7

Set the Fill to be none and the Stroke to be black with a 2-point thickness. It is very important that the fill is none so all paths are visible all the time. Draw all the construction lines of one side of the garment. Because the garment is symmetrical, which is usually the case, we will create the other half by using Reflect. Don't draw the buttons yet nor the buttonhole tab for the collar, as these will be created with symbols later on.

20

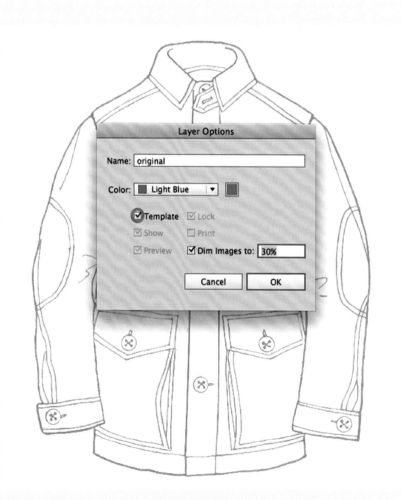

PROJECT
THIRTEEN—
ILLUSTRATOR:
THE BLOB AND
ART BRUSHES

PROJECT
FOURTEEN—
ILLUSTRATOR:
FLATS

PROJECT FIFTEEN—
ILLUSTRATOR: ALL
THE TRIMMINGS

PROJECT SIXTEEN—
ILLUSTRATOR:
LAYOUT

PROJECT
SEVENTEEN—
ILLUSTRATOR:
PRESENTATION

PROJECT
EIGHTEEN—
PHOTOSHOP:
PRESENTATION

CASE STUDY:
PRINTFRESH
STUDIO

CASE STUDY:
C&A DESIGNERS

Use the pen and pencil tools and use the drag to copy technique (**option/ alt + command/control**) you have learned to create parallel lines such as on the cuffs.

Note that you can draw your paths freely with an emphasis on getting good smooth curves and without needing them to stop on other paths. You do not need to worry about having garment sections connected, as this is easily done later. The different stroke attributes can also be added later. **(fig. 21)**

While drawing use as few anchor points as required to follow the shape of the garment. To create a new unconnected path use the **A** key to switch to the Direct Selection tool, and then **P** to switch straight back to the Pen tool, and then start your new path. Simple clicks with the Pen tool create straight segments between two points in a path; clicking and dragging creates curved segments. Use control arms where needed to adjust the curves of paths. Hold

down the **command/control** key to temporarily change the Pen tool to the Direct Selection tool. With this tool you can move the individual point or control arm (direction line). Release the **command/control** key to revert to the path tool. **(fig. 22)**

In Illustrator CC, by default, the Pen tool displays a "rubber band" preview so that when you move the mouse (or digital pen) pointer across the artboard, a path stretches out from the last placed anchor point to the current location of the pointer. This version of the Pen tool may not be convenient in that it requires you to click the escape key (**Esc**) in order to stop showing the preview and to end the path, so you might want to turn this feature off in the Illustrator Preferences. Select the Selection and Anchor Display tab and clear the Enable Rubber Band for Pen Tool tick box.

21

22

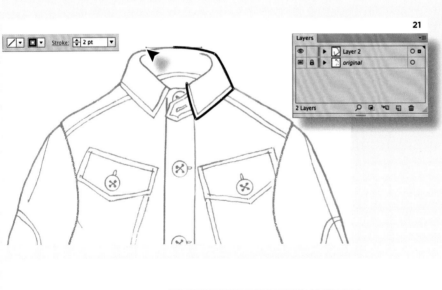

Direction line/control arm

Unselected anchor point

Corner point

Smooth point

Unselected anchor point

Selected anchor point

The Pencil Tool

You can use the Pencil tool as well as the Path tool to draw the paths in the design. The Pencil tool can be used for lines in a more sketchy and loose style. Anchor points are set down as you draw with Illustrator determining where they are positioned. However, you can adjust any of these points once the path is complete. The number of anchor points set down is determined by the length and intricacy of the path and by the tool's tolerance settings. Those settings also control how sensitive the Pencil tool is to the movement of your mouse or tablet and digital pen.

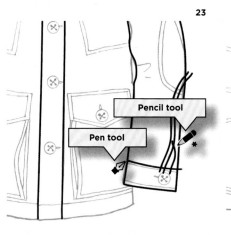

23

Pencil tool

Pen tool

23
Draw lines beyond those they cross rather than trying to draw them to exactly fit.

24

24
Use the drag to copy, option/alt + command/control to create parallel lines.

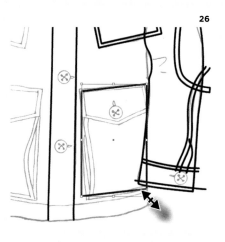

25

Offset Path

Offset: 1 mm
Joins: Miter
Miter limit: 4
☑ Preview   Cancel   OK

Guide path

Offset path

25
For the elbow patch draw a path between the two sketch lines and use the offset command to create a path running around this guide path, offset by 1 mm. This will create two perfectly parallel curves—note the inner curve is tighter than the outer and this is what Offset Path correctly creates. Copying and resizing never matches the paths as well as offset can do automatically. Delete the inner path you used as the guide.

26

26
Draw the pocket shape with the rectangle tool and use the Selection tool (shortcut the "V" key) to rotate and resize it to match the sketch.

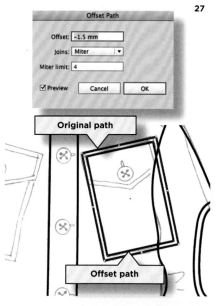

27

Offset Path

Offset: -1.5 mm
Joins: Miter
Miter limit: 4
☑ Preview   Cancel   OK

Original path

Offset path

27
Use the Offset command again to create the inner stitch lines on the pockets. Enter -1.5 mm as the distance. Because the rectangle is a closed path the minus value places the new path inside the original. Because you will turn your paths into a Live Paint Group for editing, at this stage you can draw your paths freely, with an emphasis on getting good smooth curves and without need to prevent them crossing other paths.

PROJECT
THIRTEEN—
ILLUSTRATOR:
THE BLOB AND
ART BRUSHES

PROJECT
FOURTEEN—
ILLUSTRATOR:
FLATS

PROJECT FIFTEEN—
ILLUSTRATOR: ALL
THE TRIMMINGS

PROJECT SIXTEEN—
ILLUSTRATOR:
LAYOUT

PROJECT
SEVENTEEN—
ILLUSTRATOR:
PRESENTATION

PROJECT
EIGHTEEN—
PHOTOSHOP:
PRESENTATION

CASE STUDY:
PRINTFRESH
STUDIO

CASE STUDY:
C&A DESIGNERS

14.8

Select All with **command/control + A**. All paths are selected but not the sketch because it is on a locked layer.

14.9

Press **option/alt + command/control + X** to create a Live Paint Group from the selection. Note the larger than normal squares that appear along the bounding box.

With Live Paint groups things are quite different from the standard way of working. Paths don't behave in the normal way; no paths are behind or in front of any other. Instead paths all exist in the same plane and divide the surface up into areas, any of which can be colored, regardless of whether the area is bounded by a single path or by segments

of multiple paths. You won't be coloring using Live Paint here but as a technique it is worth exploring. We will explore the novel way Live Paint groups shift the control onto appearance—not their construction—as defining elements in the drawing. The best way to understand the change is to get started working in a Live Paint group. **(fig. 28)**

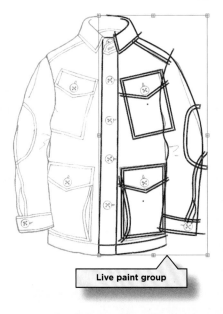

28

Live paint group

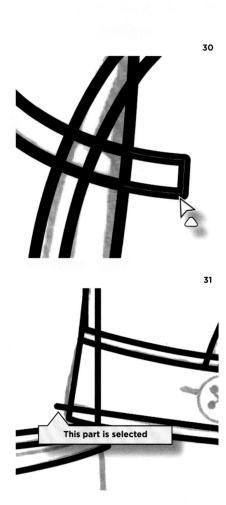

29

This part to be deleted

30

31

This part is selected

29
In the image above the actual anchor points on the paths are shown and those for the paths of the elbow patch are arrowed. In the classic way of working you would cut the path for the elbow patch with scissors to remove the unwanted bit or possibly use the divide objects below command.

30
With a Live Paint group the Live Paint Selection tool recognizes the unwanted section because it is already cut by the line that crosses despite there being no anchor points in this area.

31
When you click on a path section highlighted by the Live Paint Selection tool it takes on a gray crosshatching to indicate it is selected (red highlighting indicates a region is selected). Use the delete key to remove the unwanted section.

14.10

Use the shortcut **shift + L** to switch to the Live Paint Selection tool. As you move over your drawing the tool will offer to select regions or paths. The white triangle indicates a path can be selected and the black triangle a region. At this stage you need to select all the unnecessary path sections in your drawing and delete them. Live Paint is so flexible that you can switch back to the Direct Selection tool (shortcut **A**), move an anchor point, and then switch back to Live Paint Selection tool by clicking **shift + L** and then resume editing the group.

14.11

When you have trimmed off all unwanted lines select all the paths of the drawing with the selection tool (**V**) or use **command/control + A** and Reflect to create a mirrored copy. As previously explained, use the **option/alt** key to specify the reference point for the axis. Click Copy rather than Okay. Move the copy to line up precisely with the original sketch. Delete any duplicated paths that are not needed. **(fig. 32)**

14.12

Select all the paths with the Selection tool (**V**) or use **command/control + A** to select all. Because two Live Paint groups are selected—the original and the copy—a new Merge Live Paint button appears in the options bar in the application header. This allows you to merge the two groups into one. Click on the merge button. Add any paths that are needed to complete the drawing, such as the back collar lines that are best drawn separately. **(fig. 33)**

32

33

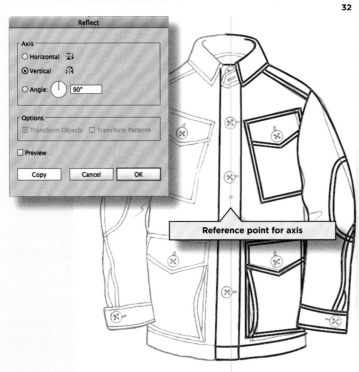

Reference point for axis

PROJECT
THIRTEEN—
ILLUSTRATOR:
THE BLOB AND
ART BRUSHES

**PROJECT
FOURTEEN—
ILLUSTRATOR:
FLATS**

PROJECT FIFTEEN—
ILLUSTRATOR: ALL
THE TRIMMINGS

PROJECT SIXTEEN—
ILLUSTRATOR:
LAYOUT

PROJECT
SEVENTEEN—
ILLUSTRATOR:
PRESENTATION

PROJECT
EIGHTEEN—
PHOTOSHOP:
PRESENTATION

CASE STUDY:
PRINTFRESH
STUDIO

CASE STUDY:
C&A DESIGNERS

14.13

Now you can change the paths that need different stroke thicknesses. Use the Live Paint selection tool to select one path section and hold down shift to select additional paths. Click again on a path with shift held down if you added it by mistake. Using the Live Paint Selection tool allows you to select sections of paths that were not originally connected—ideal for creating an outline path around the whole garment shape. With a selection of path segments selected adjust the stroke thickness to see this applied in the drawing. Change the outside edge of the garment drawing to a thickness of 4 points. **(fig. 34–35)**

14.14

Start selecting the paths that are stitch lines and changing their attributes in the stroke window to dashed line with 3 points dash and 2 points gap. This is an easy way to indicate stitching. Note that the scale is actually much larger than the stitches would be in reality. **(fig. 36)**

14.15

With all the stitching defined you can revert the paths back to their normal behavior. A number of features and commands in Illustrator are not allowed within Live Paint and **Select → Same → Stroke Weight**, which we want to use next, is one of them.

Select the whole Live Paint group and click on the Expand button in the options bar at the top of your workspace. This area is called the Control Panel in Illustrator; the same thing is called the Options Bar in Photoshop. Sometimes Adobe's labeling of parts in the applications is very inconsistent and can be confusing, as was explained at the beginning of the book.

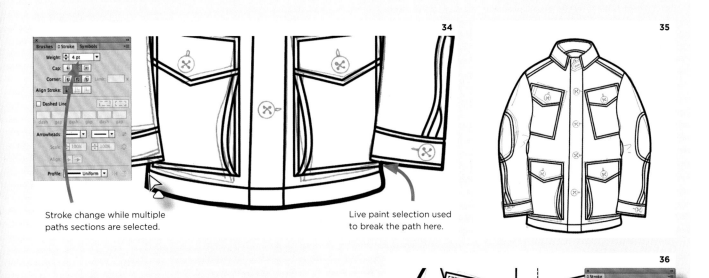

34

35

Stroke change while multiple paths sections are selected.

Live paint selection used to break the path here.

36

14.16

Select any of the paths that have a 4-point stroke. Go → **Select** → **Same** → **Stroke Weight**. All the paths with 4-point stroke are selected. Press **command/control + J** to join up the paths as one.

14.17

Open the Symbols window. In the Symbols window you have some symbols loaded by default. Click on the first symbol there, hold down **shift**, and click on the last symbol. And then click on the trash can button to delete them all (they are only deleted for the current document). It will be tidier to use only symbols related to the garment. Access the symbols menu by clicking on the button in the top right corner and go → **Open Symbol Library** → **Other Library...** Locate the file button and pocket symbols library in the project folder. **(fig. 37)**

14.18

A new button and pocket symbols window opens. First drag a buttonhole symbol out of the window and scale it down to fit a drawn version in the sketch. Then drag the button symbol from the button and pocket symbols window. Scale this and position it appropriately over your single buttonhole to correspond with the sketch.

14.19

Select both the buttonhole and button and drag into the Symbols window. (You can't drag into the library window.) **(fig. 38)**

Okay the dialog window that opens. You don't have to specify anything here. You now have created a combined buttonhole and button symbol alongside the symbols for the separate elements. Symbols make sense in fashion flats because you can modify all instances in one go. So you can change the color or fill of a symbol and update all together, as you will see. **(fig. 39)**

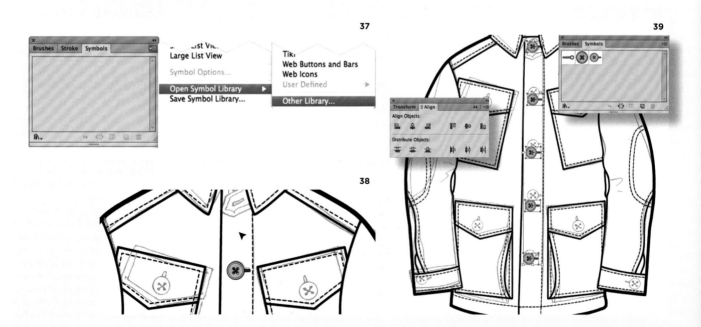

37

39

38

PROJECT
THIRTEEN—
ILLUSTRATOR:
THE BLOB AND
ART BRUSHES

**PROJECT
FOURTEEN—
ILLUSTRATOR:
FLATS**

PROJECT FIFTEEN—
ILLUSTRATOR: ALL
THE TRIMMINGS

PROJECT SIXTEEN—
ILLUSTRATOR:
LAYOUT

PROJECT
SEVENTEEN—
ILLUSTRATOR:
PRESENTATION

PROJECT
EIGHTEEN—
PHOTOSHOP:
PRESENTATION

CASE STUDY:
PRINTFRESH
STUDIO

CASE STUDY:
C&A DESIGNERS

14.20

Using the drag to copy method (select, **option/alt**, and drag) position further copies (actually instances because this is a symbol) down the front of the coat. Select all these symbols. Open the Align window and use the Vertical Distribute Center button to create equal space between your buttons. By default, Align is relative to selection; if it has been changed in your application, change it in the Align window options drop-down menu. Make more copies of the button and buttonhole by dragging with **option/alt** held down and position the copies over the pockets and cuffs. Rotate the symbols as necessary.

14.21

Now the collar tab needs to be made. Elements like this can be made and saved as symbols if you think you will need them again. Symbols can always be scaled and edited to suit a new usage. For drawing the collar tab make sure Fill is still none in the Toolbar and draw a rectangle as near as possible in height to the size of the tab in the original sketch. With the Path tool (**P**) add another point in the middle of the left side of the rectangle. Pull this point out with the Direct Selection tool (**A**) to make the pointed end of the tab. **(fig. 40)**

Select all three points on the left side and use Vertical Distribute Center again to ensure the middle point is equal distance from top and bottom. **(fig. 41)** Select the whole shape with the Selection tool (**V**). Use Offset to create the inner line that will be the stitch line. Use the same –1.5 mm distance for consistency. Illustrator remembers the units last used in the window. With the Direct Selection tool select and then drag the left side of the inner shape to beyond the edge of the outer. Select both shapes and then define as a Live Paint group (**command/control + X**). Switch to the Live Paint Selection tool (**shift + L**) and delete the overhang on the right-hand side. Editing using the Live Paint Group method is often easier than using the scissors tool. **(fig. 42)**

14.22

Select the whole Live Paint group with the Selection tool and then move the collar tab to the position of the sketch version. Rotate, using one of the corner control points of the bounding box, to match the angle of the sketch version.

40

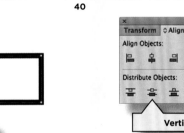

41

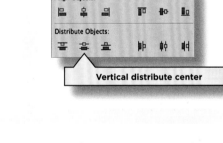

Vertical distribute center

42

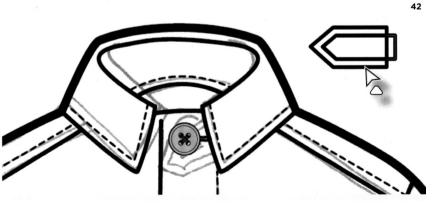

14.23

Erase the sections of the paths that are not needed, the paths in the collar tab that overlap the collar. Use the eraser tool and note that because there is a selection—the Live Paint Group—the eraser only affects the selected paths and not the other paths surrounding. **(fig. 43)** The original sketch layer has now been made invisible.

14.24

The tab should look like it sits behind the collar. Click on the Expand button to return the paths to normal behavior. We need ordinary paths now to join up the cut end of the tab. Press "**A**" to switch to the Direct Selection tool, click on one of the anchor points on the cut end of the tab, and, then holding shift, click on the second anchor point on the cut end. Press **command/control + J** to join the ends of the path. **(fig. 44)**

14.25

Make sure fill is uppermost in the Toolbar, click "**X**" to swap the fill and stroke position if necessary. Click on white in the Swatches window or select White in the Fill drop-down menu in the Control Panel. The collar tab should now appear as a black stroke outline with a white fill.

14.26

Click with the Direct Selection tool on any part of the inner path and click on the dash box in the Stroke window. Illustrator remembers the dash settings for the stitch effect and applies these. Alternatively use the Eyedropper tool to copy the attributes of an existing stitch line. **(fig. 45)**

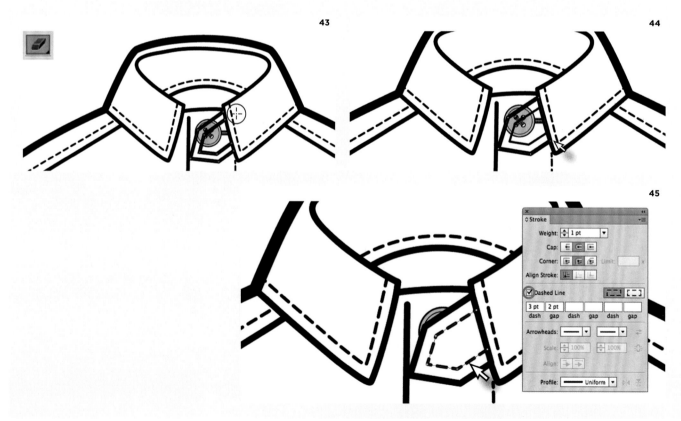

43

44

45

PROJECT
THIRTEEN—
ILLUSTRATOR:
THE BLOB AND
ART BRUSHES

PROJECT
FOURTEEN—
ILLUSTRATOR:
FLATS

PROJECT FIFTEEN—
ILLUSTRATOR: ALL
THE TRIMMINGS

PROJECT SIXTEEN—
ILLUSTRATOR:
LAYOUT

PROJECT
SEVENTEEN—
ILLUSTRATOR:
PRESENTATION

PROJECT
EIGHTEEN—
PHOTOSHOP:
PRESENTATION

CASE STUDY:
PRINTFRESH
STUDIO

CASE STUDY:
C&A DESIGNERS

14.27

The garment drawing is nearing completion. With the construction details in place a little indication of the fabric stiffness can be added with some shading and creases. Placing the shading on its own layer enables it to be easily hidden when needed and to automatically darken whatever color or pattern is placed in the garment below. Make the original sketch layer visible again. It will be a guide to placing the shading marks. Create a new layer above the layer that your garment is drawn on. Using the Pen tool, draw some simple paths in similar positions to those in the original sketch and any more that you feel are needed. Use the Width tool to alter the thickness of the path and to make the lines more expressive. **(fig. 46)**

14.28

Having finished drawing all the shading marks you will now adjust the transparency of the shadow layer. Open the Transparency window. On the shadows layer click on the radio button on the right side in what Adobe calls the Target Column. When clicked this appears as a double ring, indicating that the entire contents of the layer (or sublayer if picked) are targeted and the appearance of all objects can be changed as one. In the Transparency window change the mode to Multiply, so that the shadows will realistically overlay any color below, and change the opacity to 30 percent so the shadows are not too strong. **(fig. 47)**

14.29

To further organize your flat you could move all the stitching to a separate layer. Select one stitch line and use the **Select → Same → Stroke Weight** command to select all stitching in the design. Create a new layer and name it Stitching. Drag the little square in the selection column, indicating all the selected stitch paths, to the new layer.

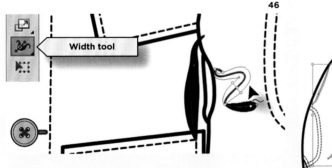

Width tool

46

47

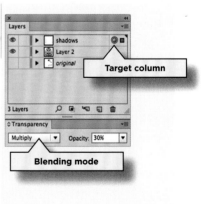

Target column

Blending mode

14.30

Now to color the coat. With the Direct Selection tool double click on the outline of the garment, the thickest stroked path around the edge of the garment. Have Fill uppermost in the Toolbar. Either double click on the fill square and select a suitable brown from the color picker or click on a brown in the Swatches window. The coat becomes brown except for the collar tab. If, when the coat outline is filled, it obscures the other lines, send it to the back of the layer by immediately going to **Object → Arrange → Send to Back**. For the collar tab select the same brown fill. Note that the shadows in the design show as darker brown on the brown coat. The actual browns used in the design are shown here for exact matching and you can create color swatches with the same CMYK values. **(fig. 48)**

14.31

You can now add some color detail to the design by creating regions of contrasting color and changing the button material to a more interesting horn finish. To change the color of areas such as the pocket sides, double click on one of the paths and launch Isolation Mode. There you can easily change the color of the area you want. **(fig. 49)**

14.32

With the color changes finished exit Isolation Mode. The final detail in the design is to change the button material to horn. If you spend time creating various symbols and custom brushes in Illustrator to represent zippers, pulls, and lace then, because they will be vector, they are easily adapted and changed to fit new designs. So the time is well spent. Make the layer with the buttons the active layer. Go **File → Place** and load the Horn.psd file. Resize the place image to about 20 mm by 20 mm to get closer to an appropriate size. Drag the resized images into the Swatches window to create a fill swatch. Delete the original horn image, as it is no longer needed.

14.33

Double click on one of the button instances in the design. By default, a warning dialog box tells you that you are about to edit the symbol definition and that this will be applied to all instances. This is what you want to happen. (If you want to you can click on the tick box to never see the warning again.) An Isolation mode for the symbol launches. Zoom in to see the button elements clearly. Double click on the button itself to isolate that. Remember the button and buttonhole symbol is made from two separate original symbols. Isolation mode helps you drill down to the specific bits you need to alter. Click on the outer circle of the button. Ensure the Fill is uppermost in the Toolbar, and click on the horn

49

50

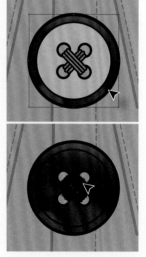

48

C=56 M=56 Y=72 K=42   C=35 M=69 Y=91 K=34

PROJECT
THIRTEEN—
ILLUSTRATOR:
THE BLOB AND
ART BRUSHES

PROJECT
FOURTEEN—
ILLUSTRATOR:
FLATS

PROJECT FIFTEEN—
ILLUSTRATOR: ALL
THE TRIMMINGS

PROJECT SIXTEEN—
ILLUSTRATOR:
LAYOUT

PROJECT
SEVENTEEN—
ILLUSTRATOR:
PRESENTATION

PROJECT
EIGHTEEN—
PHOTOSHOP:
PRESENTATION

CASE STUDY:
PRINTFRESH
STUDIO

CASE STUDY:
C&A DESIGNERS

material swatch in the Swatches window to make this the fill. Click on the inner ring of the button and change this, too, from gray to the horn fill. The button thread is too light for the coat so select this and change it to a darker color.

When you have finished the changes click the escape key to exit Isolation Mode. Note that all buttons have updated to the same attributes. **(fig. 50)**

You could, of course, use the same technique of bringing in an image and creating a fill swatch to create all sorts of pattern and material variations on the fabric and details of your garment. Once the initial drawing is done design variations are very quickly developed. **(fig. 51)**

PROJECT REVIEW

REVIEW

This has been a complex project but you have covered an enormous amount of what you need to draw professional looking, flat garment designs and you have gained experience in many advanced techniques. Although you concentrated on a single garment style the techniques relate to all other styles. You should feel that previous projects have given you confidence with the tools and techniques in simpler applications and now in flats many of them come together to build the complexity needed in designs. The only other techniques you need to know are constructing trims and details using brushes and objects, and these are covered in the following supplementary project.

PRACTICE

As mentioned at the beginning of this project in order to practice the drawing skill and to become relaxed, separate the designing from the drawing initially. Select some images of existing styles that interest you and practice recreating these as flats trying to describe the garment accurately and clearly. Explore ways of representing various fabrics or graphics in your designs. Check any fabric swatches in Photoshop with the Offset Filter to see how they repeat. You want to avoid awkward bands, which could occur when made into a pattern swatch in Illustrator.

51

PROJECT FIFTEEN—ILLUSTRATOR: ALL THE TRIMMINGS

15

In the previous project you drew a garment in Illustrator and added Live Paint to your tool set. With practice you should be able to draw convincing flats. The final step to making truly professional flats is drawing all the various trims that will enhance your designs.

The preceding projects emphasized customizing tools and creating custom brushes in particular. Custom brushes offer great opportunities for expressing your personal style, but they become truly essential when you want to create professional designs. Custom Brushes, Symbols, and Fills are the tools required to furnish the important details in your design. Doing this work in Illustrator means that these trims are forever editable; they can always be tweaked, reused, and adapted so it is worth investing the initial time to get an impressive result.

52

PROJECT
THIRTEEN—
ILLUSTRATOR:
THE BLOB AND
ART BRUSHES

PROJECT
FOURTEEN—
ILLUSTRATOR:
FLATS

**PROJECT FIFTEEN—
ILLUSTRATOR: ALL
THE TRIMMINGS**

PROJECT SIXTEEN—
ILLUSTRATOR:
LAYOUT

PROJECT
SEVENTEEN—
ILLUSTRATOR:
PRESENTATION

PROJECT
EIGHTEEN—
PHOTOSHOP:
PRESENTATION

CASE STUDY:
PRINTFRESH
STUDIO

CASE STUDY:
C&A DESIGNERS

ILLUSTRATOR: ALL THE TRIMMINGS

In this project you will:
- Create Pattern Brushes and add these to garment drawings.
- Learn how to use Clipping Masks to precisely control where your pattern brushes appear in a garment shape.
- Practice using Live Paint Groups and learn how the Live Paint Bucket tool can be used to quickly define shapes in a drawing.

Outcome
You should have learned some of the techniques for adding precise garment details to drawings and for giving a professional finish to flats. You should understand the ways to create more complex pattern brushes with multiple tiles.

Aim
To show how the fundamental techniques in Illustrator, such as stroking a path, become very powerful tools when combined with more complex artwork. To introduce the more advanced versions of custom brushes needed to draw professional flat designs. To show how a single technique is used to render a huge amount of the trims needed to be depicted.

Project files are available at
www.bloomsbury.com/hume-textile-design

Pattern Brush Trimmed by a Clipping Path to Create an Elasticized Waistband

Symbols can be used for repeated individual objects like sequins, buttons, or pockets. Art brushes can be used for indicating drape, creases, and gestural marks. Pattern brushes can be used for more complex stitches such as overlocking, and for continuous elements such as ruching, ruffles, smocking, cords, elasticized waistbands, and zippers. Pattern brushes act like a very elaborate stroke applied to a path. More than one brush tip, or Tile, can feature in the same Pattern Brush. So a zipper pattern brush can have a beginning, middle, and end tile reproducing the details of the particular zipper.

Pattern Brushes conform to any path you draw and with a brush applied to a path, the path can be altered and the brush will redraw to match the changes. The size of the brush itself can be altered by clicking on the brush tip in the Brushes window and by the stroke size. A Clipping Mask can be used to exactly control where the brush appears, for example, to make ribbing drawn with a pattern brush fit neatly inside a collar.

15.1

From the project folder open the file named Mens Sports Shorts.

15.2

The file has four layers. Make the two layers named stitches and creases invisible. This is to make things clearer when using the Shape Builder tool.

15.3

On the layer named brushes select the path crossing the waist area with the Selection tool. **(fig. 53)**

15.4

Go **Object → Path → Offset Path...** and enter 4 mm as the offset. The offset shape will become both the waistband and a clipping path for the elastic waistband brush. **(fig. 54)**

15.5

Create a new layer. Select the original path you used to create the offset shape and move it to this layer using the Direct Selection tool. Make that layer invisible.

15.6

Select all the shorts drawing that is visible by dragging a box to enclose it with the Selection tool. Define this selection as a Live Paint Group by pressing **command/control + option/alt + X** and use the Live Paint Selection tool (**shift + L**) to remove the overhanging bits of the waistband that you don't need. Remember, click once with the tool on the path, look for the white triangle beside the tool cursor to confirm a path is selected and the gray crosshatching across the path. Then press the delete key. **(fig. 55)**

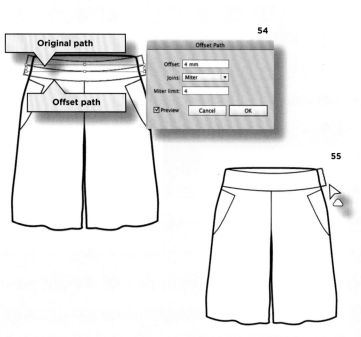

PROJECT
THIRTEEN—
ILLUSTRATOR:
THE BLOB AND
ART BRUSHES

PROJECT
FOURTEEN—
ILLUSTRATOR:
FLATS

**PROJECT FIFTEEN—
ILLUSTRATOR: ALL
THE TRIMMINGS**

PROJECT SIXTEEN—
ILLUSTRATOR:
LAYOUT

PROJECT
SEVENTEEN—
ILLUSTRATOR:
PRESENTATION

PROJECT
EIGHTEEN—
PHOTOSHOP:
PRESENTATION

CASE STUDY:
PRINTFRESH
STUDIO

CASE STUDY:
C&A DESIGNERS

15.7

If your swatches palette only has black, white, and none then add a couple of colors to your swatches window. The choice of colors doesn't matter, but to get the best out of the Live Paint Bucket you need to have a few extra colors in Swatches. Select the Live Paint Bucket tool (**K**). It is part of the Shape Builder group in the Toolbar. With the Live Paint Bucket you can paint regions and paths of a Live Paint Group with the current fill and stroke. With sufficient colors in Swatches the tool pointer will display three color squares; the center one is the current fill or stroke color and the other two squares are the adjacent colors in Swatches. You can access the other colors, and colors next to these, by pressing the left or right arrow key on your keyboard. The default setting is to fill a region or face and you can switch to stroke by holding down shift. Use the Live Paint Bucket tool to fill the back waistband, front waistband, and the two pockets. Live Paint is doing the work of turning individual paths into objects. **(fig. 56)**

15.8

Press the **V** key once to switch to the Selection Tool. Click on the Expand button in the Control Bar to release the Live Paint Group. Then press **shift + command/control + G** twice to ungroup everything.

15.9

Open the Brushes window if not open. Look for the brush tile on the artboard, it is to the left of the drawing of the shorts. This brush tile is a small group of paths that has been drawn so that the right side will connect up with the left and repeat smoothly to describe a waistband. Select this brush tile with the Selection tool (**V**) and drag it into the Brushes window. Select pattern brush as the option in the dialog box that opens. **(fig. 57)**

15.10

Make the layer with the original waistband path visible again. The ends of the path should appear beyond the solid waistband. Click on the path to select it. Click on the new brush in the Brushes window to apply the brush to the path. You should just be able to see the brush applied behind the solid waistband. Note: You do want the waistband in front. **(fig. 58)**

58

Click on brush to apply

57

56

15.11

With the path still selected hold down shift and click within the solid waistband front (the solid waistband will become the clipping mask for the stroked path). **(fig. 59)**

Press control or the right button on a mouse and click again on the waistband front. From the menu that opens select Make Clipping Mask. Clipping masks allow you to precisely control how much of a brush or pattern is shown; they act as a mask clipping the underlying artwork to their shape. **(fig. 60)**

15.12

In the Brushes window click on the brush to open its options window. With Preview ticked adjust the scale slider to get the ideal size.
(fig. 61)

15.13

Make all layers visible to check how things look together. Select one of the pocket shapes with the Selection tool (V). To create the effect of shadow in the pockets open the Gradient window. Double click on the left-hand gradient slider and change this to a light gray (if the sliders are not apparent, click on the gradient bar to reveal them). Single click on the other slider and change its opacity to zero creating a fill from gray to transparent. When you have something that looks realistic,

switch to the Transparency window and change the mode to Multiply to make the gradient darken what is behind it. Select the other pocket, switch to the Eyedropper tool (I) and click on the finished pocket to apply its attributes to the other one. The shading needs to be reversed, so click on the Reverse Gradient button in the Gradient window. **(fig. 62)**

15.14

For the back waistband you will create a new pattern brush of your own. Make the brushes layer the active layer. Have black as the stroke color and no fill in the Toolbar. Select the Line Segment tool (\), hold down **option/alt** and click to draw a path 6 mm long. Have the stroke be 0.25 points.

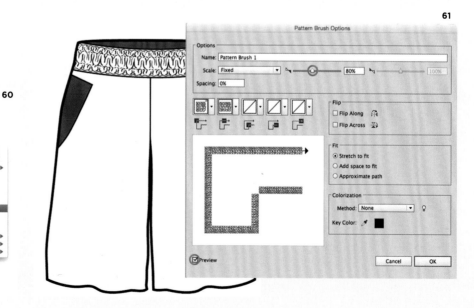

Brush applied

59

60

61

PROJECT THIRTEEN— ILLUSTRATOR: THE BLOB AND ART BRUSHES

PROJECT FOURTEEN— ILLUSTRATOR: FLATS

PROJECT FIFTEEN— ILLUSTRATOR: ALL THE TRIMMINGS

PROJECT SIXTEEN— ILLUSTRATOR: LAYOUT

PROJECT SEVENTEEN— ILLUSTRATOR: PRESENTATION

PROJECT EIGHTEEN— PHOTOSHOP: PRESENTATION

CASE STUDY: PRINTFRESH STUDIO

CASE STUDY: C&A DESIGNERS

15.15

Go **Effect → Distort and Transform → Zig Zag**. In the Zig Zag window change the size to Relative and 2 percent, make the ridges 13 per segment, and the points smooth. "Okay" the window to close. An uneven number of ridges ensures that the path can repeat properly. **(fig. 63)**

15.16

Go **Object → Transform → Move** (**shift + command/control + M**) and select the horizontal distance as zero and the vertical distance as 0.5 mm. Click Copy rather than Okay. Immediately press **command/control + D** 15 times.

15.17

Select all the paths and drag into the Brushes window. Choose Pattern Brush as the type of brush. In the document select the brushes layer and draw a path across the area of the back waistband.

15.18

Click on your new pattern brush in the Brushes window to apply it to the path. To trim the pattern to the shape of the back waistband repeat the same procedure as you did with the front waistband. With the path still selected, press **shift** and then click inside the back waistband shape. Then press **control** and click again in the back waistband. From the menu that appears, select Make Clipping

Mask to trim the brush to fit the back waistband. **(fig. 64)**

15.19

If you want to fill your garment shape with fabric, textures, or patterns then the outline of the garment should be bottommost in the stacking order of elements so that all detail will show on top. Select Layer 5, rename this fill, and move this layer to the bottom of the layer order. On the outline layer select just the outer garment outline with the Direct Selection tool. In the Layers window move the little square in the selection column, indicating the selected object, down to the fill layer. **(fig. 65)**

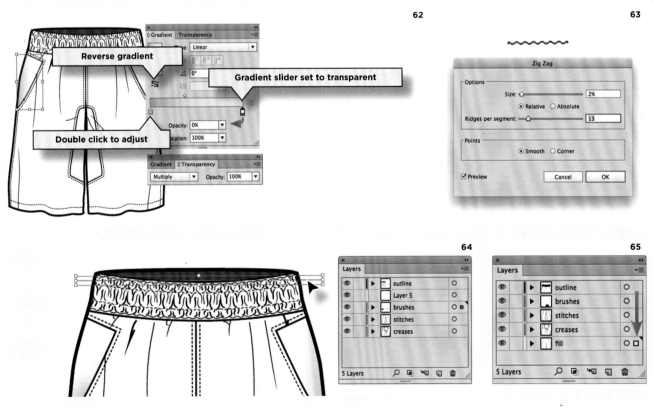

62

63

Reverse gradient

Gradient slider set to transparent

Double click to adjust

64

65

15.20

Go **File → Place** and find the Marl.psd image in the project folder. Click Place. When the marl image loads drag it into the Swatches window. Delete the original marl image. Click on the outline in the fill layer, ensure that fill is uppermost in the Toolbar, and click on the marl swatch in Swatches to apply this as the fill. **(fig. 66)**

The elasticized waistband was made with a pattern brush using a single pattern tile. This is the way many trims are made in Illustrator. The ribbed collar in the illustration, for example, is made from a pattern brush with a single pattern tile trimmed by a clipping mask. **(fig. 67)**

Both frills on the skirt illustrated are similarly single tile pattern brushes. **(fig. 68)**

Other brushes have additional tiles for the beginning and end of the path. The most complex pattern brushes tend to be for zippers and areas where tiles are required for all the sections of the zipper. Although Illustrator CC now has automatic corner generation for pattern brushes for most brushes, for trims distinct tiles need to be made. To complete this project the draw cord for the shorts needs to be added.

66

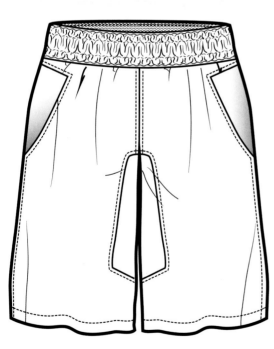

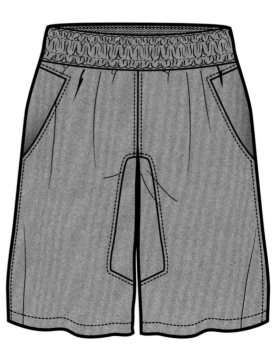

PROJECT THIRTEEN— ILLUSTRATOR: THE BLOB AND ART BRUSHES

PROJECT FOURTEEN— ILLUSTRATOR: FLATS

PROJECT FIFTEEN— ILLUSTRATOR: ALL THE TRIMMINGS

PROJECT SIXTEEN— ILLUSTRATOR: LAYOUT

PROJECT SEVENTEEN— ILLUSTRATOR: PRESENTATION

PROJECT EIGHTEEN— PHOTOSHOP: PRESENTATION

CASE STUDY: PRINTFRESH STUDIO

CASE STUDY: C&A DESIGNERS

67

Pattern tile for brush

68

Pattern tile for brush

Pattern tile for brush

69

Pattern tile for brush

A Pattern Brush with Three Pattern Tiles: Braided Cord

In the options window on any Pattern Brush spaces are shown for five tiles—for the sides, inner corner, outer corner, start, and end of the pattern. If you are making a pattern brush with a single tile, as you did with the waistband, then by default this becomes the side tile, which normally makes up most of any pattern brush. For the cord we want a rounded end, which requires a tile for both the start and end tiles. All tiles need to connect up with each other seamlessly so the beginning and end tiles need to connect seamlessly with the side tile. Of course, if the braided cord was not a significant part of the design or you thought you would never need this particular brush again then a much simpler version would be fine, but the same requirements apply to any brush where you need the beginning or end finished neatly.

15.21

In your mens sports shorts document create a new layer, have this layer at the top of the layer stack, and call it cord.

15.22

From the project folder open the file called Braided cord. Note the document and objects in it are very small. It makes sense to have the elements of a brush close to the scale that they will be used in a design before converting to a brush. Otherwise the stroke thicknesses can get scaled down so small that the brush looks disproportionately finely drawn. Zoom in on the objects. Select the three objects and copy all three (**command/control + C**), switch to the mens sports shorts document, and paste them on the cord layer (**command/control + V**). Unfortunately "Place" is not the easy way to bring the artwork in here.

15.23

The objects for the start and end of the brush need to be dragged separately into the Swatches window. **(fig. 70)** From there they can be selected as pattern tiles in your pattern brush options. After you create a pattern brush, you can delete the pattern tiles from the Swatches panel if you don't need them for additional artwork. Hover the pointer over the new swatches to check what names they have been given by Illustrator.

If you created a pattern swatch for the marl texture, Illustrator would have called it New Pattern Swatch 1, so the two new swatches are New Pattern Swatch 2 and New Pattern Swatch 3. You can change the names by switching to list view or opening the pattern options window.

15.24

Select and drag the remaining object, the straight section of the cord, directly into the Brushes window. Select Pattern Brush as the brush style.

15.25

In the options window for your new brush there are five Tile buttons. Two are already filled in. The second one, the Side Tile, has been filled with the artwork you dragged into the Brushes window. The first tile position, the Outer Corner Tile, displays a possible option that Illustrator has constructed from the Side Tile. The other tiles are currently showing None with a drop-down menu alongside each that allows you to select a choice from the Swatches window.

Click on the Start Tile and from the available swatches, identify, and then click on, the swatch that is for the start of the brush. The artwork should now appear in the tile button. Click on the End Tile button and from the swatches choose the artwork for the end of the brush. Under the tile Fit options, Stretch To Fit will be suitable for the cord. It lengthens or shortens the pattern tile to fit the object. "Okay" the window to exit. **(fig. 71)**

70

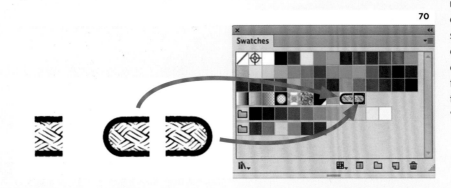

PROJECT
THIRTEEN—
ILLUSTRATOR:
THE BLOB AND
ART BRUSHES

PROJECT
FOURTEEN—
ILLUSTRATOR:
FLATS

PROJECT FIFTEEN—
ILLUSTRATOR: ALL
THE TRIMMINGS

PROJECT SIXTEEN—
ILLUSTRATOR:
LAYOUT

PROJECT
SEVENTEEN—
ILLUSTRATOR:
PRESENTATION

PROJECT
EIGHTEEN—
PHOTOSHOP:
PRESENTATION

CASE STUDY:
PRINTFRESH
STUDIO

CASE STUDY:
C&A DESIGNERS

You could ask Illustrator to offer an option on the inner corner tile but as there will not be any corners when drawing the cord this is not needed.

15.26

You have now created a pattern brush, and you will use that brush to create an Art Brush to go with the Pattern Brush. The drawstring for the waistband can be drawn with just the Pattern Brush but the Art Brush will be good for adding in the knots on the end of the cord and it is easy to make from the Pattern Brush. Using the Pen or Line tool draw a straight horizontal path about 6 mm long. Click on your new Pattern Brush to apply it to this path. Drag the path with the brush applied into the Brushes window. This time select Art Brush as the style of brush, select Stretch to Fit in the Scale Options, and click Okay to exit.

15.27

To draw the drawstring on the shorts you need to draw paths with the Pen or Pencil tool. You can see the individual paths in Outline view in the illustration. **(fig. 72)** You can adjust the stroke thickness of the paths to change the size of the cord or resize the brush itself in the Brush Options window. Before drawing the path you can draw two eyelets for the cords using the Ellipse tool, Offset Path command, and then either the Shapebuilder or Pathfinder tool to create a ring with an empty center. Fill the ring with a gradient for a metallic effect.

15.28

On the cord layer draw a path between the two holes of the eyelets and then a convincing knot. For tied ends use the Art Brush and make any adjustment needed to the thickness of the cord using Stroke or the Brush Options window. **(fig. 73)**

The final part of this trimmings project examines how the invisible bounding box controls what becomes the tile in pattern brushes.

71

Pattern Brush Options

Options

Name: Tie-Cord

Scale: Fixed   100%   100%

Side tile   New pattern swatch 2

Swatch selector

Flip Across

Start tile   End tile

etch to fit
Add space to fit
Approximate path

Colorization

Method: None

Key Color:

Preview   Cancel   OK

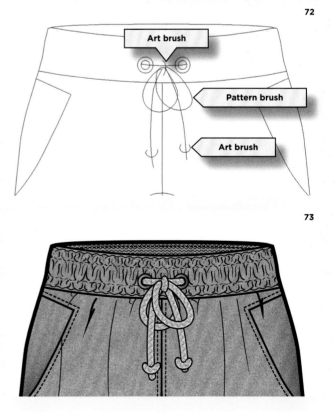

72

Art brush

Pattern brush

Art brush

73

A Pattern Brush for a Zipper

Before Adobe radically overhauled the pattern making in Illustrator the common technique for cutting artwork into a repeat swatch was with a rectangle with no fill and no stroke. This invisible rectangle was behind all other artwork and when the artwork was dragged to the Swatch window this invisible rectangle defined the repeat rectangle. This technique is still the ideal one for controlling the pattern tile in brushes. Often the artwork for a tile needs to be cut into an exact repeating unit. The unit we need for the repeating teeth in the zipper requires one complete tooth on one side and two half teeth the other. You could use paths to cut though the teeth artwork but you would need to expand the appearance of the strokes to cut through them. But none of that is needed with the invisible box method. **(fig. 74)**

15.29

Open the file called Zipper artwork from the project folder. You will first create the closed teeth zipper brush. Draw a rectangle that is the exact width and height of the zipper bottom stop. Drag a copy of this, holding down shift to keep it exactly aligned and position it behind the teeth unit. Adjust the width so it exactly cuts the teeth into a repeating section. When you have the rectangles correct for size make sure that they are at the back of the artwork. Use **Object → Arrange → Send to Back** if you need to. Remember the rectangle must not have any fill or stroke. **(fig. 75)**

15.30

With the zipper teeth artwork and the invisible rectangle selected drag them together into the Brushes window. Select Pattern Brush as the style. This creates a pattern brush of continuous zipper teeth. Draw a line about 4 mm long and apply the new brush. Now you will add the bottom stop.

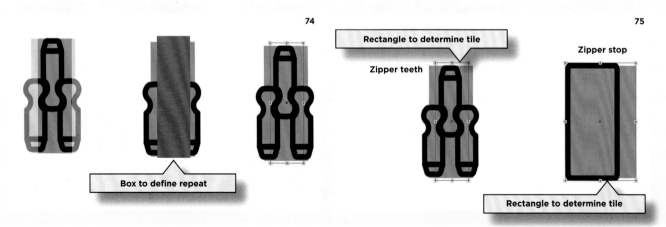

74

75

Box to define repeat

Rectangle to determine tile

Zipper teeth

Zipper stop

Rectangle to determine tile

PROJECT
THIRTEEN—
ILLUSTRATOR:
THE BLOB AND
ART BRUSHES

PROJECT
FOURTEEN—
ILLUSTRATOR:
FLATS

**PROJECT FIFTEEN—
ILLUSTRATOR: ALL
THE TRIMMINGS**

PROJECT SIXTEEN—
ILLUSTRATOR:
LAYOUT

PROJECT
SEVENTEEN—
ILLUSTRATOR:
PRESENTATION

PROJECT
EIGHTEEN—
PHOTOSHOP:
PRESENTATION

CASE STUDY:
PRINTFRESH
STUDIO

CASE STUDY:
C&A DESIGNERS

15.31

There is another method for adding tiles to a pattern brush, but you have to be good with your aim! Instead of creating swatches you can drag the artwork for tiles directly into the row of tiles for the pattern brush. Select the artwork, this time the bottom stop of the zipper and drag while holding down the **option/alt** key onto the space for the Start tile. **(fig. 76)**

The bottom stop of the zipper is the start tile here because the zipper is going to be the end tile. Press Okay in the options window. A second dialog box opens; it asks you whether you want to apply the changes to existing brush strokes. Choose to leave the existing strokes unchanged. A new version of the brush is created below the original. But you can add to this second brush without generating another duplicate.

15.32

Some designers add zipper sliders as symbols to designs and others add them to the zipper brush itself. For this brush you will include the slider. Place the artwork for the zipper slider on top of your strip of zipper teeth on the artboard. Place a rectangle behind this artwork that includes the entire slider and that cuts the last zipper tooth at the exact same place on the left-hand side as the original zipper teeth unit. Remember when you drag into the brush window that the rectangle must have no stroke and fill. **(fig. 77)**

15.33

Drag the zipper, teeth, and rectangle group while holding down the **option/alt** key onto the End Tile of the second version of the brush. This time the new tile is added to the existing brush without generating a duplicate. **(fig. 78)**

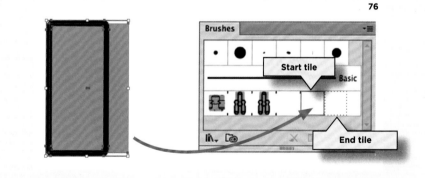

76

77

Rectangle to determine tile

78

15.34

Now make a brush for the open zipper using the single zipper tooth artwork. This is already an exact single unit. Create an invisible rectangle for the small end stop that is the same height as the tooth unit. Add the end stop as the end tile for the open zipper. **(fig. 79)**

15.35

From the brushes window drop-down menu select Save Brush library... and save your new zipper brush library so you can use it in other files. Give the file an appropriate name and either save it in the same location as Adobe's default brushes or to a convenient location of your choice.

15.36

Open the file named Cropped Biker Jacket from the project folder. In the Brushes window open your new Brushes library. Draw suitable paths in the design for the zippers and apply your two brushes as appropriate. To reverse the direction of an individual stroked path select it and click on the small Options of Selected Object button in the brushes window. With preview on try the two flip options. **(fig. 80)**

79

79
Complete brush applied
to a path.

80

PROJECT
THIRTEEN—
ILLUSTRATOR:
THE BLOB AND
ART BRUSHES

PROJECT
FOURTEEN—
ILLUSTRATOR:
FLATS

**PROJECT FIFTEEN—
ILLUSTRATOR: ALL
THE TRIMMINGS**

PROJECT SIXTEEN—
ILLUSTRATOR:
LAYOUT

PROJECT
SEVENTEEN—
ILLUSTRATOR:
PRESENTATION

PROJECT
EIGHTEEN—
PHOTOSHOP:
PRESENTATION

CASE STUDY:
PRINTFRESH
STUDIO

CASE STUDY:
C&A DESIGNERS

81

PROJECT REVIEW

REVIEW
You do not need to learn numerous techniques for creating trims. Pattern brushes, alongside symbols, achieve most things. Time has to be spent looking at trims and seeing how the necessary simplification should take place. Then the techniques in this project can be used to represent construction detail in a clear and convincing style. Your own interests will determine what actual trims you need to render and these techniques will enable you to achieve high standards of finish in your own work.

PRACTICE
Select some trims from the real world and experiment in reducing these trims to simple representations using pattern brushes. Translating actual trims is very good practice, and remember good practice is to make as few elements as is needed to achieve a convincing effect.

You do not need to learn numerous techniques for creating trims. Pattern brushes, alongside symbols, achieve most things.

PROJECT SIXTEEN—ILLUSTRATOR: LAYOUT

16

There are many times when you need to lay your work out in an ordered manner: bringing inspirational material together to frame your thoughts and clarify your thinking, explaining to others the background to a design story, illustrating key themes and showing how they are realized in your collection.

Whether the means of presentation is print on large boards, an A4 portfolio, a digital tablet, or via the web, the material needs structure that subtly indicates that, through reflection, a convincing visual argument has been developed that concludes with your persuasive designs.

Without some underlying structure in a presentation, elements can jump about randomly distracting the viewer and thereby working against your desire to appear professional

PROJECT THIRTEEN—ILLUSTRATOR: THE BLOB AND ART BRUSHES

PROJECT FOURTEEN—ILLUSTRATOR: FLATS

PROJECT FIFTEEN—ILLUSTRATOR: ALL THE TRIMMINGS

PROJECT SIXTEEN—ILLUSTRATOR: LAYOUT

PROJECT SEVENTEEN—ILLUSTRATOR: PRESENTATION

PROJECT EIGHTEEN—PHOTOSHOP: PRESENTATION

CASE STUDY: PRINTFRESH STUDIO

CASE STUDY: C&A DESIGNERS

In design, grid formats are ubiquitous. They give structure to visual material. While books have been written entirely on grid designs for layout, in this project, you will simply create a single gird to enable a balanced composition and as a possible template for a number of related presentation boards. Without some underlying structure in a presentation, elements can jump about randomly distracting the viewer and thereby work against your desire to appear professional.

ILLUSTRATOR: LAYOUT

In this project you will:
- Use the grid tool to create a structure for presentation boards and to create color chips.
- Make a grid and transform it into guides and layout images related to the grid structure.
- Use the Eyedropper tool to sample colors for the mood board and use the Type tool to give titles to color chips.

Outcome
You should have a presentation board displaying design and color inspiration, color chips, and garment sketches in an ordered composition. In professional practice a presentation would have the inspiration and the design displayed on separate boards, but for this project your presentation board will be a very abbreviated version. From the project you will create a potential template document with a grid structure that will help you present your own work in a systematic way.

Aim
To introduce the use of grids as good practice in presentation boards. To show how an underlying grid structure can balance disparate images in a coordinated and convincing manner.

Project files are available at www.bloomsbury.com/hume-textile-design

16.1

In Illustrator create a new A4 document, call it Mood Board, and select Print as the profile because you want a reasonable ppi. Make the units millimeters. Select landscape as the orientation; often this better suits presentation both on screen and on paper.

16.2

Because it makes sense to have the guides for the layout on a layer to themselves, rename Layer 1 "Guides." Double click on the name in the Layer window to rename it.

A margin should be set around the document to avoid clipping elements of the document in printing. It is also better, design-wise, that the text not be too close to the margins of the document. You could pull guides out of the rulers and manually, with some calculations, set these up, but in this exercise you will use Offset Path to do it more automatically.

16.3

Make sure the object fill is set to none and the stroke to black in the Toolbar. Have the whole document visible. Select the Rectangle tool and, going from top left down to bottom right, drag out a rectangle to exactly match the dimensions of the document. If you select Smart Guides from the View menu (**command/control + U**) they will aid with this.

16.4

With your drawn rectangle still selected go to **Object → Path → Offset Path** and select 15 mm as the amount (negative values put the path inside the current path). When you okay the offsetting, the original rectangle is no longer selected because the new offset rectangle becomes the selected object. The original rectangle remains; it is just a bit difficult to spot. **(fig. 82)**

16.5

Have the rulers displayed on the artboard (**command/control + R**). Click within a ruler and drag out a guide to line up with each side of the offset box, horizontal guides from the horizontal ruler and vertical guides from the vertical, unless you want to be super slick and hold down the **option/alt** key as you are dragging a guide to switch its orientation. If you drop a guide in the wrong place use a selection tool to move it and if it won't move use **option/alt + Command + ;** to unlock the guides, as they can be locked by default.

16.6

With the four guides in place, delete the offset rectangle, as it is no longer needed. If you find it difficult to select this rectangle, as it has no fill, then it will be easier if you temporarily hide the guides that are sitting on its edges. This is a very useful action to learn and the shortcut is **command/control + ;** (**command** plus **semicolon**). Delete the inner rectangle and then make the guides visible again by using the same shortcut—**command/control + ;**.

82

TIP

Converting elements to guides means they can be part of your document helping with the layout, but as guides they will not print when you send the document to a printer.

PROJECT THIRTEEN— ILLUSTRATOR: THE BLOB AND ART BRUSHES

PROJECT FOURTEEN— ILLUSTRATOR: FLATS

PROJECT FIFTEEN— ILLUSTRATOR: ALL THE TRIMMINGS

PROJECT SIXTEEN— ILLUSTRATOR: LAYOUT

PROJECT SEVENTEEN— ILLUSTRATOR: PRESENTATION

PROJECT EIGHTEEN— PHOTOSHOP: PRESENTATION

CASE STUDY: PRINTFRESH STUDIO

CASE STUDY: C&A DESIGNERS

16.7

Select the original rectangle that is at the edge of the document and then go **Object → Path → Split into Grid**. Have Preview on and enter 3 rows and 3 columns and 0 gutter. **(fig. 83)**

Although the Split into Grid command can add guides, we actually want to convert the nine rectangles grid itself into guides. In Illustrator you can convert any path to be a guide, so now, with the grid still selected, use the shortcut **command/control + 5** to convert the grid to guides. If you click outside the grid to deselect it you will see that it is now the standard turquoise color of a guide.

16.8

Lock the layer guides by clicking in the space next to the eye icon to toggle the lock on. Create a new destination layer for your images and then go **File → Place...** and select the Glasses file from the project folder. It is important to link the file rather than embedding it in the layout, so select the Link tick box then click Place. Position the image with its top in line with the top left-hand guide box. Do not resize the glasses image or any other image in this exercise. **(fig. 84)**

Linked Artwork

Linked artwork is connected to the document but remains independent, which results in a smaller document. You can use the linked artwork many times without significantly increasing the size of the document, and if the original artwork is altered you can update the changes to any of the

linked versions. You can modify linked artwork using transformation tools and effects but you cannot select and edit individual components of the artwork.

When you export or print the document, the original artwork is accessed, creating the final output at the full resolution of the originals. You may have to manually direct Illustrator to the originals if you change the location of your files and the link gets broken. If you move or copy the document to another location and fail to include the linked artwork then Illustrator will not be able to display the images. As "cloud" resources become more and more common it is important to properly manage the location of linked files.

Remember, do not resize the glasses image, or any other image in this exercise.

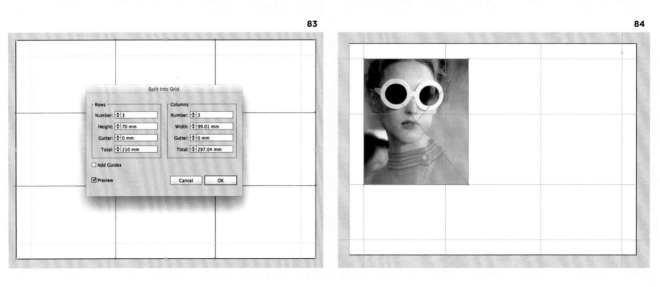

83

84

16.9

Change the fill color in the Toolbar to a color other than white. With the Rectangle tool draw out a rectangle that lines up with the edge of the glasses image at top, bottom, and left but lines up with the second vertical guide in the document. This rectangle will become a clipping mask for the glasses image. **(fig. 85)**

16.10

10. Select both the glasses image and the filled rectangle either by dragging a box over them with the Selection tool or by clicking the image first with the selection tool and then, while holding down the shift key and clicking on the filled rectangle, with the Selection tool. Release the mouse or pen and then the shift key. Now with both objects selected hold down the **control** key and click with the mouse (or right click a two-button mouse). The context menu pops up and from that menu select Make Clipping Mask. The topmost object of a pair becomes the mask for the object below. (In the Adobe world a mask is the opposite of the normal usage, in that the mask reveals rather than hides.) The glasses image becomes clipped to the rectangle. The complete image is still there so it could be moved within its mask at some later time. **(fig. 86)**

16.11

Go ➔ **Place** and select the Macaroons in the project folder. Place the image in the bottom left box of the grid and create a mask to fit the grid rectangle exactly. **(fig. 87)**

85

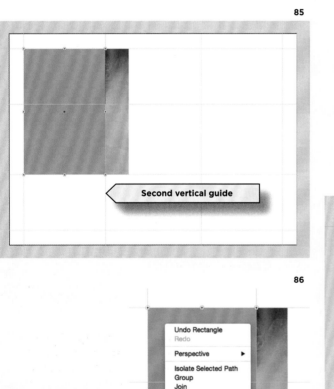

Second vertical guide

86

87

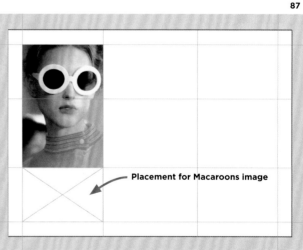

Placement for Macaroons image

PROJECT THIRTEEN— ILLUSTRATOR: THE BLOB AND ART BRUSHES

PROJECT FOURTEEN— ILLUSTRATOR: FLATS

PROJECT FIFTEEN— ILLUSTRATOR: ALL THE TRIMMINGS

PROJECT SIXTEEN— ILLUSTRATOR: LAYOUT

PROJECT SEVENTEEN— ILLUSTRATOR: PRESENTATION

PROJECT EIGHTEEN— PHOTOSHOP: PRESENTATION

CASE STUDY: PRINTFRESH STUDIO

CASE STUDY: C&A DESIGNERS

16.12

Once the clipping mask is in place, use Isolation Mode to get the macaroons into the ideal position. **(fig. 88)**

If you need to move an image within its mask or edit the shape of that mask, Isolation Mode is the ideal method. If you double click on an object you will jump into isolation mode, which does as the name implies: makes only the layers and elements of the current selected object editable while locking all other objects in the document. The gray header bar that appears at the top of the document window and the dimming of the rest of the document indicate you are in isolation mode. In Isolation Mode you should be able to click on the image on its own and move it to an even, centrally aligned position. When the image is in the correct position click on the Back One Level arrow in the left-hand corner of the Isolation Mode header to move back out of the sublayers progressively or press the escape key (**esc**) to immediately exit.

16.13

Go **File → Place** and select the Painting Image. Place the Painting image exactly in line with the bottom horizontal grid line and the second vertical guideline (right edge of glasses image) to match the position shown here. You do not need to use a clipping mask on this image.

16.14

Create a rectangle to fill the space above to the Painting image in the grid. Have the rectangle line up with the top grid line and with the right edge of the painting. Using the method shown in Stage 7 of this project, divide this new rectangle into four equal, horizontal strips. Specify four rows and one column and no gutter. Select individual strips and use the Eyedropper tool to change the color of these color chips to sampled colors from the mood board images. **(fig. 89)**

88

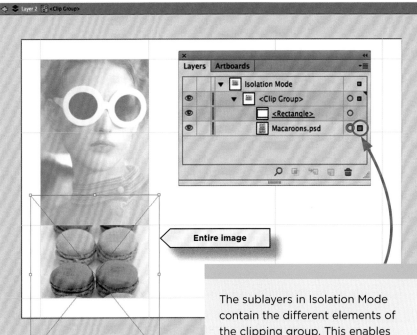

Entire image

The sublayers in Isolation Mode contain the different elements of the clipping group. This enables you to select them individually to edit. The Macaroon image is shown selected and its position within the clipping group can be altered with the Selection tool.

16.15

Lock the layer. Create a new layer and label it Text. Have the Character window open (Window ➔ **Type** ➔ **Character**). In the Character window select a suitable font (strictly speaking, it's actually a typeface) from those available on your computer and one that is suited to the feel of the mood board. In the drop-down menu you see the font name previewed in the actual font style.

16.16

Select the Type tool in the Toolbar. The pointer changes to an I-beam within a dotted box. The small horizontal line near the bottom of this I-beam marks the position of the baseline on which the text rests. With the type tool, click on top of the first color chip. You will be using Point type. With Point type a line of text begins where you click and expands as you enter characters. Each line of text is independent and the line expands or shrinks as you edit it.

This makes it a useful way to add a few words to artwork. Type a title for the chip. The particular font you use determines what specific type size you will need in order to get the right look. Remember that the type size needs to be big enough to ensure legibility wherever the mood board might be viewed but not so big that the type itself has unwarranted emphasis in the layout. With the Type tool, create labels for all four color chips. **(fig. 90)**

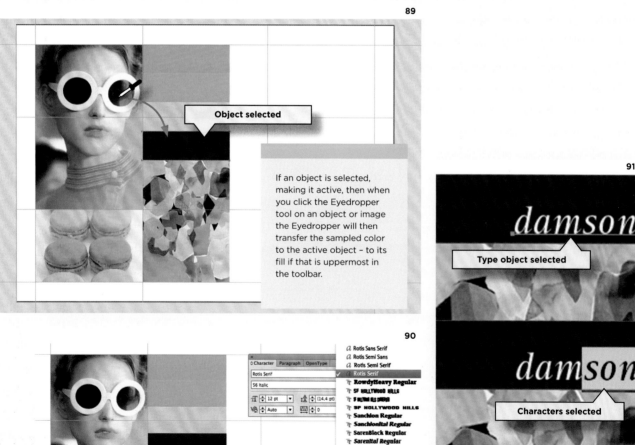

89

Object selected

If an object is selected, making it active, then when you click the Eyedropper tool on an object or image the Eyedropper will then transfer the sampled color to the active object – to its fill if that is uppermost in the toolbar.

91

Type object selected

Characters selected

90

16.17

To change the color of the type, click once and change the fill color in the Options bar. To change the wording of the type, position the pointer in the word and then double click to select that word. **(fig. 91)**

16.18

To align the chip titles select them all, open the Align window, and click on Horizontal Align Right. With the chip titles still selected drag horizontally to position them close to but not touching the right edge of the chips. **(fig. 92)**

16.19

To change the mood board ground color to be other than white, you can select a suitable color and draw a rectangle to the size of the artboard. You could put this on a separate layer and lock that layer so that it won't be moved inadvertently. You won't be using the grid for the next section so click **command/control + ;** (**semicolon**) to hide the guides.

16.20

Have the layer for images the active layer again. Go **File → Place...** and load the Stripe image. Up to now images have been added to the document by placing a version of the image along with a link to the actual file. This time, if you load the Flat Sketch artwork as a linked placement it will not be flexible enough, as you will not be able to use a component of the image as a clipping mask. Linked images don't allow for that kind of editing.

16.21

If you place the Flat Sketch image as an unlinked placement then you still have to release the automatic clipping masks that are generated by the placing process. The simplest thing to do is open Flat Sketch as another document, select all and group (**command/control + G**), and copy over to your Mood Board document.

16.22

Select the Flat Sketch group and position to fit on the mood board and over the Stripe image.
On the mood board we want to show a plain dress and a patterned dress. You could ungroup the Flat Sketch then select the amber colored skirt plus the Stripe image and use the dress as a clipping mask. That's fine, but if you wanted to move the Flat Sketch you would have to remember that it is now ungrouped. It is better practice to just move the Stripe image into the Flat Sketch group and then make a clipping mask from within the group. All the components of any artwork are displayed in the Layers window and, as you have seen in previous projects, it is easy to push objects from one layer to another. **(fig. 93)**

melon

sorbet

frost

damson

92

Align

Align Objects:

Distribute Objects:

Horizontal align right

Distribute Spacing:

0 mm

Align To:

93

Expand arrow

Flat Sketch Group

type

images

<Group>

<Group>

<Path>

Amber dress

stripe.psd

<Path>

<Path>

<Path>

<Path>

painting.psd

<Clip Group>

<Clipping Path>

Macaroons.psd

<Clip Group>

ground colour

Guides

4 Lay...

Selected art column

16.23

In the Layers window click on the expand arrow of the images layer—the tiny triangle before the layer icon. In the stripe image sublayer click in the Selected Art Column on the extreme right. This selects all artwork on that sublayer. Now push the little square, signifying the selected artwork, up into the Flat Sketch group layers above. Moving it up one layer is enough; don't push it too far because the Stripe sublayer needs to be below the amber dress sublayer. You need the Stripe image to be below the amber dress in the group because the amber dress will make the clipping mask.

16.24

With the Direct Selection tool, not the Selection tool, click on the amber dress in the document to select it. Hold the **shift** key and click on the Stripe image. Hold down control and click anywhere on the artboard to bring up the context menu. Select Make Clipping Mask from the context menu. The Stripe image now appears inside the dress outline. **(fig. 94)**

16.25

You could use isolation mode to move the Stripe image around within the clipping mask, but a simpler method is to click on the clipping group with the Direct Selection tool. The options bar at the top of the document then shows details of the clipping group plus two buttons. One button is to edit the clipping path and the other is to edit the contents. Clicking on the Edit Contents button allows you to reposition the stripe image within the clipping mask and clicking on Edit Clipping Path allows you to add a stroke to the path or even change its shape. **(fig. 95)**

16.26

The layout of the mood board is finished. Because the drawing in the Flat Sketch is vector any of the paths could have Art Brushes applied as strokes at any time to give them a more sketchy character. **(fig. 96)**

It makes visual sense to have a group of presentation boards with a consistent structure. You have seen in this project that the grid was used to harmonize components without making them all fit exactly within every box of the grid. The structure doesn't have to be slavishly rigid for the viewer to recognize consistency in layout.

94

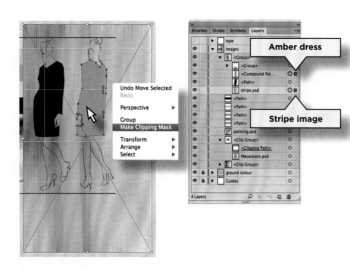

95

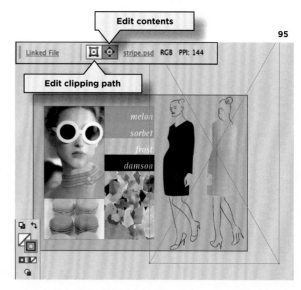

PROJECT
THIRTEEN—
ILLUSTRATOR:
THE BLOB AND
ART BRUSHES

PROJECT
FOURTEEN—
ILLUSTRATOR:
FLATS

PROJECT FIFTEEN—
ILLUSTRATOR: ALL
THE TRIMMINGS

**PROJECT SIXTEEN—
ILLUSTRATOR:
LAYOUT**

PROJECT
SEVENTEEN—
ILLUSTRATOR:
PRESENTATION

PROJECT
EIGHTEEN—
PHOTOSHOP:
PRESENTATION

CASE STUDY:
PRINTFRESH
STUDIO

CASE STUDY:
C&A DESIGNERS

Templates

Once you have established a useful layout you can save this in Illustrator as a template to enable you to create multiple presentation boards that share the same format. Delete the elements and layers that you will not need in the future template then go **File → Save as Template...**
By default, Illustrator will offer to save your template in its Templates folder within the application folder. You might choose to save your template in a folder where you save designs. To create a new document based on a template, go **File → New** from Template and find and select your template.

PROJECT REVIEW

REVIEW

In this project you practiced designing with a grid structure, a fundamental of assured layout. You placed a number of differing images in a composition where the underlying grid structure balanced them. You learned about linking files in documents and you used layer organization to move components into groups. You used clipping masks to edit the images and to insert images into shapes. You used the eyedropper tool to sample colors from images to create color chips and used the text tool to give the chips titles. You should understand that any grid is an aid to design and not a constraint.

PRACTICE

Delete the image and text layer and save the document with the colored ground and grid layer as a template. Using the same grid structure create a mood board using images you have collected and show some of your own work in context on the mood board. Clip the images to follow the grid structure where necessary to create a balanced composition. After practicing with the project grid, consider a grid structure that you would like to devise for your own presentation work.

96

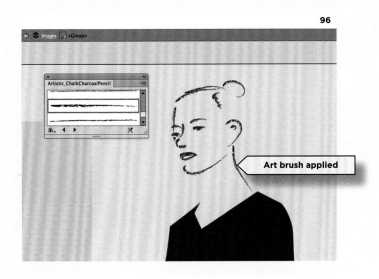

Art brush applied

PROJECT SEVENTEEN—ILLUSTRATOR: PRESENTATION

17

Effective ways of presenting your designs are clear layout and illustrating your work in context. In presentation good communication is key, and smart layout allows your work to be judged properly while context assists the viewer in evaluating the designs realized.

Layout describes the organized approach to visual presentation. As you saw in the layout project, Project Sixteen, an underlying structure does not need to be obvious to signal a systematic and creative approach.

Presenting in context is relevant to all aspects of textile and fashion design, embracing anything from showing a coordinated collection of garments together, to visualizing a textile installation simulated in its architectural space. Examples that reflect your design's intended or potential use can help you evaluate their strengths even before you begin to present them to others.

Various choices need to be made in the actual documents that are presented. If you are sending your material to print on paper for mounting on boards then you should have kept all design material at a high enough resolution to withstand close scrutiny. Low-resolution images such as 72 ppi can be passable on a screen but can look pretty poor and insubstantial when printed onto paper. Having linked files in documents ensures (as long as the links aren't broken by bad management of your files) that the documents will have small file sizes but will print with all imagery at high resolution.

PROJECT
THIRTEEN—
ILLUSTRATOR:
THE BLOB AND
ART BRUSHES

PROJECT
FOURTEEN—
ILLUSTRATOR:
FLATS

PROJECT FIFTEEN—
ILLUSTRATOR: ALL
THE TRIMMINGS

PROJECT SIXTEEN—
ILLUSTRATOR:
LAYOUT

**PROJECT
SEVENTEEN—
ILLUSTRATOR:
PRESENTATION**

PROJECT
EIGHTEEN—
PHOTOSHOP:
PRESENTATION

CASE STUDY:
PRINTFRESH
STUDIO

CASE STUDY:
C&A DESIGNERS

You can generate a second set of documents for digital presentation. Moving through PDF versions of your design documents in a presentation will undoubtedly be faster and smoother than the complete multi-layered Photoshop files.

Always keep your original design document in its native format so that editing is always possible and no information is lost. You might want to change things at a much later stage and need to have all elements in place and editable. Consider that a presentation document is a version of this original that is made to accommodate the need for easy emailing or sharing with a colleague without Photoshop or Illustrator. See the next chapter for more on the practice of exchanging files.

If you are doing a presentation that involves layout with a considerable amount of copy then you might consider another Adobe product— InDesign—although, ordinarily, you can create all you need using the multiple artboard feature in Illustrator. Artboards are also now available in Photoshop. Artboards in Photoshop are a special type of layer group and function as individual canvases within a single document.

Multiple artboards are very useful for creating multiple page PDFs and for organizing artwork for different formats. You can create additional artboards with duplicate artwork rearranged to suit web viewing rather than print or to accommodate a switch from landscape to portrait orientation.

From the Artboard window you can create additional artboards and duplicate artboards. And you can organize the order in which they print by changing their order in the stack. With the window menu you can adjust the on-screen space between artboards and alter their general layout, dimensions, and display options. The Artboard tool allows you to manually adjust an artboard's dimensions and position. Remember that artboards define printable regions so material has to be on an artboard to be printed, but you can also position material so that it is cropped by the artboard boundary. **(fig. 97)**

97

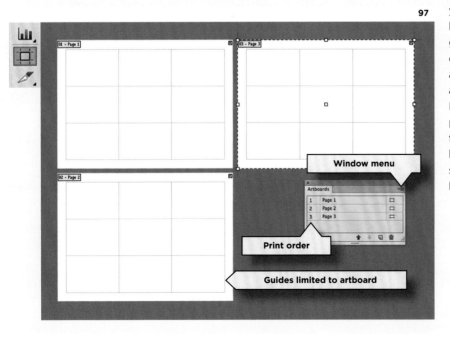

Window menu

Print order

Guides limited to artboard

Vertical and horizontal guides can be added to any individual artboard, but they will also span any other artboard that is in line vertically or horizontally. If you create your own guides as you did in Project Sixteen these will be included in the duplicated artboard without the problem of overflowing the artboard boundaries and cluttering up the workspace.

You can create a duplicate artboard that reproduces all the currently positioned artwork and layers. The format of the new artboard can then be changed, for example, from A4 landscape to portrait. In the example shown here the original layout design was recomposed to suit the new orientation and because images are only cropped by clipping masks additional material can easily be revealed to suit the new format. The background color can also be dropped in preparation for printing on paper. **(fig. 98)**

Prints, weaves, dye effects, and fabric can be defined as fills and applied to garment shapes as fills.

Often it is better though to use a clipping mask on the material and use that to fit it to the garment shape. Copy the garment shape or part of it to a new layer and apply it as a mask to the artwork. A clipping mask allows you to fine tune the position of the artwork whether it is a graphic, texture, or fabric scans. **(fig. 99–100)**

Remember that any embellishments to your presentation sheets should not draw attention away from your designs; rather they should support the designs. In the example shown of the Wondrous World presentation designer Helen Chan used enlarged versions of the embroidery flower motif from the garment designs as a pattern in the background. Note also the written descriptions of the items are clear, but done in gray and not black so as not to distract from the garments themselves. The color chips in rabbit silhouettes is an effective playful twist. **(fig. 101)**

98

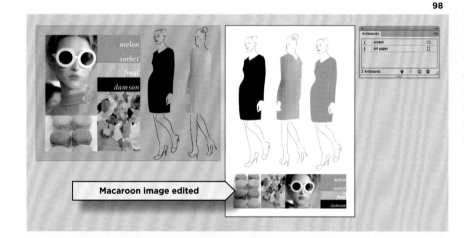

Macaroon image edited

99

Graphic clipped by a mask

100

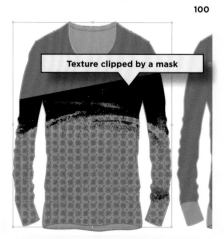

Texture clipped by a mask

PROJECT
THIRTEEN—
ILLUSTRATOR:
THE BLOB AND
ART BRUSHES

PROJECT
FOURTEEN—
ILLUSTRATOR:
FLATS

PROJECT FIFTEEN—
ILLUSTRATOR: ALL
THE TRIMMINGS

PROJECT SIXTEEN—
ILLUSTRATOR:
LAYOUT

PROJECT
SEVENTEEN—
ILLUSTRATOR:
PRESENTATION

PROJECT
EIGHTEEN—
PHOTOSHOP:
PRESENTATION

CASE STUDY:
PRINTFRESH
STUDIO

CASE STUDY:
C&A DESIGNERS

101

WOndROuS WOrlD

KNITTED CARDIGAN WITH 3D FLOWERS & FRILL DETAIL

CHIFFON LOW WAIST PLEATED DRESS

FRILLY JERSEY/TUNIC WITH
BRODERIE ANGLAISE BUNNY APPLIQUE

JERSEY/BRODERIE ANGLAISE T-SHIRT

CHIFFON TIERED & FRILLY SHIRT

LEGGINGS WITH BRODERIE ANGLAISE
& BUTTON TRIM

BRODERIE ANGLAISE DRESS WITH 3D FLOWERS

PROJECT REVIEW

REVIEW

For evaluating textile designs in context you will
need a suitable, simplified representation of where
you see those textiles being utilized. You could
trace this shape from an existing image by hand
or, if the original image is suitable, use Illustrator's
Live Trace tool to create a simple vector version
of the image.

Even quite basic shapes can be very effective
at representing your designs in context, enabling
you to evaluate your own designs and inspiring
ideas about variations. For fashion, presenting your
garment ideas together can enable you to evaluate
strengths and weaknesses in the collection. Build
on the strengths and don't be reliant on too little
exploration and design development. Use the
presentation sheets to assess your work and to
prompt ideas for variations and additions.

PRACTICE

Using a template from Project Sixteen create a
number of presentation sheets of your work. Make
sure that the presentation sheets tell a coherent
design story, that the viewer will understand the
context and find the designs presented persuasive.

PROJECT EIGHTEEN—PHOTOSHOP: PRESENTATION

18

Photoshop is not as well suited to layout as Illustrator. Although there are very useful guides and rulers in Photoshop, and you have used them frequently in previous projects, it does not have the same access to grids as illustrator does. But because Photoshop and Illustrator make such good companions you can create your grid structure in Illustrator and open it up in Photoshop. Actual guides in the Illustrator file are not imported into Photoshop so keep any grid simply as paths. You can then layout your Photoshop artwork on layers above the imported layer.

Photoshop may be less flexible for layout than some other applications but it is eminently suited to visualization and to representing designs in context. You can superimpose your designs on photos and use masks to control what is shown and what is clipped or hidden. Extremely realistic simulations are possible in Photoshop but, obviously, a balance has to be struck between how much effort and how much realism is warranted. The time spent on making images more elaborate than necessary could be spent instead on new designs.

PROJECT
THIRTEEN—
ILLUSTRATOR:
THE BLOB AND
ART BRUSHES

PROJECT
FOURTEEN—
ILLUSTRATOR:
FLATS

PROJECT FIFTEEN—
ILLUSTRATOR: ALL
THE TRIMMINGS

PROJECT SIXTEEN—
ILLUSTRATOR:
LAYOUT

PROJECT
SEVENTEEN—
ILLUSTRATOR:
PRESENTATION

**PROJECT
EIGHTEEN—
PHOTOSHOP:
PRESENTATION**

CASE STUDY:
PRINTFRESH
STUDIO

CASE STUDY:
C&A DESIGNERS

Photoshop offers a very useful tool for presentation—Layer Comps. "Comps" is an abbreviation of the word composition and the tool allows multiple compositions of a page layout within a single Photoshop file. In Project Eight, Fills, Textures, and Layers in Chapter 2, Layer Comps were introduced to manage colorways; they can also be used to explore and record different arrangements of your artwork.

In Layer Comps you can take a snapshot of the state of the Layers window at a specific time and record three types of layer options, the layer visibility, layer position in the document, and layer appearance. History in Photoshop records "states" of the document and allows you to return to a previous state. These states, however, get deleted when you close a document and the best History can do is preserve a text log of your actions. Unlike History states comp versions of your document are retained in the saved file and can be used to record earlier versions.

Multiple layouts are also now possible in Photoshop following the introduction of Artboards. As mentioned elsewhere in this book, there is usually more than one way to achieve the same thing in Photoshop. Both Layer Comps and Artboards can be exported as multiple page pdfs. With exporting layer comps the individual layer comps become the pages, with exporting artboards the individual artboards become the pages. Layer Comps allow you to make large or small adjustments to compositions and to instantly shift between these variations for evaluation while artboards allows you to see all the composition variations you have made laid out simultaneously. There are advantages to both methods.

Resolution is a factor in the quality of your visualization. Low-resolution images from the web are likely to compromise the quality of your work so selection of appropriate images is important. Any drawing or photo of sufficient resolution and definition could be suitable, as long as the area where you want to put your pattern or graphic does not have a pattern or a lot of texture already.

Remember that if you want people to respect the copyright on your work you equally have to respect the copyrights of others and be mindful about how you source your images.

PRESENTING YOUR DESIGNS IN CONTEXT WITH PHOTOSHOP

In this project you will:
- Practice placing designs in context using the original shading and lighting in an image to create verisimilitude.
- Use Clipping Masks and Blending Modes to control the placement and appearance of artwork in context.

Outcome
You should have examples of designs that are in context and you should be able to easily change the size and placement of the project artwork and your own. The potential success of a design can be evaluated and options explored by seeing it in context.

Aim
You should understand that using the same fundamental techniques that were explored in many of the previous projects it is easy to achieve professional representations of your work in context. Paths and Clipping Masks are once again shown to be essential tools. Using Paths delivers precise results and Clipping Masks ensure the process is flexible and always editable.

Project files are available at
www.bloomsbury.com/hume-textile-design

Here we present an ideal method for showing your surface pattern designs in context. There are other methods of representing your patterns in drawings or in photographs, such as using Bucket Fill, but this method is the most flexible. Any drawing or photo of sufficient resolution and clarity could be suitable as long as the area where you want to put your pattern is free of imagery already. An area of white with shading is ideal. You might have to manipulate the image beforehand to remove the color if you can't find something suitably white.

Artwork in a Homeware Context
You want your artwork to appear to exist in the same 3D space that a photo recorded. For convincing realism you need to analyze the direction of the planes in the image so that you can place your pattern in alignment with these planes. In this exercise, using the Simple Dining Chair file, you can divide the planes of the fabric into those that are vertical (red) and those that are horizontal and receding (green). **(fig. 103)**

102

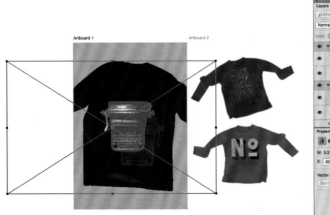

102
A Photoshop document with two artboards. Smart objects allow for nondestructive editing; the resizing of the image does not remove or alter data permanently.

PROJECT THIRTEEN— ILLUSTRATOR: THE BLOB AND ART BRUSHES

PROJECT FOURTEEN— ILLUSTRATOR: FLATS

PROJECT FIFTEEN— ILLUSTRATOR: ALL THE TRIMMINGS

PROJECT SIXTEEN— ILLUSTRATOR: LAYOUT

PROJECT SEVENTEEN— ILLUSTRATOR: PRESENTATION

PROJECT EIGHTEEN— PHOTOSHOP: PRESENTATION

CASE STUDY: PRINTFRESH STUDIO

CASE STUDY: C&A DESIGNERS

18.1

Open the file named Simple Dining Chair. Using the Pen tool draw a path that carefully follows the outline of the seat of the chair (the area shown green in the illustration). To create a completely unbroken path at the final stage, position the Pen tool over the first (hollow) anchor point, look for a very small circle to appear beside the Pen tool pointer. This indicates that you are close enough to the first anchor point and if you now click the mouse or digital pen then the path will be closed. Remember from Project Four, if you make an abrupt change in direction when drawing a path you may have to use the control arms or "direction lines" on anchor points to adjust the curve segment.

From the Paths window menu select Save Path and call this path Seat. If you have any paths in a document it is good practice to have both the Layers and Paths windows visible simultaneously. To remove a docked window, drag it out of the dock group by its tab or title bar. If a path remains active in a document (highlighted in the Paths window) then using the delete key will not delete what you think you have selected but will instead delete that active path. (See the help section at the end of this book for more detail on Photoshop hierarchy and paths.) **(fig. 104)**

18.2

In the Paths window select New Path by either clicking on the New Path button at the bottom of the window or by selecting it from the window menu. Repeat Stage 2, this time drawing around the whole outline of the chair fabric. Save the finished closed path as Complete. **(fig. 105)**

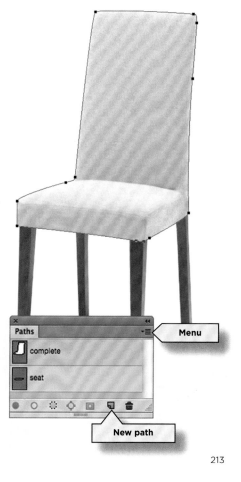

105

103

104

18.3

Open the Stripes and Dots file from the project folder. Go **Edit → Define Pattern...** to define the whole Stripes and Dots document as a pattern.

18.4

Switch to the Simple Dining Chair document. Create a new destination layer for the pattern fill. With this layer active go **Edit → Fill...** and from the dialog window select Pattern as the contents and go to the last entry in the Pattern fill list (sometimes called the pattern well), which should be the stripes and dots pattern. Have the Mode as normal and the Scripted Pattern unticked. Click Okay to fill the pattern across the entire layer, Layer 5. Go to the Paths window

and make the path for the complete chair fabric active by clicking on its entry in the path window. Use either the command in the window menu or the shortcut icon (dotted circle at the bottom of the window) to make a selection of the whole path. **(fig. 106)**

18.5

Now with the selection active go to the Layers window. Ensure the layer with the pattern fill is the active layer. Click on the very small mask icon at the bottom of the Layers window. A mask is then applied to the pattern layer based on the selection that was active. Whatever was in the selection is visible and whatever was outside is still there but hidden. **(fig. 107)**

18.6

Create a second layer and fill this one with the same pattern fill as before. Repeat stages 18.4 and 18.5 but this time use the seat path to make the selection and mask for the second pattern fill layer.

The orientation of the patterns now needs to be adjusted to match the way they would be in the 3D world. As indicated by the arrows on the chair at the start of the project the seat pattern is lying in a horizontal plane and receding, while the rest of the planes describing the orientation of the chair fabric are just slightly angled off the vertical. Consult the diagram at the start of the project if you need clarification.

106

107

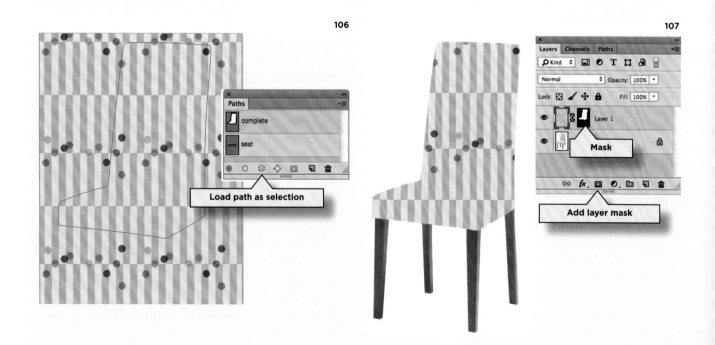

Paths

complete

seat

Load path as selection

Layers | Channels | Paths

Kind

Normal | Opacity: 100%

Lock: | Fill: 100%

Layer 1

Mask

Add layer mask

PROJECT
THIRTEEN—
ILLUSTRATOR:
THE BLOB AND
ART BRUSHES

PROJECT
FOURTEEN—
ILLUSTRATOR:
FLATS

PROJECT FIFTEEN—
ILLUSTRATOR: ALL
THE TRIMMINGS

PROJECT SIXTEEN—
ILLUSTRATOR:
LAYOUT

PROJECT
SEVENTEEN—
ILLUSTRATOR:
PRESENTATION

**PROJECT
EIGHTEEN—
PHOTOSHOP:
PRESENTATION**

CASE STUDY:
PRINTFRESH
STUDIO

CASE STUDY:
C&A DESIGNERS

18.7

Make invisible the layer with the mask for the complete fabric shape. This layer makes it easier to see the seat fabric on its own. On the seat fabric layer, click on the small chain icon that sits between the layer artwork thumbnail and its mask thumbnail. The chain icon disappears and the link is broken. This enables the two elements to be moved independently. Make sure that the four-corner highlighting is around the image thumbnail thereby indicating that it is the one of the pair that will be transformed. To switch the highlighting, click on the image thumbnail.

Now, using the Free Transform tool (**command/control + T**) rotate and squash the pattern, distorting it to appear as it would on the actual seat. Hold down the **command/control** key while selecting a middle point handle on the transformation bounding box to change the transformation to Skew and to be able to distort the pattern off at an angle. Remember to choose Rotate, move the pointer outside the bounding border (it becomes a curved, two-sided arrow), and then drag.

18.8

Now make visible the layer for the complete fabric. Break the link between the layer image and mask by clicking on the chain icon between the two. Make sure the pattern image has the highlight corners to show it is the selected one. With the Free Transform tool rotate the pattern to get the right angle (about four degrees) and hold down the **command/control** key and drag control corners of the transform box as needed to get a slight appearance of perspective.

Now the appearance is quite realistic because the pattern is conforming to how it would lay in the 3D world. At this stage the pattern can be judged accurately in context with the chair. To give the simulation a final touch of realism we can use the shading from the original photo.

108

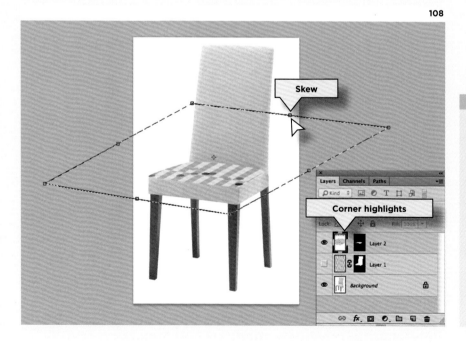

TIP

Although there is a Perspective and Skew command in Transform it is often much easier to use the modifier keys— **command/control**, **option/ alt** and **shift**—on the Free Transform box to get the results you need.

18.9

Holding down the **command/control** key click on the mask thumbnail for the complete fabric outline. **(fig. 109)**

This is the short cut for generating a selection from the mask. It's a convenient shortcut and note that neither the mask nor its layer has to be active for you to generate the selection. Have background the active layer so that the selection is applied to that layer. Use **command/control + C** then **command/control + V** to paste the section where the original fabric was in the photo onto a new layer.

18.10

Move that new layer up to the top of the stack and, for convenience, label it shading. Change the layers Blending Mode to Multiply. The colors in the shading layer are added to those on layers below creating a darkening effect. While this is a very useful technique for overlaying shading from an image onto artwork the darkening often needs a little tweaking. In practice you want a proportion of the colors in the artwork to not be shaded so that they show their true brightness. By using Levels adjustment on the shading layer and moving the white point (also known as the highlight slider) to include more light colors the shading will look better while keeping more colors true in the resulting artwork. **(fig. 110)**

18.11

With the shading layer active go **Image → Adjustments → Level** or **command/control + L**. Move the white stop in from the right to define more light tones as white on the shading layer and as a result leave more colors unaffected on the underlying image layers (the pattern fills). Watch the shading change on the patterns on the chair and when happy "okay" the Levels window to accept the changes.

109

Thumbnail

Selection active on background layer

110

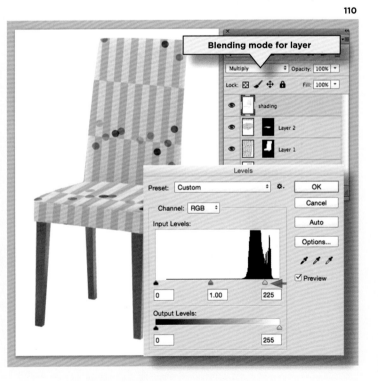

110

Blending mode is set to Multiply on the shading layer. In the Levels window the white point is moved to the left to redefine more colors as white in the shading image.

PROJECT
THIRTEEN—
ILLUSTRATOR:
THE BLOB AND
ART BRUSHES

PROJECT
FOURTEEN—
ILLUSTRATOR:
FLATS

PROJECT FIFTEEN—
ILLUSTRATOR: ALL
THE TRIMMINGS

PROJECT SIXTEEN—
ILLUSTRATOR:
LAYOUT

PROJECT
SEVENTEEN—
ILLUSTRATOR:
PRESENTATION

PROJECT
EIGHTEEN—
PHOTOSHOP:
PRESENTATION

CASE STUDY:
PRINTFRESH
STUDIO

CASE STUDY:
C&A DESIGNERS

Fashion Contexts—
Fabric in a Sketch

Presenting your fabric ideas in your own fashion sketches is an easy way to make your designs more compelling. Color, texture, and pattern added to your garment designs make them more persuasive, while showing your textile designs in a fashion context, however approximate, can demonstrate and enhance their effectiveness.

In the next section you will use a mask to present a pattern in a garment sketch. This time the mask will be a little more complex and reflect some of the problems with photos of figures. Project Eight, Fills, Textures, and Layers, provided plenty of detail about placing patterns into sketches so here it only remains to introduce the use of shading in sketches.

Shading adds realism to your sketches and gives an indication of drape and handle in the proposed fabric. A little shading can be quite effective so don't labor over it too much—you are enhancing a sketch and not trying to make it look absolutely 3D.

Using the layer structure in Photoshop it is easy to create and manipulate the shadows on their own layer and leave all other artwork intact. Don't draw anything directly on the sketch or patterns—there is no need and it will restrict your options later. You can be quite loose drawing the shadows with a large soft brush and then neaten them up with a soft eraser brush afterward.

18.12

Make sure the checkerboard grid indicating transparency is turned off in Preferences, otherwise it will be too distracting. Load the file named evening from the project folder.

18.13

Choose some scanned-in fabric or a pattern of your own design and put it on a layer of its own in the evening document. A linked image file will work the same as an embedded file in this exercise. Have the layer with the fabric the top layer and invisible.

18.14

The original style sketch is on the layer named outline. Make that the active layer and select the Magic Wand tool. Have the Magic Wand selection tool options set to Contiguous and not set to sample any other layer than the active one (sample all layers unticked).

"Contiguous" means sharing a common border or touching so the selection includes all colors touching the one you clicked until it reaches another color not included by the tolerances range. Transparency also counts as a color so if you click somewhere in the dress the selection runs to the borders of the dress where it encounters black. Black is too dissimilar to be included even if the tolerances are set at the maximum of 255. Equivalent colors beyond the black outline such as in the handbag are not included when contiguous is ticked because they are not touching. **(fig. 111)**

18.15

With the selection active, switch to your fabric layer. Click on the Selection to Mask button at the bottom of the Layer window. Make your fabric layer visible. **(fig. 112)**

111

112

18.16

Create a new layer above the fabric layer and label it shading. Set its Blending Mode to Multiply so that you immediately see the shadow effects on the artwork. You could use the selection from the dress to constrain your shading to the dress shape or just draw freely and clean up afterward with the Eraser tool. Select a suitable sized soft brush, set the color as dark gray, and paint in some shadows in the appropriate places. Gray is preferable to black, as you do not need stark shadows that hide too much of the fabric detail. You may even want the shadow to have a tint of the fabric color, which is easy to do with Hue adjustment.

18.17

With your shading on its own layer it's easy for you to experiment with different variations on the fabric on underlying layers. In whatever way you alter the fabric the shadows will always be effective. **(fig. 113–114)**

With a sketch prepared and shading in place different ideas about fabric placement can be quickly explored and evaluated. You can represent fabric ideas in photos of garments as well as sketches of garments. Photos offer opportunities for very realistically rendered images of designs on figures but figures offer more complications than images of objects. The edges of a person may be a bit more difficult to define, and hair can be particularly tricky in a selection. However, because Photoshop is, in essence, a photo retouching application, there are tools to help with these problems.

113-114
With a sketch prepared and shading in place different ideas about fabric placement can be quickly explored and evaluated.

113

114

PROJECT
THIRTEEN—
ILLUSTRATOR:
THE BLOB AND
ART BRUSHES

PROJECT
FOURTEEN—
ILLUSTRATOR:
FLATS

PROJECT FIFTEEN—
ILLUSTRATOR: ALL
THE TRIMMINGS

PROJECT SIXTEEN—
ILLUSTRATOR:
LAYOUT

PROJECT
SEVENTEEN—
ILLUSTRATOR:
PRESENTATION

PROJECT
EIGHTEEN—
PHOTOSHOP:
PRESENTATION

CASE STUDY:
PRINTFRESH
STUDIO

CASE STUDY:
C&A DESIGNERS

Fashion Contexts—
Fabric in a Photo

18.18

Open the file named Kirsten 04. Here is an example of a common problem with photos. The plan is to put a print design onto the white top of the model. When you look you can see a clear distinction between the top and everything else in the photo. But if you try and select the white top with the Magic Wand, Quick Selection tool, or by Color Range then Photoshop struggles to distinguish between what are in effect similar greys in the top and the surrounding background.

Photoshop makes selection entirely on color and not subject matter. Often photos do not have an ideal contrast between the subject and the background for selection purposes. So for making most of the selection it is most effective to use the Pen tool. It can often be faster than a lot of fiddling with other selection tools. It is one of the fundamentals of Photoshop because it is of service in so many situations.

18.19

With the pen tool draw a path around the body and sleeves of the white top. When you get to where the hair is, just cut across where you imagine the hidden shoulders to be. You will use another tool to sort the hair out. Come back to your starting point and close the path. Change the name of the work path to Top. Renaming is another way of saving a work path. **(fig. 115)**

18.20

From the Paths window make a selection from this path, click on the Path to Selection button at the bottom of the Path window. Now go to the command **Select → Refine Edges (option/alt + command/control + R)**. This allows you to paint the wispy area of the hair into the selection. In Photoshop it is often convenient to resolve difficult selections with a combination of tools. When a figure has hair touching clothing, as often happens in photos, you don't want too hard-edged a mask in that area. Refine Edges is the ideal way to get a good result. It makes sense to outline the garment manually where you can define it more effectively than Photoshop and then have Photoshop's aid in resolving the hair boundary where Photoshop can do a pretty impressive job.

115

Make selection from path

18.21

In the Refine Edges window leave View Mode as the default setting and with the Refine Radius tool, which acts like a paintbrush, draw strokes over the hair, following the direction of the large strands. Have your settings in the window set as shown in the accompanying image. As you paint over the hair, the area becomes white or partially white indicating that it is being excluded from the selection and the potential mask. Even when you are not very exact about covering all the fine hair the results with this tool are very impressive. You can always fine-tune the results as well because, as it's a nondestructive process, you can always re-edit things by tweaking the related mask. **(fig. 116)**

18.22

Click Okay to exit the window when you have removed most of the hair from the selection. As a precaution, save the selection as an alpha channel because you don't want any chance of losing all that work. Go → **Select** → **Save Selection...** Don't bother to give the selection a name in the dialog window that opens just "okay" the window to close.

18.23

Open the Channels window. Below the default color channels your selection has been saved as an alpha channel and called Alpha 1. The default color channels represent each of the color components of an image. For example, an RGB image has separate channels for red, green, and blue color values. That they share the same window with the alpha channels can sometimes be a bit confusing for the beginner.

Alpha channels are, in effect, masks that have not yet been associated with any layer. Masks and channels are gray scale images so they can be edited with painting tools and editing tools just like any other image. Areas painted black on an alpha channel are protected and subtracted from the selection, and areas painted white are editable and added to the selection. Often painting to adjust a selection or mask is easier than struggling with Lassos or Magic Wands.

18.24

Open the file named Grainy from the project folder. You can also use artwork of your own at this stage. Select all of the artwork (**command/control + A**) and then copy (**command/control + C**). Switch to the document named Kirsten. Press **option/alt + shift + command/ control + V** to paste into the Kirsten document (or select **Paste Special → Paste Into** from the Edit menu, as it is a fairly longish shortcut!). The artwork will be placed on a layer with the active selection translated to a mask.

116

PROJECT
THIRTEEN—
ILLUSTRATOR:
THE BLOB AND
ART BRUSHES

PROJECT
FOURTEEN—
ILLUSTRATOR:
FLATS

PROJECT FIFTEEN—
ILLUSTRATOR: ALL
THE TRIMMINGS

PROJECT SIXTEEN—
ILLUSTRATOR:
LAYOUT

PROJECT
SEVENTEEN—
ILLUSTRATOR:
PRESENTATION

**PROJECT
EIGHTEEN—
PHOTOSHOP:
PRESENTATION**

CASE STUDY:
PRINTFRESH
STUDIO

CASE STUDY:
C&A DESIGNERS

18.25

Rename this layer Grainy. Change the layer Blending Mode to Multiply so that it mixes with the shading from the figure's top in the actual photo. Note that the hair looks convincingly like it is actually sitting on the grainy artwork. However the shadows in the top do not come through very strongly, which can happen with heavy patterned artwork. The solution is to make a separate shadow layer and stick this at the top of the layer stack in the same way as with the drawn shadows in the previous exercise.

18.26

Click on the grainy mask thumbnail to reload the selection. Make the background layer the active layer. Use this selection to copy the model's top in the photo onto a new layer—**command/control + C** then **command/control + V**. Move this layer up to the top of the stack. Rename it shading and change its Blending Mode to Multiply.

18.27

For further fine-tuning click **command/control + L** to open the Levels window. Ensure preview is ticked and adjust the sliders to boost the contrast in the shading in the image.

18.28

Once you have a good useful selection it can be used, as here, to finesse the shading and to explore adding additional effects to the artwork. In the illustration a gradient has been added to a new layer and masked with the same selection. **(fig. 117)**

Most pattern fills or graphics added to figures in photos look convincing enough with shadows overlaid. Presenting designs this way requires only a limited realism and it is unlikely you will ever have to do something that meticulously imitates reality. The objective is to enable judgment of the design. On occasion you might need to add another effect where the artwork is a stripe or a very pronounced geometric that still looks too rigid in the image. You could use the Displace Filter to distort the artwork. Displace uses a map that is a gray scale version of the destination surface. Black areas become the low points and the light areas the high points of the contours in the distortion. However the results of the displacement map are very dependent on the tones being in the right place in the original image. An alternative technique that is easy and not dependent on any image is to use the Liquefy Filter.

117

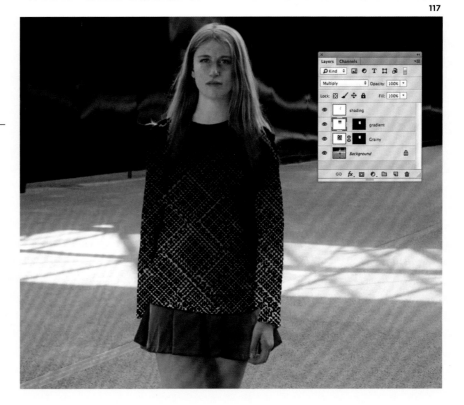

Liquefy was originally an add-on for Photoshop that later got adapted into the application. Ordinarily used for doing idle caricatures of faces by distorting photos, it always had lots of potential in other areas. It is a quick way for making small adjustments to motifs and is a really interactive way of distorting artwork so that it matches a photo.

18.29

In the example illustrated you can see that the rigidness of the artwork undermines the work of the shading. This technique applies to any artwork you want to distort in context. For working on a pattern you need to see the actual artwork masked but you don't want to distort the mask as well, so break the link between artwork and mask. Make the artwork the active part and draw a selection bigger than the masked area. If you don't make a selection, Photoshop will load the whole of the document into the Liquefy window, which is not what you need. You create a selection bigger than the mask so you can draw material into your distortion from beyond its edges. **(fig. 118)**

18.30

Go **Filter → Liquefy...** The Liquefy window opens with your selection framed. Click on Advanced Mode to show the additional settings. It is helpful to have Show Backdrop on so you can see the artwork in context and get an idea of the places where you should distort it. If you have your shading on a separate layer and it's conveniently labeled then you have the ideal layer showing as a guide in the Backdrop settings. **(fig. 119)**

118

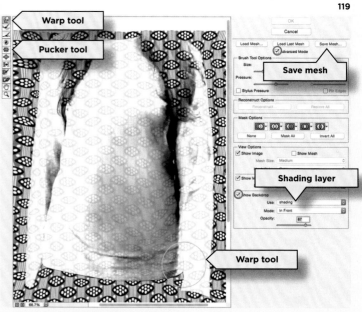

119

PROJECT THIRTEEN— ILLUSTRATOR: THE BLOB AND ART BRUSHES

PROJECT FOURTEEN— ILLUSTRATOR: FLATS

PROJECT FIFTEEN— ILLUSTRATOR: ALL THE TRIMMINGS

PROJECT SIXTEEN— ILLUSTRATOR: LAYOUT

PROJECT SEVENTEEN— ILLUSTRATOR: PRESENTATION

PROJECT EIGHTEEN— PHOTOSHOP: PRESENTATION

CASE STUDY: PRINTFRESH STUDIO

CASE STUDY: C&A DESIGNERS

18.31

In the Liquefy window the Warp tool is an excellent tool for pushing sections of the artwork in particular directions to simulate draping and creasing. The Pucker tool lets you shrink areas to simulate recession, for example, what would happen to motifs at the edge of a sleeve. Again a few bold strokes can be very effective and all that you need. **(fig. 120)** There is even a Reconstruction tool that allows you to undo the distortions you made in any area. Liquefy is a very useful Filter with a lot of options to explore and you can even save the actual distortion mesh you created in using the various tools and apply it again at any time to any other pattern you place in the image.

120

PROJECT REVIEW

REVIEW
As Photoshop was designed as a photographic manipulation application, it is well suited to creating professional renderings of your artwork in context. Results are dependent on the foundation image so a good sketch or decent quality photo is important. Once you have established your masks and created a layer to give the impression of shading then the document can be used as many times as you want to see your designs in context. The goal is to enable the designs to be evaluated and hopefully move toward execution in fabric, so the degree of realism is only as much as is needed for this purpose.

PRACTICE
Source a suitable image that relates to the context you see for your designs. Alongside this you could also select one or two images that offer quite a different context from the obvious choices to give you the opportunity to appraise your work from a very different angle. Create the necessary masks and shading layers as in the exercise and then experiment with changes in scale and combining different artwork with changes in the placement and any division of area.

CASE STUDY:
PRINTFRESH STUDIO

Printfresh is a Philadelphia-based design studio that creates designs for print, graphics, embellishment, and embroidery. Founded in 2006 by Amy and Leo Voloshin the studio is dedicated to producing smart, commercial and trend-focused designs for the likes of Gap, Abercrombie & Fitch, Urban Outfitters, Mango, Zara, and H&M. The studio combines initial hand painting on paper with CAD design development and specializes in presenting the finished designs made up into fabric.

With designers skilled in design development on the computer, the studio is able to offer the services of color separation and reduction and to deliver artwork ready for production.

Amy Voloshin, the creative director, first began using Photoshop in high school for photography and graphic design projects. When she went to college she began to use the application for her textile design work. She had always loved drawing and painting and then saw the benefit in using Photoshop to quickly experiment with hand-created work, the exciting possibilities offered to modify the initial image and explore color, contrast, and the mix of elements.

Amy reflects that her use of Photoshop has changed dramatically with time. "When I first began in the industry I would do everything by hand. I started as a design assistant at Urban Outfitters doing both print design and apparel design. I would do 'pencil repeats,' that is, drawing the outline of the design motifs and then cutting and pasting to create the repeat, erasing and redrawing the edges and using a photocopier to change the scale. For meetings with our director and buying teams I would create the colorways by hand painting with gouache and a single colorway would take many hours.

These days with Photoshop I am able to design quickly, do repeats in minutes, and generate many colorways almost instantly. Using the pattern offset tool simplifies dramatically what I used to have to do through the actual cutting and taping of the designs together. Using Photoshop tools like Replace Color, the Magic Wand, and Fill make changing colors much easier.

I like to hand paint initially to begin my process—working from reference images of flowers, vintage textile designs, or abstract textures. Once I have painted my motifs out, I like to scan in the images, and then clean them up in Photoshop and it is there the design process then begins. The next steps include scaling, coloring, and creating a pattern."

121

122

PROJECT
THIRTEEN—
ILLUSTRATOR:
THE BLOB AND
ART BRUSHES

PROJECT
FOURTEEN—
ILLUSTRATOR:
FLATS

PROJECT FIFTEEN—
ILLUSTRATOR: ALL
THE TRIMMINGS

PROJECT SIXTEEN—
ILLUSTRATOR:
LAYOUT

PROJECT
SEVENTEEN—
ILLUSTRATOR:
PRESENTATION

PROJECT
EIGHTEEN—
PHOTOSHOP:
PRESENTATION

**CASE STUDY:
PRINTFRESH
STUDIO**

CASE STUDY:
C&A DESIGNERS

123

124

125

123–125
Examples of the initial stages
of mark-making and painting
out motifs.

121–122
Printed fabric examples.

Design Development

"I discovered digital painting techniques within the last few years, and I really enjoy creating brushes in Photoshop. Brushes allow you to get complex effects easily and efficiently and I particularly enjoy some of the dramatic effects that the Art History Brush tool provides. It allows you to mix photographic techniques while still providing a hand-done quality.

Photographic florals have been a huge trend in recent years and the Art History Brush tool has allowed us to mix our hand-done aesthetic with that trend of the moment. There are great features in the brush tools where you can play with the type of brush tip you are using whether a watercolor brush, oil paint, and so forth, and where you can vary the length and opacity of your individual strokes.

In our studio we do a lot of preliminary sketching before committing to the final design. Photoshop is great for being able to work up quick digital sketches and collages of images to communicate with each other about the layout concepts that we have. The industry has changed dramatically over the last 10 years. It used to be very common for studios to hand-paint and heat press designs, which allowed for very little revision. Now that everything is digital you have the ability to revise and refine motifs and designs. We work at a very rapid pace between 12 and 20 original designs per artist each week, so the ability to communicate and collaborate digitally is essential.

For the preliminary sketching we mostly use micron pens and fine tipped "sharpies" for line work, and ink and watercolor for more expressive pieces. We then scan this artwork in and clean it up in Photoshop. We use Photoshop for all of our final print designs.

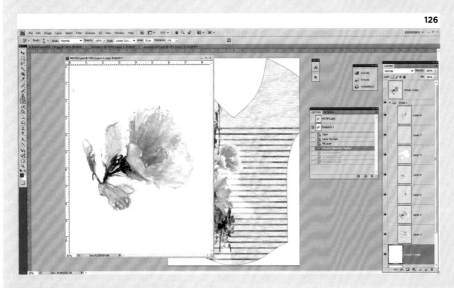

126

126–127
The Art History Brush tool enables painting with stylized strokes, using the source data from a specified history state or snapshot. The Art History Brush tool uses that data along with any options you set to apply the material with a particular handwriting.

127

PROJECT
THIRTEEN—
ILLUSTRATOR:
THE BLOB AND
ART BRUSHES

PROJECT
FOURTEEN—
ILLUSTRATOR:
FLATS

PROJECT FIFTEEN—
ILLUSTRATOR: ALL
THE TRIMMINGS

PROJECT SIXTEEN—
ILLUSTRATOR:
LAYOUT

PROJECT
SEVENTEEN—
ILLUSTRATOR:
PRESENTATION

PROJECT
EIGHTEEN—
PHOTOSHOP:
PRESENTATION

CASE STUDY:
PRINTFRESH
STUDIO

CASE STUDY:
C&A DESIGNERS

Occasionally if we are going for a more graphic appearance or if cleaner designs are on-trend we may take the artwork into Illustrator and use Live Trace. But, because our studio is known for a more organic hand-done appearance, we tend to do most of the cleanup of the drawing or painting in Photoshop, which helps us maintain the original character of the design. We will sometimes use Illustrator to create very graphic geometric motifs but always end up bringing them into Photoshop to do the final layout.

As well as developing the layout and composition within Photoshop more character can be added to the design with custom brushes, useful for textured line work, dotted designs, and especially for ikat designs. We used to do a lot of embroidery designs and we would do some of the stitch work using brushes in Photoshop. We found that Illustrator is the better place for doing the stitching designs since you are able to manipulate the spacing, thickness, and appearance much more easily." **(fig. 129–130)**

128

130

129

128
Developing colorways for a design.

227

Commercial Colorways

"At Printfresh we work in small groupings of distinct themes—for each design theme we create four unique print designs. Within that grouping we show a range of colors. Typically there will be a design that is neutral (meaning tans/beige/browns), a black and white—which may have gray tones—and then a warm and a cool design.

We find that in the United States blue tends to be a very popular color. Blue color combinations and coral combinations are always immensely popular in the US women's apparel market. At the stage that an apparel company approaches us they have often created their own color concept for the season. They look for print concepts that will fit with their own color boards; therefore we work in the formula of neutrals, warms, and cools since those will always fit into the way their collection will be divided. Later clients make changes to the design as needed. As we track the design to see how it turns out in production we often see designs that were purchased in a more colorful manner changed to a more basic color combination such as black and white with only an accent of color.

Our CAD division also does a lot of work with clients regarding colorways. For some of our clients, if a print performed especially well for them they may have reason to recolor that print for a different season. For example, for spring they might have done a floral print in shades of pink and coral, but for fall (autumn) they might do it in browns and warm tones.

There was a time when we used to "style" all of our prints for presentation to clients, that is, sew them into garment shapes. But, after trying many things and consulting with our top clients, we have found that when they are shopping for print, the garment shapes do not matter to our clients.

In fact, sometimes they find the garment shapes distracting. We now only show our prints in garment length rectangular swatches. We do not do multiple colorways of an individual print unless a client, who has purchased that print, requests our CAD team to produce different colorways for them. In that case we will either send them a digital colorway, or print on paper or fabric, depending on their needs.

To create the majority of our prints we use inkjet printing but we do use some screen-printing as well depending on the desired look. Our embroideries and embellishment, however, are made up completely with actual, real-world embellishment materials.

We will sometimes print out a stripe or another simple print behind our embellishments to add depth, but we do not print out faux embellishment. We use specially treated fabrics that react to our inks and dyes in the inkjet printers. We have always worked with the same types of printers but tried a number of different ink and dye solutions, as well as many different types of treated fabrics before we found what gives us the very best results."

PROJECT
THIRTEEN—
ILLUSTRATOR:
THE BLOB AND
ART BRUSHES

PROJECT
FOURTEEN—
ILLUSTRATOR:
FLATS

PROJECT FIFTEEN—
ILLUSTRATOR: ALL
THE TRIMMINGS

PROJECT SIXTEEN—
ILLUSTRATOR:
LAYOUT

PROJECT
SEVENTEEN—
ILLUSTRATOR:
PRESENTATION

PROJECT
EIGHTEEN—
PHOTOSHOP:
PRESENTATION

CASE STUDY:
PRINTFRESH
STUDIO

CASE STUDY:
C&A DESIGNERS

131

"At the stage that an apparel company approaches us they have often created their own color concept for the season. They look for print concepts that will fit with their own color boards; therefore we work in the formula of neutrals, warms, and cools since those will always fit into the way their collection will be divided."

CASE STUDY:
C&A DESIGNERS

C&A is one of the biggest fashion retailers in Europe with about 37,500 employees and more than 1,575 stores across 21 European countries. With around 2,000,000 visitors a day to its stores the company aims to offer quality and responsible fashion at affordable prices.

Pauline Ainslie, Unit Leader Fashion Coordinator at C&A, leads a team of 50 designers working in this demanding environment.

"Apart from the occasional exception we never really use full artistic figure illustration. A combination of 'no need' and 'no time.' Everyone is adept at 'reading' a more functional technical drawing and I feel this is the important skill to develop while training. A good skill, too, is to be able to rough sketch or thumbnail—this is particularly useful during the workshop part of the process where design and buying get together to determine the range. Matching the buyers' wants and needs, the number of options/price points, replacement of previous best sellers with the designers proposed new trend direction, and general inspiration will all be discussed in the meeting. It is very useful to leave the meeting with a rough sketch ranged to quickly show a number of items, tops to bottoms ratio, color balance, etcetera, so that everyone has a visual record and so that they have a clear idea of the range when they brief textile and graphic designers.

When the range is translated into CAD, designs are either developed from rough paper sketches or, in the majority of cases, go straight into Illustrator—especially for boyswear where the shapes change less. Designs are not done to exact scale. The designers naturally use a different style across older, younger, and baby. That is down to the individuals drawing style more than a specific requirement though. All required measurements are put on the specs."

PROJECT
THIRTEEN—
ILLUSTRATOR:
THE BLOB AND
ART BRUSHES

PROJECT
FOURTEEN—
ILLUSTRATOR:
FLATS

PROJECT FIFTEEN—
ILLUSTRATOR: ALL
THE TRIMMINGS

PROJECT SIXTEEN—
ILLUSTRATOR:
LAYOUT

PROJECT
SEVENTEEN—
ILLUSTRATOR:
PRESENTATION

PROJECT
EIGHTEEN—
PHOTOSHOP:
PRESENTATION

CASE STUDY:
PRINTFRESH
STUDIO

CASE STUDY:
C&A DESIGNERS

Filipa Cipriano, Graphic Designer for Baby Boy's Wear

"When I first started designing I used Photoshop, then Illustrator became my main design tool. Photoshop was great for textures and brushes and a lot of photo imagery techniques, but with Illustrator the quality of the image, shapes, and color is fantastic, and there is no problems with pixilation, which is very important for the printing process in terms of quality of image."

Imagery

"In Illustrator you can still do hand-drawn styles and photo images, in a more clean way, without the pixilation problems. I do use both applications depending on the techniques but I now use Illustrator 99 percent of the time. I only use Photoshop if I need to use a photo image. I scan it into Photoshop and work on it there before placing in illustrator.

My way of working is very different from a lot of designers. I hand draw a lot. I make all my textures by hand with different types of crayons, inks, and a variety of pens. Then I scan them, live trace, and expand them in illustrator.

My main tools in Illustrator are the pencil tool, strokes tool, clipping masks, brushes and live trace, and my own swatches. I don't separate my designs into layers. I use the full page as my canvas and work on one layer only."

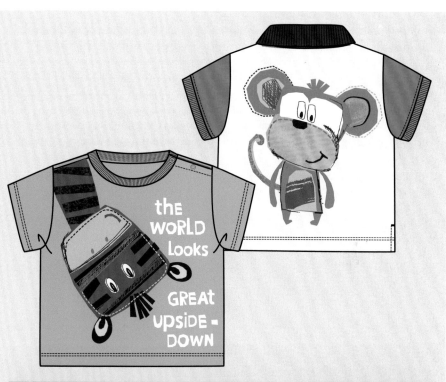

"For me it's very important to keep drawing by hand as well as drawing with Photoshop and Illustrator. And try to learn as many skills as possible, like hand embroidery, to translate into design in the applications, to make your designs as fun on fabric as on the computer.

It's very important at the moment to be able to not make everything flat looking, because Illustrator can do that sometimes. And with the trends for art works that have a lot of movement and textures, it's important to get the hand-drawing feel into it.

Whilst there is no shared library at C&A for garment styles, as everything we design is original, sometimes we have shared libraries for textures and for generic patterns.

There are not strict range guidelines, instead I have to make sure my designs are fun, humorous, and suit our client. I look at the work of artists and other graphic designers and illustrators and different techniques always grab my attention. I also look into fashion for women's wear to find techniques and styles for print.

Helen Tran, Children's Wear Designer
"I started my career using Photoshop, which I had learnt in college. It was much later on I started to use Illustrator, and it was then I saw its benefits for commercial fashion designing.

"I started my career more as a freehand designer, sketching by hand, then scanning and editing using Photoshop. Over time I have started to use Illustrator more frequently. Other than personal projects, I tend to prefer to use Photoshop for graphics artwork, creating all over prints, editing photos, creating mood boards, and collages. I find it much easier to use the editing tools in Photoshop, whereas in Illustrator I mainly draw garment shapes, creating stroke patterns, color fills, and crisp lines and shapes.

In Photoshop I like using the Air Brush and Clone tools and Transparency Effects with merging and layering for collages. In Illustrator I like the Drawing tool, the Pathfinder tool, customizing brushes and brush strokes, and clipping masks. I create a few custom brushes, but mainly I adapt from similar or previously used brushes. As my CAD work has developed I have added variable strokes, contrast shadows, and more curvy lines to create movement and a less flat drawing look."

PROJECT
THIRTEEN—
ILLUSTRATOR:
THE BLOB AND
ART BRUSHES

PROJECT
FOURTEEN—
ILLUSTRATOR:
FLATS

PROJECT FIFTEEN—
ILLUSTRATOR: ALL
THE TRIMMINGS

PROJECT SIXTEEN—
ILLUSTRATOR:
LAYOUT

PROJECT
SEVENTEEN—
ILLUSTRATOR:
PRESENTATION

PROJECT
EIGHTEEN—
PHOTOSHOP:
PRESENTATION

CASE STUDY:
PRINTFRESH
STUDIO

**CASE STUDY:
C&A DESIGNERS**

"The good thing about Photoshop and Illustrator is there is always more than one way to do the same job. I discover things as I test new tools using trial and error. But I would say most of the time I learn new things through work colleagues. With Illustrator I learnt on the job, so I had to learn to use it very quickly to do the work needed. It was very stressful at the start, but once I got the hang of it things were much easier, and I still learn new things about the application every day.

I am more of a garment shape designer so in designing I generally prefer using the Drawing tool in Illustrator, and this tool I use the most to draw all my garments and shapes. I use Illustrator to color and recolor garments and graphics. Doing an overview layout of a collection helps me view my collection as a whole, and it helps to see where additional ideas are needed. As a garment/shape designer I choose Illustrator as the more helpful in evaluating designs. Generally I use both applications to communicate projects with colleagues and freelance designers.

Mostly in children's wear I develop a design from a previous digital drawing, but for women's and men's wear I tend to draw from scratch depending on the creativity of the project. Within the team we are always changing and adapting shapes. It is important we keep design elements up-to-date and the

team informed so whilst designing as individuals we remain consistent with our designs across the team.

Nowadays the same drawing is enough to guide the technical team to develop a sample, and depending on the complexity or simplicity of the designs drawings can replace some sampling."

Vicky Sanders, Graphic Designer
"I started using Photoshop in secondary school; I taught myself the basics and these I then developed further in art foundation. It really benefited my work, as I could develop as a designer both by hand and digitally, and that is an industry must. I started using Illustrator whilst at university; I think that once you know one program, the second comes easily.

Photoshop opens up endless design potential. As a print designer you are able to draw elements, scan them into the computer, then use the program to manipulate and turn drawings/paintings into prints and graphics! I use Illustrator more for shape design; it's an essential tool for fashion design. I use Photoshop and Illustrator every day working as a commercial designer but like to make sure I always design by hand too, both drawing and painting.

In Photoshop the Brush tools are amazing. I also use the Selective Color tool, Brightness Contrast tool, and Hue/Saturation tool a lot to adjust hand paintings to the correct colors of a story."

"I didn't used a Wacom tablet and pen in university and had to learn how to use it fast during my first internship at a busy high street retailer. I found the coordination of it difficult at first, but after a couple of days I wouldn't be without one. It's ingenious to have the control of drawing but digitally. I always work from scratch and sometimes draw directly in the application with the Wacom, however I usually draw by hand and scan in. I think in textile prints it is important to have the feel of hand-drawn work; without this designs can look very flat. This is why I prefer to work in Photoshop generally.

I generally use Photoshop when I have the starting idea as a drawing or photo and I develop a print or create a graphic from it in Photoshop. However I sometimes use Photoshop to experiment with different ideas. I scan in some mark-making and then play around with different effects for example. With Illustrator I usually use it when I have an idea of a garment shape and then work on it.

You may have an idea but you always have to be open to other possibilities and be experimental, try new things. The different tools in Photoshop and Illustrator mean that you can create things different and sometimes better than you originally envisioned. I love to draw and paint and I incorporate this into my work as much as possible. I will scan in an artwork and then work on it in Photoshop.

I use Illustrator for evaluating whether designs work. When you put a design onto an overview, where the prints are filled into a shape and next to the rest in the collection, you can then evaluate whether or not they work and if they need any changes.

Illustrator is great for communicating with colleagues; it is a professional presentation tool. Showing designs in an overview in the way they will sit together in a store with garment shapes and prints combined is the best way of presenting a collection. We present our ideas on mood boards; these are done both by hand and digitally depending on the purpose. Whichever way chosen, I always think it's really important to show as many samples and visuals as possible to communicate ideas. Drawings can never replace sampling, but the more detailed a spec or drawing, the better the sample will be."

**CASE STUDY:
C&A DESIGNERS**

SHARING,
COMMUNICATION,
AND OUTPUT

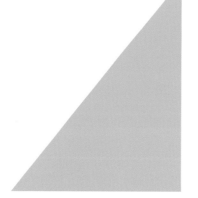

If you have Photoshop and Illustrator designs ready to transform into textiles and garments how do you manage this process professionally?

USER FRIENDLY FORMATS

As talked about in Project Seventeen it is good practice when you want to share your designs with others to create a copy and keep your original design document in its native format. If you go to a presentation with your laptop and that computer is where you created the design work make sure you have backed-up those precious files somewhere beforehand (automating this process is a good policy). Accidents happen and laptop bags get left in cafés!

Creating a PDF version is a very good option for sharing your files, as this format is specifically designed for document exchange. Illustrator will save AI files with embedded PDF readability. That means that an AI file can be opened in Adobe Acrobat Reader (freely available) and viewed.

All the super smooth and crisp vector detail of the artwork will be preserved. Acrobat also recognizes the layers in the original document so be careful if you send a file that has hidden layers that you have forgotten about. If you don't want the recipient to be able to edit your file then save it as a PDF and tell Illustrator in the dialog box when saving not to Preserve the Illustrator Editing Capabilities.

Acrobat cannot open a standard Photoshop file as it can an Illustrator file, but it can open a Photoshop PDF. Saving a file as a Photoshop PDF enables the layers, channels, and other data such as spot colors to be preserved. The layers are not accessible in Acrobat but you can reopen the file in Photoshop and the layers and channels will be all there. Again, you will need to decide whether you want to send editable versions of your files. Editing capabilities in Acrobat can be switched off as in Illustrator. Another alternative is to send a JPEG.

JPEG is a good format for compressing bitmap images. It is not so well-suited to vector, as crisp edges get softened. You can use the Save for Web window to preview the translation to JPEG at various settings.

In this window you can save at higher settings than is customary for material for websites and have the advantage of seeing and comparing the effect of the different settings. Using the same Save for Web window in Illustrator also guards against saving a CMYK image straight into JPEG format and making it unreadable by some recipients. Compressing big design files for easy file transfer will always be a balance between file size and compromising the quality of your image. In a JPEG everything in the original Photoshop document is collapsed into one image so no layers or channels are preserved.

Rather than sending a number of separate documents as your package it is better to bundle them up into a single document with multiple pages. If you are sending guidance for the making of an item you do not want any page to go astray. With a multiple-page document you can control the sequence of viewing, and all together the package looks more professional. This multiple-page document could be a slide show on a website, a downloadable multiple-page PDF, or a multiple-page PDF you send as an attachment. From Photoshop and Illustrator you can export artboards or comps as multiple-page PDFs and Adobe Acrobat Pro has excellent and easy to use tools for creating and combining multiple-page PDFs, and there are various freeware applications too.

If you present your work via a website then all your files remain on your server or on the provider's server and there is no need for actual file transfer. What you want to avoid though is low resolution and thin content presentations. Online presentation can be rather evanescent and you may have to show compromised low-resolution images to guarantee smooth viewing. In contrast, a multi-page PDF allows for rich content and digital convenience with the reinforcement of an easily printed record. You can have the PDF viewable on line and downloadable in all its high-resolution glory.

USER FRIENDLY
FORMATS | OUTPUT

THE IMPORTANCE
OF COLOR

COMMUNICATION

CASE STUDY:
A FACTORY
PERSPECTIVE

CASE STUDY:
A DESIGNER'S
PERSPECTIVE

OUTPUT

When you want to share the full quality design files with no compromise in quality or size or when you have prepared the files for production then the ideal method for sharing files is a file transfer service. A number of companies provide a platform that allows anyone in the world to send large files, typically up to 2GB per transfer. Very large files can be sent in their native format with all layers and flexibility retained and with no need for compression to shrink the file size. The transfer process is simple and you may never need to step up to the pay-for-use service. You upload the file to the company's server and you receive a link that you send to your intended recipient. They then download the file using that link. The process is simple and, in practice, a lot more efficient than sending CDs or DVDs.

In addition to file transfer services email applications are increasingly allowing for extra-large file attachments. An email application uploads the attached file to a cloud server on your behalf and if the recipient shares the same OS then the file is automatically downloaded and shown in the delivered message; if the recipient uses a different OS or mail application they instead see a link to download the attachment from the cloud server.

With the advances of digital technology the demarcation between design and production has become hazy. Designers are expected to prepare their designs in some manner compatible for the intended output.

The artwork they prepare may go all the way to production with little intervention from other professionals. That responsibility can be scary— whether a designer-maker taking on-board the production of their own work and possibly packaging up their designs for a manufacturer at some remote site or a designer in a large organization preparing all the material and guidance for sampling. The actual output can be extremely varied and the detailed requirements of that production understandably beyond a designer's experience. So what do designers need to know and what is their ideal preparation and attitude?

Whether working for themselves or for a company designers need to proof their work wherever possible. Proofs create an accurate prediction of the final output. The familiarity of the work on the screen can prevent the designer from seeing an error that will be painfully obvious when the work has been realized in another medium.

This can be a costly mistake, so wherever possible, print your work out on paper (likely to be the cheaper medium) to check for errors. Translation to another medium provides a contrast to the on-screen version and your established view, enabling you to see the work afresh. If you have access to calibrated printers then you will see some confirmation of how the colors will appear. If color profiles are applied to the proofing process they can adjust your desktop printer (if the printer has the capacity) to simulate the output of the production printer. If your desktop printer is calibrated to reproduce the monitor colors as accurately as possible then you will see the translation from color in the form of light to color in the form of pigment, which can be a considerable change. A weave design might look different when viewed at its actual scale rather than at some screen magnification. Very large designs can be printed across multiple sheets of paper and taped together. This will still be a valuable aid to judging the design.

When packaging the design for sampling or production the designer, to the best of his or her ability, needs to provide a factory with the material that can create the most successful outcome to the best of the factory's abilities.

The designer may be generating their artwork on nonspecialist software and then handing it on to a manufacturer that uses very different software that is tailored to their production requirements. How can the designer prepare to have a positive, predictable outcome when the procedures and setup in a factory may be very specific to that factory, possibly overseas and beyond the designer's access? Understanding what you can most appropriately do as a designer and what is more suitably left to the specialists in a factory is part of a professional and informed approach. Production is not only merely about sending files to a factory; it is also about establishing a relationship with that factory and ideally tailoring the work to exploit its strengths.

1
Production digital printing

1

USER FRIENDLY
FORMATS

OUTPUT

**THE IMPORTANCE
OF COLOR**

COMMUNICATION

CASE STUDY:
A FACTORY
PERSPECTIVE

CASE STUDY:
A DESIGNER'S
PERSPECTIVE

241

THE IMPORTANCE OF COLOR

If you are having fabric printed by a digital printer, it is good policy to see if the printer can supply color management tools, such as color profiles, so that you can anticipate (with qualifications) the output. What is actually produced on the fabric depends on the fabric itself and on the treatment it has received to prepare it for the inkjet or dye sublimation printing. So the profile, to be accurate, should be based on those specifics. The printer might supply you with a digital file of colors and a printed fabric guide. By adhering to these colors you may be able to predict the printed outcome.

When dealing with a mill, printer, or factory it is very important that they receive accurate colored standards to match to. Color is perceived before form and has serious influence on the success or failure of your design. The factory has its own ways of ensuring color matching but they will need something exact from you for the guide.

You could send them physical color swatches and clear instructions to refer to the swatches, however while that does mean that you can instantly send the digital artwork, the factory will still have to wait for the physical color swatches to arrive. If the factory has a recognized color reference, such as the PANTONE® Color specifier for Fashion and Home, then you can match the colors in your artwork to those in the specifier and you can state this in your guidance to the factory. There are a number of color specifier systems but the PANTONE Fashion and Home is especially tailored to the colors favored by these industries. It is not a theoretical or randomly generated color gamut but, instead, is one based on the evaluation of 10,000 plus products in the fashion and home markets to select the most relevant colors. And, it adds colors every few years to reflect market trends. A factory will also be able to reproduce the colors specified because PANTONE has usefully ensured that all two thousand plus colors in the Fashion and Home System are reproducible by any mill or factory, as PANTONE uses only globally available, approved dyestuffs to create their formulations. So this system is a very useful tool for specifying color quickly to a remote production site.

Problems can arise however if the recipient is not recognizing your file format. Experience shows that if there is any problem reading your file it falls to the designer to figure out what the problem is! So be aware that recipients might well not know they can open AI files in Acrobat. There may be problems, less common now, exchanging files from the Mac world to the PC, and some recipients might have very old versions of the applications. So you might have to save in older formats from your own applications. Again, make sure you save the document as a copy so you don't alter your original. If problems then arise effective communication is key.

COMMUNICATION

Unless you are using your own equipment to output, successful production of your work depends on the skill, contributions, and judgment of others. So output is not really about the machines and equipment, but more about the people and the systems in use. Following are two perspectives on the process of production.

"PANTONE has usefully ensured that all two thousand plus colors in the fashion and home system are reproducible by any mill or factory"

CASE STUDY:
A FACTORY PERSPECTIVE

Paul Turnbull is managing director of Turnbull Designs and part of a family that has been innovating in textile production since the 19th century. Toward the end of that century, William Turnbull, a machine printer, foresaw how printing could be advanced if the machine was allowed its place in artistic production. He believed that work of true value could be produced with machines, as well as with hand-craft methods, bringing "something better" to the wider public. Today Turnbull Designs, from factories in the UK and Thailand, produces the highest quality textiles and wall covering from a wide array of techniques, from the now rare process of hand block printing to the latest generation of digital printing for furnishing fabrics.

The imaginative fusion of the old and the new is seen in their innovative digital warp printing, reviving an historical technique and combining it with the latest technology. Paul is persuasive on the benefits of a good dialog with a factory:

"The final outcome is very much dependent upon communication with the client, but also between those areas of the factory that deal with the differing stages of the development process. The interpretation and translation of a design for production is often a subjective process, particularly when we are developing techniques that are difficult to simulate using CAD, or with conventionally painted artwork. In these cases there is often an absence of a specific 'target' piece of artwork, and the process relies more upon

interpretation, which results in several different possible paths to take. Some of the technically complex techniques that can be employed in sampling cannot be meaningfully simulated using normal CAD programs. This is particularly the case when we are mixing techniques, such as print with foil, or using resist/discharge to create effects. In these cases CAD can be used to a certain point but, after which, it is a case of describing the potential outcomes to the customer. So an active dialog with the customer is essential, through meetings, but also using email, image transfer, and, in some cases, video conferencing.

Some printing companies present themselves as basic manufacturers focused on simple reproduction, and this is particularly true of digital, where the approach could be simply

2
The revived warp printing technique used to produce a "shadow tissue".

USER FRIENDLY
FORMATS

OUTPUT

THE IMPORTANCE
OF COLOR

COMMUNICATION

**CASE STUDY:
A FACTORY
PERSPECTIVE**

CASE STUDY:
A DESIGNER'S
PERSPECTIVE

outputting a scanned image directly onto fabric. This characterizes the lower areas of the market, and in the case of digital, the 'bureau' printers using pigment systems. Whilst the differential between some producers may merely be price, where we aim to distinguish ourselves is the ability to work with our clients to employ the compelling subtleties and details required to compete at the middle and upper end of the market.

Our input might be in the interpretation of the rendering of the design file itself and helping with color balance, through to helping to develop the print-mark and overall appearance to suit a particular cloth. We would not be presumptive enough as to tell our customers what they should do with a particular design; it is more of a collaborative approach, to work together towards creating the best product. It is not a matter of making a 'one off sale,' as we have a vested interest in the success and longevity of a collection.

Sometimes developing the design leads to two versions emerging—the version the client originally envisaged and a second version, sampled alongside, that shows the design with a slightly different interpretation. Demonstrating these possibilities is a key part of what we do. We clearly have a shared objective in achieving patterns that enjoy long-term success. Many go on to become classics, transcending fashion, and continuing to sell for decades.

3

3
Production screen printing

Problems with Artwork

We are quite often given artwork by companies that historically would have had design studios and that now believe that technology enables them to do without.

Someone may instead do something with a very basic app and unfortunately with so little understanding of the technology that they can supply something that is unfinished and unresolved. They may think they are giving us a file that is production ready but we know there are obvious problems with it, for example, there are *design lines*, gaps, they have taken a low resolution scan, or they worked with very poor quality images, and yet regrettably their expectations are for a high quality outcome. It is obviously misguided for people to take over parts of the process unless they have a suitable understanding of that process and can execute the necessary work to a high standard. Whilst the widespread use of CAD has made a positive contribution to many areas of design, it does appear that in many cases key planning stages are often omitted, and the quality of artwork itself can lack finesse and show a marked contrast to archival pieces.

At the preliminary stage it is critical to make people aware if there are any issues, be they aesthetic or technical, rather than let them travel undetected to the later stages. By helping our customers with the detail and nuances we hopefully achieve a quality and finish for the product that provides the best chance of success, where prints compete with not only other prints, but also with different forms of decorative fabrics, such as Jacquard weaves and embroidery.

Professional pride comes into the process too. Turnbull has a long history of manufacturing and we are always mindful of how the future will judge our contribution. So if the customer hasn't thought of the potential of a particular outcome we do feel duty bound to make our contribution in this area. And it reflects the level of the market that we are in, where we are being measured not against a company 10 miles down the road but against, say, a company in Italy. There is an international, high standard of aesthetic and technical endeavor."

What Paul calls the "corporate DNA" is present both at the UK site and also at their unit in Thailand. They see the ideal artist in the technical studio in Thailand, as in the UK, as being someone that possesses both the traditional design skills, such as being able to paint, and the ability to excel in the use of computers. Though most important assets are seen as an enquiring mind coupled with the desire to create interesting and special new developments.

At the specialist production unit in Thailand, computer controlled "wet and dry" screen-printing delivers the layered color and the superior depth of print and clarity not obtained with higher speed "continuous printing."

The company uses high performance vat dyestuffs for the screen and block prints, and applies the same fastidious approach to design to their warp-printing, block-printing, and technical textiles. The studio artists are art school graduates, who have honed their skills within the working environment. Traditional craft skills such as hand-color separation are widely used and are particularly important for recreating the subtle effects of fine-line drawn outlines and historical reproductions of antiques toile fabrics.

4

USER FRIENDLY
FORMATS

OUTPUT

THE IMPORTANCE
OF COLOR

COMMUNICATION

CASE STUDY:
A FACTORY
PERSPECTIVE

A DESIGNER'S
PERSPECTIVE

245

5

4
Hand block printing production

5
Preparation of separations

6
Color adjustment of production
artwork

THE DESIGN DEVELOPMENT PROCESS

"Recently we developed a design in conjunction with the Ralph Lauren design team in New York, where the brief was to recreate the variation in print-mark as often found on the reverse of hand-block printed documents. Developing the artwork involved introducing into the design file a series of cloth effects and fine tonal variations adapted to suit the individual colorways. So the resulting file for the blue version is different from the file for the pink/green version and this fine-tuning of the 'tone work' is ideally suited to digital printing. The nuanced nature of the resulting colors beautifully expresses the Ralph Lauren country house look of comfortably aged, informal elegance.

We had meetings with Ralph Lauren in New York to develop designs. When we first started working with them from the second or third meeting they saw we were discussing issues together in such detail that they needed to share the bigger picture with us. Now from the outset they try to introduce us to the way they are thinking, so we are quite privileged to be taken into their confidence on the design vision but it does definitely help. Having an understanding of how the product sits as part of a wider look helps us communicate more effectively within our internal team. We are saving time in the long run while delivering more precisely what they want."

"They see the ideal artist in the technical studio in Thailand, as in the UK, as being someone that possesses both the traditional design skills, such as being able to paint, and the ability to excel in the use of computers."

6

CASE STUDY:
A DESIGNER'S PERSPECTIVE

Juliette van Rhyn has considerable experience designing products manufactured in varying materials, in disparate factories, and brought all together to form a coordinated range.

7

"The trickiest thing with working with factories in the Far East is that people there have amazing skills but often the language barrier prevents precise communication.

This is why factory visits are so crucial: they offer a chance to meet face-to-face, build relationships, and address technical issues directly. As a designer filling in gaps in technical knowledge can dramatically improve how I choose to brief artwork, comment on colors, and adjust template layouts. The best product is created when a clear division of expertise is established early on: the design team leads creative direction and the factory offers technical guidance and anticipates any sampling problems from the start.

Product development is an area where you can have limited control at times. Working on products that are made in different factories and have varying lead times can mean a juggling act of sampling and approval. Altogether it can be quite a task to achieve matching colors and print quality across a diverse range that all has to go to production on time. To avoid potential issues, I find it useful to request color swatches and samples at an early stage of development, especially for long lead-time items like decorated ceramics. It can help to establish

which colors are possible to achieve and which ones will be problematic. This, in turn, can influence the print design itself.

There is always a balance to strike between achieving the most beautiful product possible, whilst understanding when there are likely to be technical restrictions and time constraints. Buyers have high demands placed on them to achieve certain margins and production dates, whilst designers have the responsibility to maintain the aesthetic standards of the brand. If there have been setbacks during sampling, sometimes it will have to be decided whether the product is commercially acceptable or not. Whilst it might not live up entirely to the dreams of the designers, if deemed commercially acceptable then it can still be signed off for production.

Juliette's experience is that when briefing textiles, factories accept TIFF artworks created in Photoshop. However when briefing hard product, some factories prefer to receive artwork in Illustrator format. Based on this, if the original artwork is created in Photoshop, she will develop a second parallel version in vector format.

Live Trace does not pick up all of the information you might want in the artwork. Corners can become overly smoothed, edges can be spiky, and the overall effect can look too rigid. With a fine texture in the artwork, it might translate poorly. To overcome this, I would usually do an initial live trace on each separated color layer, and then go back through with the Pen tool to meticulously tweak the anchor points in order to make a more refined version that is truer to the original."

USER FRIENDLY
FORMATS   OUTPUT   THE IMPORTANCE
                            OF COLOR   COMMUNICATION   CASE STUDY:
                                                                A FACTORY
                                                                PERSPECTIVE   **CASE STUDY:
                                                                                    A DESIGNER'S
                                                                                    PERSPECTIVE**

Rather than leaving this translation process to the factory, Juliette has always done this extra stage herself and says that in her experience, "Sometimes the factory's Illustrator retracing is excellent but if the original TIFF artwork is sent to two factories each could create subtly different interpretations in their vector format. This might result in prints looking slightly different across products in the same range, which would be unacceptable.

If I have control over both formats of the artwork it ensures that suppliers, whether working with either vector or TIFF files, will receive something consistent. Depending on the product and print technique, the factory might still go on to trace the separations in specialized production however, from my perspective, I will have provided a uniform starting point. This helps to establish as much consistency in briefing across hard and soft products as possible.

With factories in Portugal, India, China, and the United Kingdom I brief them all in the same way. I use Photoshop to create and edit the artwork, to put the artwork into repeat, make colorways, and to separate colors ready to be engraved.

To make a print as ready for a factory as possible, I always ensure the design is 'clean' (i.e., it only contains [the specific] colors that will be used to engrave the screens). To avoid anti-aliasing the artwork, I use the Pencil tool rather than the brush, as well as indexing the file to avoid any other stray colors creeping in. The file is then ready to be separated into layers representing each color in the print (usually no more than 12 if rotary printing) and to be sent off to the supplier. The factory will convert this file using specialist software so that it is ready to engrave on rotary screens, but by supplying such precise artworks the possibility for variation between factories is kept to a minimum.

When using factories overseas, tighter control over how artwork is briefed can ultimately save an enormous amount of time. I would normally send out hard-copy briefs of the print with large color chips (the color chips are often cut up and used by the various teams in the factory), as well as information by email regarding print technique, substrate, number of colors in the print, and any special instructions if applicable. For example, if there is

a texture in the print I might ask the factory to pay particular attention to it when printing to ensure it is visible.

In my experience, supplying both AI and TIFF formats of artworks, sending out detailed briefs, and working with factories to understand technical limitations have all proved useful tools in developing products both in the United Kingdom and overseas. Whilst this degree of preparation can be time consuming, I have found it crucial if the product range is to match in terms of color and print quality. It definitely requires quite a degree of organization and precision."

TIP

It is clear from these professionals' perspectives that establishing a good relationship with whoever is involved in producing your work is very important; but of course not always easy or indeed possible. However, as a factory is likely to make amendments to your work to fit their actual production methods it is crucial that they understand what is essential about your design. You need to convey that clearly. So communication is key in achieving a successful outcome.

8

7
Refining artwork

8
Selecting color standards

SOME ADVICE ON THINGS THAT CAN TRIP YOU UP IN PHOTOSHOP AND ILLUSTRATOR

When you don't seem to be drawing anything in Illustrator, there are two possible causes.

When Illustrator will not allow you to draw anything at all look at your Layers window. You may have a layer active (shown highlighted) but a blank space in the visibility column rather than an eye to denote visibility. Illustrator quite logically won't allow you to draw on a layer you can't see. You might have a layer visible and be intending to draw on that layer but if it is not the active selected layer then Illustrator will not draw on it. Make either the visible layer the active one or turn on visibility for the currently active layer.

When you are drawing an object in Illustrator and you release the mouse or digital pen and the object disappears, check that you actually have a stroke or fill attribute selected in the Toolbar. With neither stroke nor fill assigned, the object will be there but will be hidden. Smart guides will try and give you a clue that the object is there but invisible if your cursor passes over it. To draw the object correctly, select an appropriate fill or stroke in the Toolbar, but before drawing your object afresh, select "Outline View" to see if you have already drawn hidden versions of the object, which you may need to delete. By default, Illustrator sets the view so that all artwork is previewed in color with the strokes and effects shown.

However, you can choose to display artwork solely with Outlines (or Paths) visible. Viewing artwork in Outline shows any objects on the artboard that may be invisible under Preview Mode. Without any Paint attributes assigned these objects are not displayed in Preview. With complex artwork, switching to View will also speed the redraw time.

To view all artwork as outlines, go **View → Outline**. Choose **View → Preview** to return to previewing your artwork in color with attributes.

WAITING DIALOG BOXES

If the computer beeps (as long as the sound is on) and will not allow you to do anything, see if there is a dialog box open somewhere on the screen waiting for an enter/return or an okay or cancel response.

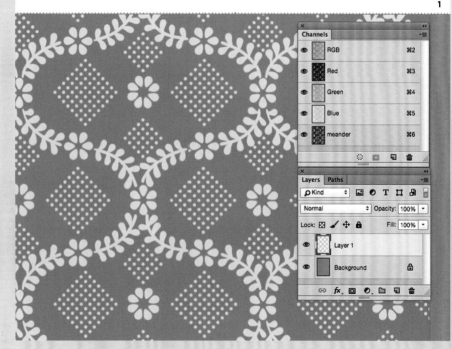

ALPHA CHANNELS IN PHOTOSHOP

Alpha channels are very helpful but not if you don't notice whether they are active or not.

In the example shown the RGB channels that compose the image are not active and consequently the Background Layer and Layer 1 are not active either and are grayed out. If you do start painting the material will go onto the alpha channel 1, as this is the only active channel. Alpha channels are for saving and editing of selections and are different from image channels but very importantly they live together in the same window and affect each other. At least one of the individual RGB channels (or CMYK) needs to be active (selected) to allow painting onto the image itself. **(fig. 1)**

If you edit a selection as a channel remember to make sure the RGB or CYMK composite channel is active when you want to start editing the file again.

MORE ATTENTION FOR CHANNELS

In the example illustrated if you try to select the brown square with the Magic Wand, the whole document is selected even though the tolerance on the Magic Wand is as low as 2 in this case. This is because, again, you are actually clicking in the alpha channel and not the layers and because the alpha channel is the only active space. The alpha channel is entirely the same color white, so all of it is selected. **(fig. 2)**

THE ALL-IMPORTANT HIERARCHY IN PHOTOSHOP

Sometimes deleting appears to do nothing, but it may be that Photoshop has deleted what you did not expect. In the example shown if you were to press the delete key to delete the selection in the brown rectangle this action would not happen.

Instead the currently active points on the work path would be deleted. This is because Paths comes first in the hierarchy in Photoshop. The application first applies the command to active paths it finds before active selections; here the work path was still active. This is why I emphasize making sure paths are not active when they are not needed. De-activate the work path by clicking in the gray area below in the palette and better still save it first within the document The work path is temporary and you must save it to avoid losing its contents. If you deselect the work path without saving it and start drawing again, a new path will replace the existing one. **(fig. 3)**

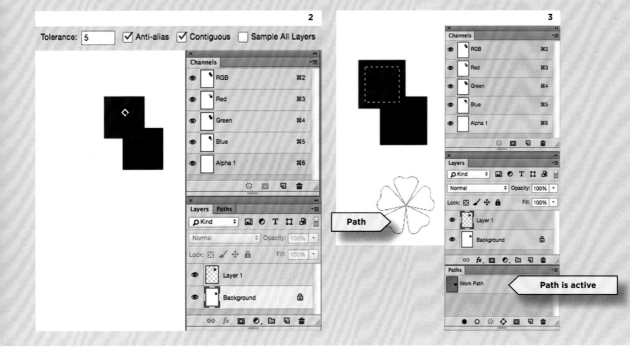

APPLIED BRUSH STROKES GET SQUASHED

Illustrator can resize an object and that object's attributes together. So Brushes applied as strokes are scaled down or up along with the object. Linking objects and attributes scaling is an option; alternatively, you can also scale objects without scaling those attributes.

Both ways are useful, and naturally Illustrator gives you the freedom to choose. By default the strokes and effects are not scaled along with objects. To change this, either go **Preferences → General** and select "Scale Strokes and Effects" or scale using the **Transform → Scale** command, and then in the Dialog window click the tick box to "Scale Stroke and Effects." You can also change the setting in the Transform window using the options drop-down menu. Once you have changed this setting, it applies, until you change it again, to any manual scaling to an object using the bounding box or using the Scale tool. **(fig. 4)**

TRANSFORMING PATTERNS IN ILLUSTRATOR

This is not actually a problem but a short cut that it is not a well-known and does very effectively speed up adjusting designs. To transform only the pattern and not the object when using a Transform tool, hold down the tilde key (~) while dragging. The borders of the object will appear to be transformed, but when you release the mouse the borders snap back to their original position leaving only the pattern transformed. You can also easily move the pattern within the object by holding down the tilde key and dragging the pattern with the Selection tool.

LINES BETWEEN REPEATS IN ILLUSTRATOR

On occasion, in Illustrator, very fine lines can appear between the tiles of your repeat pattern fill. Sometimes this can merely be Illustrator making a mistake in the screen rendering. If you zoom further in and the lines disappear then this indicates the problem is only in the display at certain magnifications.

If the lines persist at different magnifications then the problem is with the document itself. Using the Pattern Options window to make repeats should ensure that all tiles match up exactly. So unless you have used a different method of doing the repeat the problem lies elsewhere. If you have a background rectangle in the artwork and it happens to be fractionally smaller than the repeat tile this might be producing the lines. If there is no background rectangle or if the rectangle is larger than the repeat tile then the cause of the fine lines between tiles is likely to be anti-aliasing. Illustrator may be applying anti-aliasing to the edge of the artwork that forms the repeat tile, anti-aliasing being the default setting in preferences. **(fig. 5)**

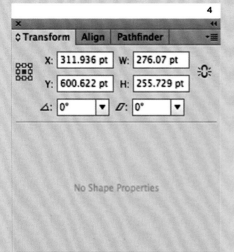

TIP | **Anti-aliasing**
Anti-aliasing is the technique the computer uses to minimize aliasing—or jagged or blocky patterns—where, owing to the resolution of the image, the underlying pixels would be evident. Anti-aliasing smoothes the jagged edges of artwork by softening the color transition between edge pixels and neighboring pixels. In the case of the pattern fill, Illustrator is attempting to soften the transition between the individual tiles and the background, which is empty.

The anti-aliased artwork setting in preferences should normally only apply to how Illustrator displays objects in Preview mode on your artboard. It shouldn't normally affect how artwork is exported, but in the case of pattern fills, if you save a document with an object containing a pattern fill with visible lines between tiles and you open that document in Photoshop then Photoshop ensures that those lines caused by anti-aliasing will be made visible, and often they are made even more visible by Photoshop. As these lines can ruin your careful repeat work make sure you check the repeats in Illustrator for the hairline dividing lines. It is actually better to leave anti-aliasing on in preferences in Illustrator so you spot the problem and to turn it off in the Import window in Photoshop.

Even with anti-aliasing switched off in Illustrator, Photoshop will add it back in if it is left ticked in the Import window of Photoshop. And even if anti-aliasing is off in Illustrator preferences, copying and placing or dragging from Illustrator to Photoshop will still produce those visible lines. So, good practice is to import with anti-aliasing unticked in the Import window. This is a small but important detail to pay attention to in order that it doesn't ruin repeat work and worse still get translated into production artwork. **(fig. 6)**

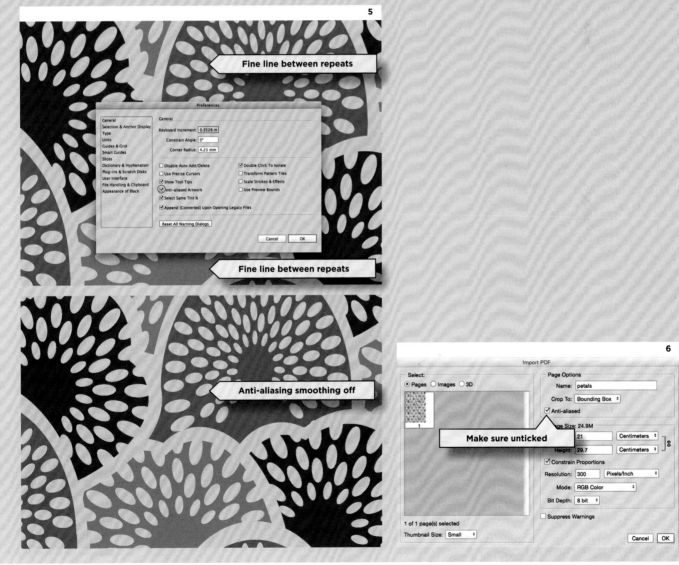

WRONG DEPTH, WRONG SIZE

If the option to convert your image to indexed color is grayed out, it is probable that either the image is in CMYK color and you will have to first change it to RGB, or your image is set at too high a bit depth.

Bit depth specifies how much color information is available for each individual pixel in an image. The more bits of information per pixel, the more available colors for that specific pixel. Photoshop has gone on to accommodate images with very high levels of bit depth, in addition to 8-bit or 8-bpc (bits per channel) images, that now contain 16 bpc and 32 bpc, known as high dynamic range or HDR images. If your image is other than an 8-bit image you will have to change it to 8 bit to allow the conversion to index color. Go **Image →
Mode → 8 Bits/Channel**.

If you copy between documents and the material appears much larger or smaller than you expect then check that the documents have the same resolution. Mistakes can occur when you enter a figure, for example 300, as pixels per centimeter rather than pixels per inch (the more common). There is a big difference between physical size of the same document at the resolution or 300 ppi and at 300 ppcm.

SELECTED COLORS CHANGE TO GRAYS IN ILLUSTRATOR

In Illustrator you may find that your color selection inexplicably changes to a grayscale equivalent when you try to use it in your document. If you select a color from the Color Picker you will see it change to gray in the Toolbar when you exit Color Picker. The first solution is to select the Color window from the Windows menu or click F6. From that window's options menu you will probably see that Grayscale is ticked; select instead the color space you want to use, RGB or CMYK.

If the color choices are grayed out in the options menu then it may be because you have used Image Trace on an image with Grayscale as the method. This will have given you many objects individually requiring to be changed to RGB or CMYK if you want them in color. The easiest method for this will probably be to use **Edit → Edit Colors →
Recolor Artwork...** and introduce the color to all objects that way.

A very good method to change the color mode of individual objects is to select an object then to Shift-click the color map area at the bottom of the Color window, that is, the horizontal rectangle below the sliders filled with the actual color space representation. Every Shift-click will toggle through the next color space in the list.

PICTURE CREDITS

LEVEL ONE

Project One—Photoshop: Layers and Custom Brushes
Images author's own

Project Two—Photoshop: New Ways of Drawing
Images author's own

Project Three—Photoshop: Scanning Drawings
Images author's own

Project Four—Photoshop: Paths and Brushes
Images author's own

Project Five—Photoshop: Stripes and Weaves
Images author's own

Case Study: Wallace Sewell
Images courtesy Wallace and Sewell, all images © Wallace and Sewell

LEVEL TWO

Project Six—Photoshop: Repeats and Colorways
Images author's own except Brocatel, design William Morris, courtesy of the William Morris Gallery. Golden lily design William Morris, courtesy of the William Morris Gallery. Willow Bough design William Morris, courtesy of the William Morris Gallery

Project Seven—Color Theory in Practice
Images author's own

Project Eight—Fills, Textures, and Layers
Images author's own except page 88 and 99 images courtesy of Samantha Fynes © Samantha Fynes

Project Nine—Illustrator: Paths to Fashion
Images author's own

Project Ten—Simple Geometry in Illustrator
Images author's own

Project Eleven—Repeat Patterns in Illustrator
Images author's own

Case Study: Nadine Bucher
Images courtesy Nadine Bucher, © Nadine Bucher

Project Twelve—Illustrator: Photoshop and Filters
Images author's own except Shibori image 116 the work of Motochiko Kitano Shibori images 117, 118 and 119 courtesy of narablog.com

Case Study: Tord Boontje
Images courtesy Tord Boontje, © Tord Boontje

LEVEL THREE

Project Thirteen—Illustrator: The Blob and Art Brushes
Images author's own

Project Fourteen—Illustrator: Flats
Images author's own except page 163 courtesy Helen Tran, image and design © C&A

Project Fifteen—Illustrator: All the Trimmings
Images author's own except page 182 courtesy Helen Tran, image and design © C&A

Project Sixteen—Illustrator: Layout
Images author's own except page 199 courtesy Peut-Être magazine, glasses by Tsumori Chisato © Peut-Être

Project Seventeen—Illustrator: Presentation
Images author's own except pages 208, 209 courtesy Helen Tran, image and design © C&A

Project Eighteen—Photoshop: Presentation
Images author's own

Case Study: Print Printfresh
Images courtesy Printfresh Studio, © Printfresh Studio

Case Study: C&A Designers
Images courtesy of Helen Tran pages 230, 232, 233
Filipa Cipriano page 231
Vicky Sanders pages 234, 235, image and design © C&A

Sharing, Communication and Output
Images for a Factory Perspective courtesy Paul Turnbull Design, © Paul Turnbull Design

A Designer Perspective
Images courtesy Juliette van Rhyn, © Juliette van Rhyn

INDEX

ACKNOWLEDGMENTS

I would like to express my gratitude
to all the contributors to the book
who kindly gave up their time to be
interviewed. They candidly shared their
experience and insights, and allowed
their work to be featured.

Pauline Ainslie
Tord Boontje
Nadine Bucher
Helen Chan
Filipa Cipriano
Samantha Fynes
Bruce Malcolm
Nathalie Malric
Juliette van Rhyn
Vicky Sanders
Emma Sewell
Paul Turnbull
Amy Voloshin

I would like to thank Nicholas Rodgers
for giving me the opportunity to teach
at Norwich University of the Arts where
working with the students sowed the
seeds for this book.

The publishers would like to thank
Tamara Albu, Cindy Bainbridge,
Georgina Hooper, and Toni Nordness.